"Dale's story is a bold reminder that no life should be treated lightly. In the weighty matters of justice and mercy, Dale chose to follow Jesus, who sided with the poor, the dispossessed and despised. I hope what you read here impassions you to do the same."

Sister Helen Prejean, CSJ, author, *Dead Man Walking* and *The Death of Innocents*

"This fascinating life story describes a profound personal journey leading to deep spiritual transformation. I was deeply moved in reading it, and I am delighted to highly recommend it."

Francis MacNutt, co-founder, Christian Healing Ministries; author of the bestselling *Healing* and many more

"My longtime minister friend offers a collection of high-definition snapshots of the sinful nature of man. But Dale makes it clear that all humankind, not just criminals, is suffering on "death row," waiting for Judgment Day. Thankfully, my friend doesn't leave us there—alone, facing the sentence we deserve for our sins. Dale writes about a gracious God, who through the death and resurrection of our Lord Jesus Christ, forgives us of our sin and delivers us from the fear of death and dread for the hereafter. By the end of this quick but not easy read, tears of shame for my sins gave way to tears of joyful hope for myself and others. The contents are based on the truth of the Word of God and will pierce your inner being like a double-edged sword—and judge the thoughts and intents of your heart."

Ken Cooper, founder, Ken Cooper Prison Ministry; author, *Held Hostage*

"A gripping narrative, a personal testament to the reality of unbought grace and its constant power to transform the lives of those who dare to accept it."

Charles E. Rice, professor emeritus, Notre Dame Law School

"With the transparency of a converted heart, the brilliance of a top legal mind, the honesty of his own personal struggles and understated moral outrage, Dale takes us to the radical edge of following Jesus fully. Travel with him from elite board rooms to the sights, sounds and smells of Florida's death row. Your life will be challenged and—be prepared—it may well be changed.

Don Williams, Ph.D., pastor and author of thirteen books

"Dale Recinella was a successful, high-flying lawyer until God took him by the scruff of the neck and let him know He had other plans for his life. If ever we needed a prod to reexamine our self-centered, materialistic lives, this book would do it. Dale doesn't preach. He simply tells his remarkable story from riches to rags, which—in the economy of God's kingdom—was actually a journey from emptiness to abundance. Dale has often asked himself, 'Did Jesus really mean what He said?' No one can read this riveting book without pausing to ask a similar question. And the response may well lead to a re-sorting of our own priorities."

Julie Belding, president, Baptist Women's Union of the South West Pacific; vice president, Australasian Religious Press Association

"I hope this fine book receives a wide reading. We need to put intelligence, faith, passion and justice together in the same place, and Dale Recinella does this so well—because he has lived it first!

[Fr.] **Richard Rohr,** OFM, Center for Action and Contemplation, Albuquerque, New Mexico

"This is a fascinating book that will give young people a good insight into what happens on death row in our country. By telling his own story with passages from the gospels that challenged him, Recinella invites the reader to wrestle with the question whether it is right to execute a human being. This is a must-read for high school and college students. My wife could not put the book down."

Johann Christoph Arnold, senior pastor, Church Communities International (also known as the Bruderhof)

"This is a masterful work charting a professional and spiritual journey of one of the best project finance attorneys of our generation. The book recounts a fascinating and inspiring modern-day story of the author's worldly and spiritual metamorphosis to effect God's will in his life and, hopefully, as a blueprint in our lives. The book is a challenge for everyone to find the true meaning of God's will in our lives. It is a book that few people will be able to read without being moved."

Eugene Z. Grey, senior evaluation officer, European Bank for Reconstruction and Development (EBRD), London, England

"A riveting, inspiring and heartbreaking account of what it means to try to bear witness to Christ's love on death row. Please—read this book."

Dr. David P. Gushee, distinguished university professor of Christian ethics; director, Center for Theology and Public Life, Mercer University

"To take Jesus at His word, as Dale Recinella has lived and written about, may mean a life journey that leads us in unexpected directions. The way up to heaven may likely be down the corporate ladder. A life of true freedom may mean walking into a prison. Let this powerful and gripping story of ordinary people being led in extraordinary ways inspire us all to believe that Jesus really meant what he said."

Pastor Russ Eanes, Mennonite Publishing Network, Scottdale, Pennsylvania

"This book comes with a health (or should it be 'wealth'?) warning! Dale Recinella tackles two questions that most people avoid: 'Did Jesus mean what he said?' and 'Does that mean I have to do something about it?' Joining thereby the sadly small number of inspirational people in the history of the world who have been prepared to live for Jesus without limits, to literally 'do whatever it takes to get the job done,' this is the story of how Dale, together with his wife, Susan, and their family, are willing to follow wherever Jesus leads, facing up to their fears along the way, no matter the personal cost. In the process they also have been able to use their lives to help a host of others. You were warned: Read this book at your own risk! But if you don't, you'll never have the chance to find out what the secret of the true happiness was that Dale and Susan found."

Monica King, clergy spouse and former Florida coordinator of LifeLines (UK)

Now I Walk on
DEATH ROW

DALE S. RECINELLA

A division of Baker Publishing Group
Grand Rapids, Michigan

Published by Chosen Books
11400 Hampshire Avenue South
Bloomington, Minnesota 55438

Chosen Books is a division of
Baker Publishing Group, Grand Rapids, Michigan.

Printed in the United States of America

Library of Congress Cataloging-in-Publication Data

Recinella, Dale S.
    Now I walk on death row : a Wall Street finance lawyer stumbles into the arms of a loving
God / Dale S. Recinella.
        p.   cm.
    ISBN 978-0-8007-9505-4 (pbk. : alk. paper)   1. Recinella, Dale S.   2. Catholics—
United States—Biography.   3. Church work with prisoners—United States.   I. Title.
    BX4705.R397A3   2011
    261.8'3366092—dc22
    [B]
                                                                        2010052872

In keeping with biblical principles of
creation stewardship, Baker Publishing Group advocates the responsible
use of our natural resources. As a
member of the Green Press Initiative,
our company uses recycled paper
when possible. The text paper of
this book is comprised of 30% post-
consumer waste.

 green
press
INITIATIVE

To live a life that makes no sense unless
the gospels are true . . .

To my children
Adelaide, Christopher, Jeanette,
Christina & Anthony

CONTENTS

FOREWORD

Now I Walk on Death Row is a shocking book. It will make you uncomfortable. But if you are not uncomfortable in this world, you haven't yet seen it as it is. The author has been, from the human standpoint, all the way up and all the way down, and has also come to see "up" and "down" from God's point of view—exactly the reverse of the human's.

You will come away with a much better appreciation of where and what evil is in our pretty world, and of how you can participate in the triumph of Jesus here and now.

That participation will cost you dearly in human terms, but it will also position you solidly for eternal living.

Dallas Willard, professor, School of Philosophy
University of Southern California in Los Angeles

ACKNOWLEDGMENTS

Because this book is about a spiritual journey, my gratitude first falls upon our guides, Friar Murray Bodo and Pastor Michael Foley, and upon my traveling companions: Susan, my wife and partner in ministry, and my children. The children, Susan and my longtime friend Charles Lester have soldiered through all the drafts of this work, improving it markedly. Gratitude is also due to all those mentioned in these pages who have accompanied us for portions of the trip, especially my brother Gary, Pastors Joe Maniangat and John O'Sullivan, Rev. Ken and June Cooper, David Stewart, Claude Kenneson, Peter Cowdrey, Jim Galbraith, the Community of *Sant'Egidio*, Klaus and Heidi Barth and their community and Kenny Cofield.

    I also thank all those who have been and continue to be a support for the prison ministry work God allows us to do on death row and in solitary confinement; my pastoral supervisors, Bishop Victor Galeone, Father Jose Maniyangat and the supervising state chaplains of Florida State Prison and Union Correctional Institution; Bishop John Ricard, episcopal moderator for Catholic prison ministry in Florida; my lawyer, Robert Link; and Susan Cary, a longtime assistant public defender now in private practice, who advocates for humane conditions for death row inmates and assists with their end-of-life legal needs. Others include Deacon Paul Consbruck,

Rev. David Crawford, John Corwin, Thomas Lang, Lee and Carla Chotas, Michael McCarron, Sheila Hopkins, William Beitz, William Tierney, Guido and Grazia Grenni, Giuseppe Lodoli, William and Shirley Poore, Tim Thielen, Barb Ries and the Poor Clare Sisters of Spokane, Washington, William Labre and Tim Fox, all dear friends and fonts of spiritual, emotional and temporal support. Thanks go to Brother David Manning, dear friend and regular prayer partner for a dozen years, and the hundreds of supporters around North America and the world who make up our Internet circle of prayer support.

A special note of thanks is due all those who have been and continue to be volunteers who deliver the good news cell by cell in the two most desolate and oppressive prisons in Florida: retired bishop John Snyder, deacons Ken Cochran and Edgardo Farias, Gerry McMahon, John Bourgon, Bill Burguieres and Arnold Leporati. And, of course, a very special expression of gratitude is due Mike Savage and Deacon Marcus Hepburn, who have both accompanied me inside prison walls across north Florida, from the Panhandle to Starke. Deacon Hepburn, who went home to the Lord on June 8, 2010, has left us a legacy of joyful service that inspires and challenges all who step inside a prison fence.

I wish to thank Francis and Judith MacNutt and the staff and board of their Jacksonville, Florida, ministry, where I work part-time. They have given love and support of the prison ministry through their constant flexibility in accommodating the unusual and unexpected demands on my time from the needs on death row.

Finally, deep gratitude goes to Jane Campbell, who suggested the writing of this work; Paul Ingram, my editor, and all the unseen others at Chosen Books who have helped render my memories intelligible on the written page; and Natasha Sperling and Tim Peterson and their staff, who have toiled tirelessly to shepherd this work to conclusion.

1

From Times Square to Time Square

THE BLAZING FLORIDA SUN of late summer has been cooking this building for hours. It feels like a zillion degrees as I step from the air-conditioned quarterdeck, where the staff takes their breaks, onto the actual death row corridor. The solid steel door slams shut behind me, and the electronic dead bolts engage with a resounding bang from deep inside the wall. I face a six-foot-wide concrete path, blackened and discolored from years of strong chemical cleaners, yet still slick with today's humidity and the drippings of human sweat.

Along the right are the death row cells. To the left is a string of grimy windows open to the heat penetrating relentlessly from outside the concrete exterior of the wing. From floor to ceiling a wall of steel bars, barely covered with chipped and peeling beige paint, stretches down the entire corridor, separating the concrete floor into two walkways. Between the steel-barred wall and the windows is the area called the catwalk. It is too far removed from the cells for me to minister to the men inside. One can barely reach far enough through the bars to touch fingertips in prayer. Even speaking from the catwalk requires me to shout at the men in their cells and for them to shout back. It is more than a problem of distance. It is a function of the acoustics as well.

Today I am on the gate walk, the path immediately in front of the nine-by-ten-foot cells, each holding one of the fifteen men on this corridor until Florida can execute them. A voice can be readily heard on the gate walk from several cells away. As I begin speaking to the man in the first cell on my right, several of the men on the corridor can hear me.

It is September 1998, my second week ministering on death row in Florida. The priest who has been making these rounds by himself for fifteen years walks ahead of me. The physical environment of this place has worn him down and broken his health. He needs to move on. In June I will be taking over the cell-to-cell rounds from him. In the meantime I am his shadow, learning the ropes and the names and faces of the unseen men who inhabit more than four hundred cells on Florida's death row. For me, it is a blessing that they come in small bites, fifteen cells at a time along one side of each corridor. For those men, I am a curiosity, a newbie, a green prospect. One man in particular on this corridor is determined to challenge my motives and denounce my credibility.

From his cell near the end of the corridor, he hears me enter. As I work my way from man to man, he knows from the sound of my voice that I am white. He knows from my speech patterns that I have lived a life that is socially privileged. Unbeknownst to me he is waiting, ready to give me what for. Finally, thirteen cells into the corridor, I arrive at the barred door that is the front wall of his house. He is not smiling.

"Good morning," I greet him. "I'm Brother Dale. How are you doing today?"

"Yeah, I know who you are." He dismisses my salutation in a breath. "And you are in way over your head, Mister Brother Dale. You think you know what's going on here. But you and your cracker mind don't have a clue!"

My attorney-trained brain is already in gear, collecting data on this angry new face. He is about two inches taller than I am with roughly my build. His chest and arms reveal great strength, like someone who has been working outside most of his life. He is African American, and he is angry. His eyes burn with intensity, and his lips are stretched taut. The sweat on his skin reflects a weird iridescence from the fluorescent bulb on the back wall of his cell, creating the illusion of an aura of anger.

"I'm sure you're right." My lips form the words, but my mind has already detached. I am hastily building a shadow space to think and analyze from a distance, while my body stays in the moment. Although my adrenaline is pumping, I dare not reveal fear or tension. My body is stalled in neutral while the instincts of fight-or-flight are revving in my chest.

"You don't even have a clue how right I am." He stretches his hand outside the bars of his cell with his pointed finger now just an inch from my face. His fist pumps forward punctuating each syllable. "With your cracker upbringing on the right side of the tracks, you don't know nothin' about my life or about my world."

As he leans forward, close to my face, with eyes burning, I have a split-second recollection of a movie where the bad guy has x-ray lasers for eyes. If the lifeless remnants of beige paint were not already peeling off the bars of his cell door, I think his eyes would burn the paint right off.

I find myself mechanically charting the portion of space on my side of the bars, which he has claimed through his gestures and his rage. There is barely any energy for thought. All my resources are engaged to make sure I do not challenge his claims to my space and do not step backward or wince. My instincts from street ministry and raising teenagers have kicked me into receiving mode. There is not yet an opening to respond. From my silence, he assumes I disagree.

"Don't be a rube, boy." His large arms move upward and his hands grip the cell door bars that frame the sides of my face, twisting back and forth with each breath. "You think some cracker judge put me here? You're wrong. You think some cracker jury put me here? You're wrong!"

On the heels of the tirade, his pause seems louder than his words have been. The moment has come to respond. Sounding as neutral as possible, I ask the obvious question.

"Then how did you get here?"

"I was born on this side of this door!" His head thrusts forward with each phrase, delivering the verbal equivalent of pummeling head butts. "From the first day of my life, everything put me on track for this cell on death row. I was born on this side of this door."

His words hang for a moment in the stagnant, stifling air. Although he is enraged, I do not sense any animosity toward me personally. The steel bars standing between us afford a luxury rarely available on the streets. I can step into this anger and claim it as fertile ground for the Kingdom.

"Let's assume that you are right." I speak firmly while locking my eyes on his and intentionally leaning into his space that has been extended to my side of the bars. "That means I was born on this side of this door, that I had just as little to do with being on this side of the bars as you did with being on that side of the bars."

He freezes, then steps back a half step, with his fists still firmly gripping the bars on either side of my face. My words have met an angry but open heart. With our eyes still rigidly engaged, I lean a little farther into the contested space and place my hands on the bars one space outside each of the bars he is gripping. His gesture, which originally was meant as a threat, is now reframed as an encounter.

"Here we are," I continue. "What are you and I going to do now?"

He looks puzzled for a moment. Then he drops his hands to his side, muttering a stream of expletives punctuated by glances at me and the repeated phrase "crazy white whatever."

The entire corridor is dead silent. Every ear in every cell on wing 3-Left downstairs is pushed against the bars toward the corridor. There is no doubt in my mind that the microphones in the ceiling that allow every word to be monitored in the control rooms are turned to maximum pickup. This is the moment to push the issue. But my voice must be devoid of pressure or threat.

"What are you and I going to do now?" I ask again in as neutral a tone as an Italian lawyer can muster while his heart is pounding out of his chest.

The protagonist in this drama has retreated to the center of his cell. He sets his right foot on the bunk about two feet off the floor, as though to steady himself. His right hand moves to his chin in a gesture of thoughtfulness. Finally he responds.

"I don't know. Let me think about it."

In that moment I could not imagine that six years later he would ask me to be his spiritual advisor for his execution; that I would be with him for hours each day during the last six weeks before he was killed; that I would stand next to his wife to catch her and comfort her as she collapsed, sobbing in her home when his lawyer handed her the open box of his cremains. I could not imagine the hundreds of times we would speak at the front of his cell, always ending with him shaking his head in dismay, saying, "Man, oh man. You sure are white."

In the moment all I can imagine is getting outside and getting some air. But there are at least another hundred cells to see before the priest and I exit the prison that day.

Hours later, the priest and I are standing in Time Square at

Florida State Prison to be processed through the master control room. This is the prison where the executions take place. This is the prison that holds the death house, which men are moved to when their death warrant is signed and after they are removed from the long-term cells at the death row building.

The two main corridors of Florida State Prison intersect in the shape of a huge cross. The longer prison corridor runs south to north for over a quarter of a mile. The suicide watch wing and medical clinic are housed at the southern extremity. The execution chamber and the death house make up the northern end. The shorter corridor cuts across the trunk of the cross. Its eastern end runs to the front entrance of the prison building. Its opposite end terminates at the west door. The place where the trunk of this cross intersects the horizontal transept is called Time Square. It is an intentional play on words because this is Florida's big house. This is where serving a sentence is referred to as doing big time. But it is not just a nickname. It is official. The words *Time Square* are spelled out with four-foot kelly green letters in the beige floor tile of this space.

The moment triggers a flashback to another place, another time, another life—my life more than twenty years earlier when I practiced law as a project finance lawyer in the U.S. and international capital markets. In those days there was only one Times Square in my life, and it was in the Big Apple. New York City is where the deals close because that is where the money is. As I stand with the hopelessness of the suicide watch wing to my right and the Florida death house to my left, the green tiles embedding the words *Time Square* in the floor of the cross resurrect a distinct memory.

○─○─○

I am in a conference room on the highest floors of the General Motors Building in New York City. It is the waning days of 1985. The fate of Joe Robbie's new stadium for his Miami Dolphins football team is on the line. The deal had been condemned as hopeless from the very beginning. My job is to make sure it closes.

That is not an unusual position for me. The surest way to pique my interest in a deal is to tell me that it has been deemed hopeless. Barry Frank was my law partner in Miami for several years. He knows that about me and is not shy about taking advantage of it. He calls me about the stadium deal near the end of October.

Barry's client is a huge investment bank that has reached an agreement with Mr. Robbie to finance his new football stadium for $125 million. There is one catch. The deal must close before year's end because of tax law changes. That means a very specific deadline: 2:00 P.M. on New Year's Eve, the time the fed wire shuts down. There is no room for wiggling. If the $125 million is not in the fed wire by two o'clock on December 31, the deal will not close, no professionals will be paid their fees or reimbursed for their thousands of dollars in out-of-pocket costs and the Miami Dolphins will not have a new stadium.

Barry calls me about a month before Thanksgiving. I am incredulous.

"It takes about eighteen months to put together a stadium financing," I protest, "and that is if everything goes perfectly. You are saying we must do it in ten weeks, including the holidays!"

"I know," he laughs. "It definitely sounds like your kind of a deal."

"How soon do we start?"

"I'm here in New York." He shifts into his get-the-lead-out tone of voice. "We just signed the commitment letter for the financing. Why aren't you here yet?"

"Because we haven't agreed on my fee yet. Assuming we do, when do you want me?"

"My secretary already has you booked on the 6:00 A.M. Eastern

Airlines flight out of Miami tomorrow. A limo will meet you at LaGuardia."

It is standard operating procedure. Finance lawyers are constantly in the air between south Florida and New York.

After setting the fee, we divvy up the turf. Barry is responsible for all the matters dealing with revenue and real estate. He is the best real estate lending lawyer I have ever met. That is his domain. My job is to dog the paper work and ensure that the documents accurately reflect the deals being cut at the table. With over a hundred documents, totaling thousands of pages, under constant revision, that will be no small feat. The race is on.

The site for negotiations is an enormous conference room table on an upper floor of the GM Building near Central Park, the offices of the midtown law firm that represents Joe Robbie. As I exit the limo from LaGuardia Airport and check in with the building security in the lobby, I know what to expect. All the big New York law firms seem to use the same interior decorators and furniture suppliers.

The building elevator will open up into a dedicated lobby with the law firm name in large gold, bronze or silver letters plastered across the wall. As New York law firms are crazily merging and falling apart in the 1980s, it is not unusual for the big metal letters of the new firm name to barely hide the shadows of the prior letters revealed in the fade of the wallpaper. That will not be the case with this firm. It is a mainstay among the so-called silk-stocking firms in midtown Manhattan.

Fungible art, intentionally meaningless enough to avoid offense to any potential business client, will adorn the imported textured paper on every wall. The stained and varnished veneers coating every desk in every office and in the reception lobby will be painstakingly matched by moldings of either light pine or deep mahogany around every window and every door. All the decor reflects off seamless marble floors.

The receptionist, always blond and curvaceous, will invariably speak with a voice and diction that betray her original reason for moving to New York City—to find stardom of some kind. Her meticulous business dress with an impossibly tight bodice will make it clear, however, that those futile dreams are now behind her. Just landing her MRS degree with a wealthy client of the firm is worth settling for. It happens more often than people might think.

I am not disappointed. This firm follows the New York law firm playbook. After being greeted, identified and assigned to a staff person, I am escorted quickly into a huge conference room filled with tense and angry people. The decor is brighter and more cheery than that of most conference rooms I have lived in for weeks and months at a time. The massive conference room table is hand carved from rich, dark wood. The level of varnish and polish is so deep that those sitting at the table can see their entire reflection. The monotony of thought-numbing art on the walls is interrupted by intricate brass fixtures imitating old street gaslights, by a few brass-bordered mirrors and by a wet bar at one end of the room.

Good, I think to myself, noting the presence of my favorite brands of scotch in the liquor cabinet. We are going to need that.

Joe Robbie and his lawyers are huddled around one corner of the massive table. My new clients, the investment bankers from Wall Street, are sitting with Barry directly across from Robbie's entourage. Representatives of the NFL and the various Miami and State of Florida government agencies involved in this massive project are strewn about the room randomly like cards in a game of 52 pickup. A well-known, highly respected Miami attorney represents the Florida bank that will monitor construction and disburse the $125 million to build the stadium. I know without asking that his instructions are the same as mine: Make sure the deal closes.

The political and public pressure is extreme. Miami wants a new stadium. No one is smiling.

"Did I miss the closing? Has the money already been wired?" I speak in Barry's direction but watch for everyone's reactions.

"In your dreams." Barry smirks with his boyish sardonic grin. "We have a few issues first."

"Oh good." I laugh back. "I love issues."

"Well, then, you're gonna love this deal," chides a man about twenty years my senior, sitting three people away from Barry. "Pull up a chair."

I immediately figure him for a lawyer. It turns out he is an attorney from a major Cleveland law firm and is representing the secondary lender in the deal. He and I will know each other well before this is over.

Everybody in a charcoal gray or blue pinstriped suit is a lawyer. The bankers all wear solid dark blue suits but get creative with their ties and their shirts. Almost any color tie is allowed as long as it is silk. The custom-made solid color shirts with off-color cuffs and collars are in vogue in 1985. Given enough bankers, there could actually be a lot of color in the room.

The government people wear sports coats and slacks. Joe Robbie wears whatever he wants. The uniforms are just as important at the negotiation table as they are on any other battlefield. Everybody needs to know who everyone else is so they do not accidentally shoot at their own side.

In the bigger picture, we are all on the same side. Even though the lender banks are my legal client, all of us are working here for Joe Robbie and his Miami Dolphins. This is about building Mr. Robbie a stadium. He will pay all the legal fees and pick up all the expenses if the deal closes. The real client, with a capital C, is Mr. Robbie. No one says it. Everyone in the room knows it.

"So, what is the presenting issue?" I ask in the direction of Robbie's lead lawyer while sliding between the carved wooden arms of a conference room chair.

"The State of Florida wants us to build a $20 million interchange and tollbooth for the turnpike that will feed traffic to the stadium, but they do not want to give up any of the tolls collected there to help pay down the debt."

I pause before answering in order to let Mr. Robbie complete his string of expletives.

"Blast it." I shake my head, feigning dismay and disappointment. "I should have had Barry pay for my airfare today. It looks like I'm going to have to eat it."

The State folks who pretended not to hear Joe Robbie's blue outburst now bristle at my implication that the deal will not close with such an unreasonable condition imposed by them. Before they can fire back, Barry interjects.

"Did you bring a suitcase?"

"Yeah. Five days of clothes. I left it with Barbie at the reception desk."

"No problem." He waves his hand dismissively. "There's same-day laundry service at the Essex where your room is. You can check in later."

"That depends." I speak to him but double-cock my head obviously toward the State people who want a free turnpike interchange. "Who is paying for the room?"

"I am." The lead Wall Street banker jumps in decisively to close down the banter. "And they gave me a cut rate because I told them you won't be having much time to sleep in the bed—only to use the room for showers and to change clothes."

A wave of nervous laughter moves around the table. I laugh, too, knowing full well that it is the last laugh I will have in that conference room for a while.

As the days and nights drag on, merging into an undifferentiated stream of hundreds of hours at the conference room table, I begin to feel like a street person who has moved into a high-class homeless shelter. Instead of three hots and a cot, I have an overstuffed chair with carved arms and an endless stream of strong coffee and deli sandwiches. My room at the Essex House overlooks Central Park, but I will not see it in daylight.

Each Friday night I catch the last plane out to Miami and catch the first one back on Monday morning. There have been a lot of grueling deals, but this one is taking the cake. By the second week of December we are making real progress. Then another bombshell hits. A suspected Indian burial mound has been found on the property where the stadium is to be built. That would be the end of the road for most projects. But Barry is a real estate law genius. If there is a way to work around it, he will find it. It will take time. He opens negotiations with attorneys for the Indian tribe. We continue to work on the financing as though nothing is wrong.

By the week before Christmas, I succumb to double pneumonia. A doctor is sent to my hotel room to shoot me up with miracle drugs so I can keep working from my hotel bed. My hotel room is outfitted with a speaker phone with conference capability for negotiations with parties in different cities. Couriers are assigned to run drafts of documents and changed pages back and forth from the conference room to my hotel room. It is a badge of honor to keep working on the deal no matter what.

Finally, it is late on the night of December 30. The Indian mound problem has been solved. The turnpike and television revenue problems have been solved. The ticket price issues and feasibility study issues have been solved. With fifteen hours left to deadline, the deal is where it needed to be three months ago in order to close by December 31. All the business principals wish us luck and leave for their hotels. They will be back in the morning to sign the papers if there are any to sign.

The attorney from Cleveland, the one from Miami and I are all that is left of the conference room gang. We need a massive document called a trust indenture. Because of the nature of the financing, the document would normally be about 250 pages long, typed single-space. The Wall Street lawyer who was supposed to prepare that document collapsed and is sitting in the hospital. Only now do we find out that she never even started on it because she did not believe it was possible for this deal to close. Without that document there will be no closing and no stadium. There is no way to word process such a document by morning.

"Is it possible to close on a handwritten document?" asks the Miami lawyer. "As long as the bank's obligations are clearly spelled out, my client will do it."

"It can be done," agrees the attorney from Cleveland. "But how do we make a permanent record of a handwritten trust indenture?"

"Can we include a provision that it is to be replaced by a typed document with exactly the same terms and obligate the parties to re-sign the typed version as soon as one can be prepared?" I ask in a moment of desperation. "Can we say that the typed version will supersede the handwritten one as the permanent record?"

I motion around the now empty room, barking aloud, "All in favor say aye."

We work through the night, two at a time, taking turns for the third to catch a few moments of sleep in the comfy overstuffed conference room chairs.

By nine-thirty A.M. the sole original of the handwritten trust indenture is ready for signing. Joe Robbie will arrive at noon to sign his papers. The signed authorizations from the local government officials and the State officials are being flown in from Florida on Robbie's private plane. The business principals are accumulating in the room. The money must move to beat the changes in the law at midnight. The fed wire shuts down at 2:00 P.M. on New Year's Eve. The sum of $125 million must be funded by the lenders to the trustee before that time.

The documents are signed. The authorization is given to wire the money. It is one o'clock. And we wait.

At 1:50 P.M., just ten minutes before the deadline, the trustee bank in Miami confirms that the money has been sent and is in the fed system. We are closed. The Miami Dolphins will have a new stadium.

The lawyers from our host law firm pass out champagne glasses, which their staff fill to overflowing with Dom Pérignon. The lead bankers, the representatives of the south Florida government agencies and a few other dignitaries who have slipped into the conference room for the first time for the picture-fest offer toasts and congratulations.

Joe Robbie indicates that he wants to speak. Some words of thanks from him for all of us who have almost literally killed ourselves to make this deal happen would be greatly appreciated. All the sports coats and suits of every kind in the room are standing and turned toward Mr. Robbie. He has the floor.

He says a few words of thanks to the government people and the bankers. Then he turns to the rest of us. I cannot believe my ears. He curses us lawyers for our outrageous fees and promises to refuse to pay us more than a fraction of what we claim we are owed. Spitting with anger and trailing a torrent of expletives at the lawyer-midwives who have just birthed his stadium baby, Mr. Robbie storms out.

Two hours later I board my plane to Detroit at LaGuardia. It is time to join my wife and children at my dad's home for what is left of the holidays.

"You and I are going the wrong way," offers the young stewardess who shows me my seat and motions to the empty plane. "Everyone else is coming into New York City to be in Times Square for New Year's Eve. Why are we leaving?"

Except for her and me, first class is empty. So is most of the plane.

"Some weeks can make even Detroit look good for New Year's."

She is clueless, but smiles sweetly, faithfully delivering double scotch for my left hand and Baileys for my right.

As we taxi, lift off and circle to the west, midtown Manhattan and then the World Trade Center fill my window. The jumble of the last ten weeks is filling my thoughts as the pleasant burn of straight scotch fills my throat. I know my fees and expenses will get paid. I am allied with the right people who will make sure that happens. But somehow, on December 31, 1985, that seems less important than a bigger question. There was a time when the thrill of closing the impossible deal was all I lived for. Now I feel as empty as the inside of this plane.

The cabin bell dings. We are at cruising altitude. With head resting against the inside wall of the cabin, I undo my seat belt and recline my seat. In the edge of sleep as the jet heads west toward the sun setting over Pennsylvania, a solitary thought repeats itself in my mind: *What the heck am I doing with my life?*

2

Who Is God, and Who Are We?

As the firstborn male of my generation in America, tremendous pressure to succeed is a given. My parents and grandparents
hail from the province of Abruzzi in central Italy. Mom is from the
high mountains along the spine of Italy, two train changes from
L'Aquila, where the massive earthquakes hit in 2009. Her generational
inheritance is the Onorato family, the honorable ones, from Castel
di Sangro (Castle of the Blood).

Dad is from the seaside town of Pescara, a city of fishermen
and sailors on the Adriatic. His heritage includes mercenaries like
his grandfather, Pamphillo, who spent a lifetime fighting for the
king of Italy in skirmishes between Christian Europe and the Otto-
man Empire. My soldier-of-fortune great-grandfather lived to be a
hundred years old.

Both my grandfathers, Dominic Onorato and Fidel Recinella,
came to America for freedom from tyranny and for economic

prosperity. Dominic moved the family to Detroit, where he was doing factory work in the automotive industry. He established himself as a tireless worker, with a remarkable level of personal integrity and honesty.

Grandpa Fidel started working in the brickyards in Pescara at five years old. As a young man he fell in love with Anna, a sweet and gentle woman who rarely uttered an unkind word and never raised her voice. Fidel was prohibited by his family from marrying Anna until his gaggle of sisters were married off or at least had the dowry to make marriage possible. Grandpa Fidel did his duty and earned their dowry by coming to the U.S. in 1906 to begin working here at the age of twelve. In 1917 Fidel was drafted into the U.S. Army, which brought automatic citizenship. After post-war return trips to Italy, first for marriage to Anna in 1923 and later for visits with his two young sons, Fidel moved his wife, my uncle and Dad near his work in the coal mines of West Virginia in 1927. Finally, he moved with them to Detroit when the auto industry opened the assembly lines after the Depression.

Throughout my childhood, Mom would recount the tale of Fidel and Anna with all the gravitas of a classic love story. Mom was an incurable romantic. That is my ethnic and genetic heritage: half mercenary, half romantic and all Italian.

Mom and Dad attended Northeastern High School in Detroit. As soon as he was old enough, Dad enlisted in the U.S. Navy and served in both the Atlantic and Pacific theaters in World War II. Although my parents knew of each other in high school, they really met as potential partners through their families after the war.

○─○─○

I am the eldest of eight children born to Italian immigrants in Detroit, so it is a given that I have tremendous responsibility for my younger siblings. Cindy, Jan, Gary and I are each fifteen months apart. Cindy, quiet and reserved, is sandwiched between me and Jan, the fireball. In those early years, Jan is my best friend.

With the help of the G.I. Bill, my parents are able to buy a tract home available to veterans near the northern boundary of the city of Detroit. One floor. Two bedrooms. One bath. Less than nine hundred square feet.

The periodic recessions in the auto industry are difficult, especially the deep one at the end of the 1950s. Those are eighteen tough months. We eat a lot of lentils and polenta, which is Italian for grits.

But Dad does not sit around waiting for help. Door to door he trucks every day and every night. He sells Mason shoes. Sometimes I walk with him. After miles of toting the huge samples case, the end of the day always elicits the same groan from him: "Oh, my aching back."

Finally, Ford Motor Company calls him back to work to a position at the huge new transmission plant in Livonia, the largest machining plant in the world. Things are turning around for him. In the language of his generation, he would say, "We're not on easy street, but our ship may be coming in."

It is not meant to be. My family is torn from its perilous economic perch in a moment that feels like we have been hit by lightning. It is the defining event of my childhood and of the destiny of our family. It happens in the summer of 1961.

At nine years old, I attend a two-week summer camp for boys run by the Salesian religious order of priests and brothers in Irish Hills, Michigan. It is a marvelous place, almost fantastic for a city kid. We sleep in bunk beds in real log cabins, make crafts, ride horses and swim in a real lake. Each cabin is a team and does everything together in competition against the other cabins. I have thirteen new best friends. It is heaven on earth. Then, in the middle of this paradise, there is a phone call.

All of us new best friends are doing evening KP when the brother from the administration office shows up at the steps of our cabin door. He motions for our counselor, and they speak in hushed whispers while pointing at me. Every pair of eyes in the cabin is looking at them, and then at me, and back at them. My cabinmates start whispering, too, pointing at me and shaking their heads. I find myself retreating around the corner of my bunk, as if I could disappear if I am not in their line of sight. My thoughts are racing at breakneck speed. *Did I do something wrong and not know it? Are they going to send me home early?*

"Camper Recinella." Our counselor walks straight over to me. "You must report to the rector's office now. I'll go with you."

When we arrive at the office, I am totally confused. The rector is sitting behind his desk, barely visible over the stacks of paper and small mountains of camp junk. But he does not appear to be angry. Instead he looks anxious, almost concerned. Nothing seems quite right.

"Please sit down, Camper Recinella." He speaks more softly than I have ever heard him on the camp bullhorns. "There is going to be a call from your mother. We want you to take it here."

The phone rings. The rector answers. "Yes, Mrs. Recinella. . . . We understand. . . . Absolutely. No trouble at all. . . . We are glad you will be able to speak to him. . . . He's here." He hands me the phone.

"Mom?"

"Yes, honey. It's Mom." She is crying.

"What's going on? Is everything okay?"

"There is nothing to worry about. Everything is fine." She is crying harder.

"Mom, are you coming to get me now?"

"No, that would not be a good idea." She is trying to stop crying.

"Are you at home?"

"No. We're at the hospital."

"Why?"

"Well, your sister Jan is sick. We had to bring her here." She is breaking down completely and speaking between sobs. "But everything is fine. We don't want you to worry."

"Okay. Will you and Dad be picking me up next week?"

"Your father will come to get you. I'll be home with Jan."

I hand the phone back to the rector.

"Are you going to be okay, son?" He asks with tremendous emotion.

"Yeah. I think so."

There is nothing to worry about. Everything is fine.

Maybe Mom thinks so. Maybe Mom hopes so. Maybe Mom knows better. I will never know.

As I will learn later, nothing is fine. Our life as we have known it is over.

Jan is only six years old. She will never speak another word. She will never communicate another thought. She will never walk, never run, never sing, never color, never laugh, never play. Never.

When I return home from camp, Jan is not there. Jan and Cindy have also been at a camp in the Irish Hills. Their camp is for girls and is run by nuns. Cindy has no clue as to what happened. All she knows is that Jan started running very high fevers, and they took her away in an ambulance. Then they made Mom and Dad pick Cindy up, just in case it might be catching. We have no idea what it is that might be catching, or if we already have it, too.

The reality is that my best friend and sister, Jan, has been bitten by a mosquito and has contracted a particularly virulent and deadly form of encephalitis. What Mom does not know how to tell me is that Jan is in the first phase of a horrible sleeping sickness, a disease that will turn her into a twisted and gnarled "vegetable" (as people are prone to call her) for almost 35 years.

By the time school starts in September of 1961, Cindy and I are accustomed to being ushered out of the living room so our parents can talk like adults with their friends and relatives. We constantly ask, "When will Jan come home?"

"Soon," is always the answer. "Very soon."

As children, we never think to ask if soon means she will be better or if it means the money has run out. We assume she will come home because she is better.

In October 1961 I muscle the courage to tell my parents that, as the eldest son, I should accompany Mom the next time she visits Jan at the hospital. Mom is not doing well. She is not able to drive anymore so she takes the cab to Children's Hospital. I explain that I can be a big help to her on her next visit.

Mom actually looks as if she thinks it would help to have me with her. Dad is in a fog. He is functioning with no sleep and no resources. He just nods and leaves it up to us.

I have never been in a taxi before. It seems to add excitement to this adventure. When the cab pulls out of the driveway with us in the backseat, my mother's hands are shaking so hard that she can hardly hold the carfare.

"I'll hold it for you," I tell her. I try to sound full-grown as I take the bills in my right hand and stroke her arm with my left. "It'll be fine. You'll see."

The cabbie drops us at a back entrance to the hospital as Mom has asked. She has been doing this three times a week for several months now. She knows the way. With a determination that feels more mechanical than emotional, she takes me by the hand and leads me inside, down a corridor to a remote bank of service elevators. A couple of black women are standing there by a stack of laundry taking a smoke break. They greet her and look at me knowingly. As the elevator door closes, Mom puts her hand on my shoulder.

"Jan is different now, but you're big enough to handle it." She is not looking at me as she speaks. She is looking at our reflections in the tarnished steel freight shield of the elevator door. It is not possible to know whether she is speaking to me, to herself or to both of us. "Don't be shocked. She looks very different than she did before camp."

"Okay, Mom." I try to sound adult again but inhale too loudly. "I can handle it."

The moment the elevator stops and the doors open, we are assaulted by the screams of children and the stench of human feces. Without looking at me, my mother leads me off the elevator and down the corridor to the left. It is as if my feet are moving without my awareness. The stench is catching in my throat; the noises are horrifying. People in white coats carry things I have never seen before. I do not know whether we are in a room or in a hallway. Nothing is familiar. Everything is a haze. I cannot get my bearings. If Mom lets go of my hand, I might stand there frozen and unable to move, maybe forever.

Then, suddenly, we are at a metal door. It has our family name on it. Mom pushes it open and leads me in. At first I am surprised that Jan is not in the room. There is just a bald grown-up-looking person sitting in a wheelchair. The person's legs are twisted into strange, oblique angles. The person's arms are contorted, with every finger sticking straight out, pointing at nothing. The person has no hair, and the head is covered with markings, as if someone has written on it with colored crayons during sleep. The old person in the metal chair is twisted to the side with head hung over, the mouth open and a line of drool extending almost to the floor. The person in the chair is covered with electrical wires attached by strange black circles—everywhere. The head has so many wires coming out of it that it looks as if the person has electric wires instead of hair.

Suddenly, I realize that Mom has let go of my hand, and she is standing next to the person in the wheelchair. Mom is crying and touching the person's head. Then Mom looks at me and talks to the person in the chair. "Jan, honey, do you remember your brother Dale? He's here to visit you."

I have no memories of the visit after that moment. Days later, Mom tells me I did fine, and she is very proud me. She never asks if I want to go back, and I never again ask to go.

Two months later there is big news. Jan is coming home from the hospital on my birthday, the day after Christmas. Cindy and I are sure that our prayers have been answered. To my memory, no one tells us otherwise. In fact, they might have, but we may have refused to hear it, refused to believe it. On the day of my tenth birthday, we wait in the living room with my Aunt Mary as Dad carries Jan in from the car and props her up in a wheelchair in the house. Her hair has started to grow back. There are no more electrodes. Other than that, she looks exactly as she did at the hospital. It will be more than twenty years after that day before I am able to celebrate my birthday on December 26.

My parents are consumed with physical and financial preparations. Two dormers have been installed upstairs to claim most of the attic space for a girls' room and a boys' room, sharing one precious additional bathroom. Jan is moved into a bedroom on the first floor, next to my parents' bedroom. The smells and the sounds—the very air in that room—are always with me.

The walls are painted yellow. Jan lies, slightly propped up on pillows, with a hole in her throat through which a tube, a tracheostomy, is connected to a pump, sucking fluid from her lungs to prevent pneumonia. That pump is always running. The smell of a six-year-old

child's dirty diapers is thinly masked by disinfectants and deodor-
izers. It is 1961; affordable disposable diapers are still many years in
the future. Jan is wearing good old hand-rinsed, hand-washed cloth
diapers. Cindy and I will spend many hours rinsing and laundering
those diapers, along with those of the younger siblings.

Jan's illness is a catastrophe in every possible sense of the word.
The financial, physical and psychological realities are enough to
destroy my parents and our family. But the spin that people put on
the spiritual aspects of what is happening is at least as devastating,
maybe even more so.

Good Christian people often have no idea what to do with
tragedy when it happens to good Christian people. Some assure us
that Jan's condition is God's will. Others assure us that God will heal
her if we pray enough or if we are good enough. Still others assure
us that this is punishment and retribution for mistakes my parents
have made. And worst of all, some are sure that it is a mistake. The
living death was meant for Cindy and me, that Jan has been taken
in our place by mistake.

How does a ten-year-old boy make sense out of all this? There
is a war going on inside me about who God is. Is God a sadist who
does this to a child, to my best friend? Is this really God's will? Or is
God a healer on the take who pours out love and restoration if we
can muster up enough ransom money?

Mom and Cindy and I are on our knees nightly. We fast. We
pray. We burn votive candles. We make novenas. We attend church
services many times per day.

Nothing happens. Nothing changes.

I even challenge God to man-up and correct His mistake. It
should have been me that was struck down. I am so sure of it that
in the mornings before going to school, I slip into Jan's room and
bargain with God, begging Him to correct His mistake, to take

the life that is in my body and put it into hers and to leave me motionless in that bed.

Nothing changes. Nothing happens.

○—○—○

It is now the summer of 1963. Jan requires constant care. Not just every day. Every hour and minute of every day. My dear mother, struggling to care for small children and to hold a household together, falls deeper and deeper into an abyss of physical and emotional exhaustion. The strain on her would have broken the best of women. My mother was one of the best of women. She holds it all together as long as she can. After more than two years and two more pregnancies, it all falls apart. Jan needs to be put in a home.

Cindy and I are listening from our bedrooms when the social workers come and tell my father that his only choice is to declare bankruptcy, sell the house and move with his family into the poor neighborhoods in the center city. We listen as my mother recounts in tear-drenched sobs how the doctors and the hospital staff are trying to convince her that the compassionate alternative is to just let Jan die, quietly, in her bed without food or water. Just let her die of starvation. After all, they say, there are other children in the family to care for. Life must go on. It is just one of those things.

My parents are adamant that Jan will not be institutionalized, that she will not be mercy-killed and that our family will not slip over the edge into the abyss of poverty. They seek out assistance from Roman Catholic charities, but it is fruitless. We cannot qualify for financial help because we own a nine-hundred-square-foot house.

They seek assistance from the nonprofit organizations that raise money to help children, but Jan does not have a popular disease. Also, she has no prognosis for recovery. No one will ever be able to put her smiling face on a fund-raising poster.

One night, as I am eleven years old, I sit in my bedroom, listening

to the expensively dressed director of a do-gooder agency and his
pert assistant with perfectly coifed hair and coordinated makeup.
Mom has put out tea and coffee and small cookies. My parents look
exhausted but are trying to be polite.

"You cannot escape the fact that you are bringing this problem
on yourself, Mr. Recinella." The Ken doll speaks arrogantly with a
hint of a British accent. "You are refusing to be reasonable."

"How?" sighs my dad. "How am I unreasonable?"

"It is inhumane to keep your daughter alive." The Ken doll
speaks as though no one could disagree. His Barbie doll assistant
nods emphatically at his every word. "It is your moral duty to let
your daughter die. Mercy and economic sense require it."

Dad asks the Ken doll if he has any children. He answers in the
negative. My parents thank them for their trouble and politely show
them to the door.

At the time of Jan's illness, my dad is working long hours of
overtime while also trying to complete night courses that will improve
his earning potential. Now he realizes the magnitude of the darkness
he is up against in the battle to let his daughter live until she dies of
natural causes. Each night he sits for hours, putting small amounts
of food in Jan's mouth and moving her jaws with his hands. He
accomplishes what the doctors said could never happen—he teaches
her to chew reflexively when food is put in her mouth.

They take her off the tube and remove the trach. Dad's super-
human effort is the only reason the do-gooders are not able to starve
Jan to death when she is finally placed in an adult nursing home
years later.

The pains of Jan's illness are not all financial. I accompany my
parents when they take her to the family doctors. Jan has never been
contagious; humans do not acquire encephalitis from other humans.
Still, we must enter and leave the medical offices through the alleys.

The doctors are afraid that, if any of their other patients see Jan, their fears will destroy the doctors' practice. It is the early 1960s. Nothing is handicap accessible. Frequently, I move piles of garbage or maggot-infested trash cans and boxes out of the way so that Dad can get her wheelchair through to the alley door of the doctors' office. My parents comply out of fear, afraid that if they make trouble, no doctor will agree to care for their daughter. If there is a word that rules our lives during those years, it is *fear*.

The Bible says that the antidote for fear is love. After the first few years of Jan's illness, we are at the end of our rope. God knows that we need an antidote for the fears that hold dominion over every moment of our days. God sends us the antidote of love in the form of a nurse named Rose.

In 1964 our family is introduced to a place called Rockhaven, a home for severely ill children. The rambling, pale white, single-story brick building is in a rural area south of Flatrock, about halfway between Detroit and Toledo. Rockhaven has a checkered history. During Prohibition it was a haven for illegal gambling, drinking and probably prostitution. After repeal, it fell out of use and into disrepair. Then an angel saw in its cracked walls and broken windows what no merely mortal eyes could have seen: a haven for severely ill, incurable children. The angel's name is Rose Miller.

The angel is a registered nurse who has had her fill of the State's ways of caring for such children. She decides to do something different, even at great personal sacrifice. It will end up costing her everything she has and more.

The Recinella family meets nurse Rose Miller the same way I presume every family meets Mrs. Miller—we have a seriously ill child who is not going to recover. In southeastern Michigan children like my sister Jan have two possible futures: either the State home or Rockhaven. Mrs. Miller is as thin as a rail and always wears a white nursing uniform with her trademark RN cap. She lives at the house with the children, scores of them. The image of a white-clad nurse named Rose Miller is permanently burned into my mind as a symbol of safety, compassion and refuge from an evil world.

On our first visit to that trapezoid-shaped house, the children in the beds are unlike any we have ever seen before. Seven-year-olds with beards share the building with infants with adult-size heads and children with no arms and no legs. Everywhere are babies with tubes in their sides, in their noses or in their heads. We push outside.

The children in the yard are not as sick as those inside. Some are severely autistic. Others are severely retarded. Many are seriously deformed but still ambulatory. One boy who annoys me greatly has no ears, no nose, no lips and no eyebrows. He wants to touch my ears and to pull on them. At first he is a nuisance, and I try to keep him away from me. Over time I start to understand his fascination, and I let him touch my ears just a little.

Over years of visiting Jan at Rockhaven, we realize that for many of the children there, we are their only visitors. My parents know it too. They never judge or compare. They simply remind us of how hard it has been for us, and that some people can only take so much.

On one particular visit, I am sitting with my mom at Jan's bedside. Cindy and the younger kids are playing in the fenced-in yard with the ambulatory children. Dad is meeting with Mrs. Miller to go over some insurance issues. Jan's bed is in a room of about twenty beds, all of them with children who are not able to go outside. For the eighty-some children in the home, we are the only visitors that day.

"So where are the others?" I ask with typical preteen self-assurance. "Why are we always the only ones here?"

"I don't know," Mom replies without even looking up from stroking Jan's hair. "I do know that God won't ask us what anybody else did—only what we did."

"That doesn't seem very fair to me."

"How can God not be fair?" she asks with a chuckle.

"If God is so fair, how come we are here so many weekends and nobody else is?"

"Maybe God allowed us to be brought here so we can be family for the children whose own families don't know how to be family for them."

O-O-O

In 1965, at the age of fourteen, I enter a residential seminary in Cincinnati, where I live with the friars, for high school, studying to be a Franciscan priest. The payoff, in my mind, is that if I become a priest, then God will have to heal my sister. The problem is that I am not called to the priesthood. By tenth grade, I know it; by twelfth grade, the friars know it. I am expelled five times in my senior year for such infractions as drinking and being off the property at night for dates, but the friars keep suspending the expulsions on the condition that I straighten out and fly right.

When I agree not to apply to seminary college, the friars are relieved. In reality, there seems to be no hope of going to any college at all because I took my college admission exams drunk.

Then the priest who has been my spiritual advisor since my sophomore year calls me in for an appointment. The spiritual advisor appointments are held in parlors off the foyer of the chapel, right at the very front of the seminary building. The doors are glass from top to bottom, framed with wood and covered with a translucent curtain. The four parlor rooms form a horseshoe with the building entrance in the middle of the shoe and the chapel in the center of the open side. The floor is a deeply worn but highly polished terrazzo. In the center of the space stands an ancient grandfather clock that is hand-carved in wood from the Black Forest in Germany.

When Friar Murray arrives from the cloister, I am leaning against the clock, noticing how the click of each swing of the pendulum reverberates through my whole body. He smiles and motions me into the parlor room. The couches look welcoming until you sit in them. No one is supposed to get too comfortable in spiritual direction.

The friar wants to convince me that our God is a God of mercy and of second chances. I listen attentively while thinking to myself that he is not talking about the God I know.

"I think you have beaten yourself up enough for whatever it is that you are punishing yourself for, Dale. God never desires to see you suffer. He certainly is fine with you not flagellating yourself anymore if you are ready to stop." He pauses and allows the words to sink in before asking, "Are you ready to give yourself a break?"

"Sure." I shrug with a total lack of commitment. "But what does that mean?"

"If you choose to do it, I have arranged for you to be accepted provisionally at the Roman Catholic College of the Diocese of Covington, Thomas More. It's up to you."

"What does 'provisionally' mean?"

"Good question. It means they are going to give you a chance to prove you can do the work. If you blow it off, you're out. Really out. We are Franciscans but they are diocesan. When they kick you out, you are out."

"Sure, I'll do it. I mean, what have I got to lose?"

He looks at me in prolonged silence. His intense blue eyes answer my question without saying a word.

Everything. It is all on the line.

3

"What Does It Profit a Man?"

MATTHEW 16:26

AT ORIENTATION FOR Thomas More College, a faculty member from the psychology department finds me, explains his friendship with Friar Murray and leads me to a small room where I must take a career assessment exam. He is a short, wiry man with a large, round something projecting from his left cheek, as if he had the mumps on that side and never recovered. While he runs through the questions and records my responses, with running commentary on my tone of voice and posture, it occurs to me that, if he did not have a crew cut and was not so skinny, the projection would look much smaller.

"The purpose of this assessment," he finally explains to sum up our exercise, "is to determine what you should declare as a major. It is quite clear from these scores that your strongest career track is pastoral."

"What? Is this a bad joke?" I can feel my temper about to go Italian on him.

"Pastoral. That means taking care of people emotionally and spiritually," he explains with a bit of backpedaling and a great deal of defensiveness. "That is very important. Why would that be a joke?"

"Because I'm Catholic, and I am not called to celibacy—that's why. I was just redirected out of the seminary because I like girls too much. And you want me to declare a major that will be useless unless I'm a priest?"

The discussion that ensues is not angry but not really cordial either. The doctor compromises a lot. We declare a four-year major in mathematical economics with a two-year degree in computers and operations research and a minor in a Hellenic language. That is as far from "pastoral" as I know how to get.

○-○-○

The first of nineteen part-time jobs that put me through college is head breakfast cook in the college's privatized cafeteria, which is primarily for the dorm students. The work is largely uneventful until St. Patrick's Day. In the spirit of the Emerald Isle, I put green food coloring in the oatmeal, the scrambled eggs, the pancakes and the donuts. The situation quickly devolves into a food riot, after which I am only allowed to keep my job upon a sworn oath that no deviations will ever be made from the company menus . . . never . . . ever.

Other jobs come and go, including serving as a resident assistant in the dorm and night manager of an airport discount parking and car rental lot. I run hot and cold steel stampings and am the first and, at that time, only Cincinnati driver for Federal Express out of their new service center at the airport in northern Kentucky. My third-shift adventure pushing hot-lead galleys in the composing room of the *Cincinnati Post* is especially challenging. The most physically demanding of my litany of part-time jobs is working on the railroad docks in the Teamsters Local 100 on midnight shift at Liberty Cherry and Fruit in Latonia, Kentucky.

In the course of all this life experience, including getting married in June of 1973, I am able to get a college education. In fact, there is time to be active in student government, to sit on the college board of trustees as the student representative, to work as a student pro-life activist, to publish poetry, to take down business awards and to write a thesis full of Greek mathematical symbols and three-dimensional graphs.

In the end, as graduate school looms, it all comes down to test scores, the big three: LSAT, GMAT and GRE. The first is for law school, the second for business school and the third for graduate school in general areas. I score off the charts on the LSAT and almost off the charts on the GMAT. That means law school and, possibly, a double graduate degree in law and business. All it will take is money.

The deductibles and the co-pays for my first child's upcoming delivery in June of 1974 need to be paid off. I make the trip to the union hall and beg for three months of scab work after graduation and before moving to law school, wherever that will be. They promise to do what they can.

Letters of acceptance from Harvard Law and Graduate Business Schools come without money. The admissions staff at the University of Notre Dame say they are impressed by the test scores, grades, activities and references. More than that, they have faculty who were attending the nationwide meeting of right-to-life groups at Macalester College in St. Paul, Minnesota, when I spoke on funding college student organizations. Notre Dame comes across with money.

At the awards night banquet in May 1974, the Thomas More College dean of students announces that I am the first person in the history of Notre Dame to receive a double full fellowship in two graduate schools, including living expenses. We are headed to the Golden Dome for a four-year JD/MBA, all expenses paid.

In June I am present when my firstborn is delivered. By August the union job has paid off the maternity bills, and it is time to empty the apartment in Florence, Kentucky, and move to married housing on campus at Notre Dame.

At this point, God and I have been operating at arm's length, to say the least, since graduation from seminary. It has been rare for me to make Sunday church in college. It will be rare in law school, as well. My justification is an overload of school, family and work. Too many things are on my list. When God pays the rent, then I'll have time to go to church. I do not notice that my rent and my law school tuition are being paid by Him. I am looking only at the things attributable to my efforts.

Even with the rent and tuition handled, the intense demands of a national law school and a second child on the way lead to the inevitable conclusion that it is time to end school and start life. My wife and I decide to drop the MBA portion of the program and accelerate my law courses in order to finish by December of 1976, in just two and a half years. This step opens the possibility of using a law degree in ways different from those I first imagined.

The social justice passions of President Theodore Hesburgh have infused Notre Dame with concern for the underprivileged and the downtrodden, reviving Franciscan sentiments in me that have lain dormant since seminary. Maybe it is time to try my hand at caring for the underclass. In the second year of the law program, I accept a part-time position with the two-man firm that holds the public defender contract for Berrien County and Benton Harbor, Michigan, just north of the Indiana border.

My initial assignment is to visit a new client at the jail, where he is being held until arraignment on numerous violent charges. My gait reeks with a false sense of nobility that only a newbie law clerk could manage on his first trip to the local pokey. My airs of enthusiasm wane as the guards plant me in front of a cell with a door of crisscrossing steel bars and inform me that the huge naked man, grunting and rocking in a crouch on his haunches against the rear corner of the cell, is my new client. None of the downtrodden I had heard about in seminary or seen rescued in the movies looked like this guy.

With a *harrumph* forceful enough to push a low-pitched sound out of my terror-stricken lips, I introduce myself to the new client. Frankly, he does not appear very interested. Instead, he lets loose in one motion with both a deafening shriek and a huge lunge from the rear to the front door of the cell. Before I can even think about what is happening, he grabs my tie through the cell door and vigorously and repeatedly yanks on it—hammering me again and again against the metal bars.

By the time the guards are able to cut off my tie by maneuvering a scissors between the steel bars and my severely bruised ribs, I have incurred injuries to my throat and significant purple welts in surreal box patterns of parallel and perpendicular lines from my forehead to my knees. I appear to have come out the loser in a death match with a giant waffle iron. The jailers virtually choke themselves trying to look sympathetic while stifling their convulsive laughter. My wife, a seasoned nurse at a local hospital who disapproved of the job in the first place, observes that I have the most geometrically precise bruises she has ever seen. Pity and sympathy are in short supply all the way around.

The next day I drive to the local five-and-dime to purchase a dark blue clip-on tie. Then I visit the law school placement office and delete all poverty and criminal law jobs from my prospects. I will finish the current semester-long commitment in Benton Harbor, but there will be no new interviews for me, except with multinational companies and prestigious commercial and financial law firms. My stroll on the other side of the tracks is over. The downtrodden will not tread on me again.

By the end of the spring semester of 1976, I have only one semester of law school left to complete. I head to the World Headquarters Complex of Ford Motor Company in Dearborn, Michigan, for a summer clerkship. They immediately assign me to the discretionary investment activities in the finance and insurance subsidiaries. That is logical based upon my undergraduate degrees in operations research and mathematical economics. I return to finish law school with a permanent job in my pocket.

After the fall semester of 1976, my new career takes off. The company is all-out investing in major pieces of equipment to the tune of billions of dollars. On the list are fleets of airframes, 747s, DC-10s, L-1011s and their engines. Really large ships are on the books, the new super oil tankers, oceangoing barges and the super container ships. So are telecommunications satellites, huge mainframe computer systems, drag lines, railroad cars and diesel train engines. All of these are life-size versions of every boy's favorite toys. I love it.

Enthusiasm for my new work and the parade of new feelings of self-importance are boundless. I become my job, a résumé of closed deals. I could do it forever. But forever is cut short by problems in the Middle East, the long-term aftermath of the Arab oil embargo.

All of a sudden, gasoline and gas stations are no longer convenient. Lines at service stations are miles long. People are rioting and shooting at each other over a few gallons of gasoline. The National Guard, with tanks and armored personnel carriers, are standing watch over the service stations that still have gasoline to sell.

Americans are asking previously unheard of questions: How many miles can we drive on the ten gallons of gas we just waited twelve hours to buy? How soon will we have to endure this again?

The answers to these questions are less popular with the car-buying public than the proposals to switch to the metric system. Americans want a solution that will end this pain fast. In other countries gasoline has cost several times American prices. Foreign automakers from Germany and Japan have been producing fuel-efficient cars to market in those countries for over ten years. Now they stand ready to annihilate Detroit and the American domestic manufacturing economy in one fell swoop.

The company studies the situation and determines that retooling its plants to make fuel-efficient cars will require an immediate investment of over $11 billion. The company looks down upon its vast resources with a bloodthirst for cash and sells almost all of its discretionary investments in a matter of months. It is the right move for the company. It is time for me to move elsewhere. In June 1979 I make the big move to private practice. The winning combination turns out to be a medium-size Miami firm that handles extensive transactional work for money center banks.

In the summer of 1979 the big news in Miami is real estate. There are office buildings to build in Coral Gables and the pricey new Brickell Avenue area south of downtown Miami. Also in the market are luxury condominiums on the waterfront of Biscayne Bay, on the islands and on Key Biscayne, and apartments, condos, homes and town houses all the way up the coast through Fort Lauderdale, into Palm Beach. Southeast Florida land is hot and money is pouring in from foreign investors who buy five or six half-million-dollar units at a time.

Unfortunately, the surest thing to follow a great real estate market is a lousy real estate market. The two most popular explanations for the collapse of Miami's real estate market in 1982 are totally unrelated: first, the Miami riots and, second, Vice President George Bush's task force to wipe out drug trafficking in southeast Florida. Whatever the reason, Miami real estate dives. Consequently, I am not very busy when Miami's newly directed and fast growing seaport needs help with a financing crisis. The long-range plan for the Miami Seaport envisions development of world-class cruise line business on part of its property and installation of massive ten-story gantry cranes for container ships on the balance.

In March 1982 the seaport's new venture verges on falling into Humpty Dumpty pieces. A creative financier has put together a plan to finance the gantry cranes, but the deal blows apart at the closing table in New York City.

Some local people know of my legal experience in corporate finance before moving to Miami. Out of the clear blue sky, I am summoned to a lunch meeting at the Standard Club, a site of Miami power lunches for decades before the term was invented. The questions are few. My answers are short. Basically, I say I am willing to take a look at the deal but can make no promises.

One hour later, I walk alone into a meeting with the county finance director, the assistant county attorney, the financial advisor, the assistant seaport director, the financing team and, by conference hookup, the lawyer for the company that is the equity investor in the cranes. To my shock and chagrin, I discover that these people have been told that I claimed at lunch to know what the problem is and have virtually guaranteed that I can work it out.

As I introduce myself to the tense assembly, it seems to me that the only certainty will be my fleeing Miami for a new job out west somewhere, probably Durango, Colorado, where a close friend from law school has a thriving practice in insurance defense litigation.

Six weeks later we are in New York to close the deal. This is it. If it does not close, the Miami Seaport will become another version of Star Island, which has been parceled out for high-priced homes by real estate developers. After six days of around-the-clock negotiations, the deal closes. It is May of 1982, and public finance, representing state and local governments on Wall Street and in the world capital markets, is my new law practice.

As we are gathering up and sorting the documents into sets, my secretary calls to inform me that divorce papers are being served on me at the office in Miami.

○─○─○

Almost a year later, it is now March of 1983. The route to and from the airport has become so familiar to me that I can make it in my sleep. I am barely conscious of traffic and tollbooths as I swing out of the Miami International Airport onto westbound 836 and connect to southbound 826 for the 25-mile drive to the neighborhood in south Dade County that is now home. How strange that I feel more at home on the road than at home.

My professional life flows easily from one peak to another, deal closing to deal closing. The distance from that to the disaster of my personal life seems much farther than the drive from the airport. Just four weeks ago my second wife and I moved into this sprawling ranch with a pool, just a half mile from the Atlantic Ocean. The marriage lasted less than a month. I am coming home to an empty house.

The silence that takes over after the engine stops in my driveway seems too pervasive. I can barely force myself out of the car. It takes forever to walk the twenty feet of red tile porch from the drive to the front door. I hear only the hollow ring of my key turning in the latch, followed by the strange echo of my feet against the vestibule tile. My house is empty. My soul feels empty.

There's a bottle of wine in the refrigerator and a bottle of vodka in the freezer. By the time my brother Gary arrives, I have established a beachhead on the dining room floor. Anchored cross-legged like some Hollywood Indian chief, I am sitting with my back to the emptiness of my house, gazing out the sliding glass doors to the pool, sipping wine right from the bottle and smoking a filterless Camel. There is no ashtray. The rug is doing just fine.

Gary does not sit, but stands behind, between me and the dining room chandelier, casting a long shadow before me, over me and past me. Gary is the number-four child in a brood of eight. I am the eldest. He has spent his entire life in my shadow. Tonight is his moment.

"Thanks for coming," I grunt without looking up. My eyes are rigidly locked on the pool, as though my gaze is holding it in the ground, as if even gravity cannot be trusted to hold the world together anymore.

"No problem," he answers in a tone of voice I would expect if I had just asked him to take out the garbage. "So what's the situation here?"

So what's the situation here? I mock him in my head, without daring to let him hear it.

"I'm remodeling."

"Oh sure, that must be what the problem is." He steps into my line of sight, obscuring the pool and demanding my attention. "Got any other clues as to what went wrong here?"

I want to tell him that he better get out of the way, because if the pool disappears while he is blocking my view, he will have to replace it. But instead, with my father's voice from years ago, I just sigh. "You make a better door than a window."

"Does this crash-and-burn situation look familiar?"

Oh great. Now I'm in for it. It was a mistake to call him over. Gary never said things like "What's the situation here?" or "crash and burn" until after his stint in the marines. He used to be just a nice, easygoing guy. He was the kid who followed too close when I was swinging the bat and ended up with a broken nose, and then apologized for crowding me. The marines made a man out of him. They ruined him. Now everything is serious, so serious he has gone to accounting school and earned a four-year degree. Gary hated school before the marines. Now he is a CPA working in Miami at the local firm that works closely with my law firm.

"Don't overreact, bro." I mimic his stressed tone. "It's just an empty house. Every house I ever lived in was empty when I bought it. It won't be empty for long."

"No, Dale. It's not just an empty house. It's a disaster, and not the first one. Another one. Look at you. What are you doing with your life? Your business may be fine, but what about everything else? Weren't you just all tore up in the hospital three months ago? Are you getting a picture?"

"It was four months ago." I chafe against his credibility with exaggerated sarcasm, while standing and walking to the glass door wall, leaning against it with both hands and making round circles of mist on the surface as I exhale cigarette smoke.

"Three months, four months—what's the point? If you don't care about yourself, what about your kids?" He paces behind me toward the living room.

"My kids are fine." I shrug before turning to face him and the emptiness of my house.

"Man, I used to think you were it. Big-time lawyer with a big-time practice. Summa cum laude this and magna cum laude that and law review. Big deals, big plans, big things." His hands move up and down in gestures that confirm our shared ethnic heritage, and finally they rest limply aside his hips. "I wanted to be just like you. I thought you were really something. But look at you. What good is all that if your personal life is a disaster zone? You're a wreck. Everything about you and around you is a wreck—except, of course, your big career." He shakes his head and lowers his eyes. "Dale, I don't want to be anything like you. I'm almost ash—"

He stops himself mid-word and turns away, his back disappearing into the empty space of the living room. I slide down to the floor, my back against the pool door wall, and disappear into the empty space of my thoughts. Yes, my marriages were a mess. Yes, my personal life is a mess.

As I light another Camel, it occurs to me that I have never intentionally made a stupid decision, have never intentionally chosen to do something that would end in disaster. I have always made the best choices I knew how to make. It always ends the same way. This does feel disturbingly familiar.

It was just four months ago that I was lying in Mercy Hospital. I had represented Dade County on the first lease deal to be taken to the public markets by a Florida local government, a deal that most everyone said could not be done. We had a team of top-notch financial and legal people, and we worked around the clock for the last two weeks before closing.

Closing is when Wall Street puts up the money. The day before closing, everybody meets and signs all the papers at a pre-closing so that first thing in the morning Wall Street will pay the money. In this case, $13 million to buy police cars and firefighting equipment. When we wrapped up the pre-closing at my law firm at one-thirty A.M., everything was done except for the mayor of Dade County signing some papers. I was to meet him at his office at eight. The money would move at nine.

We all left the pre-closing and went out for a two A.M. dinner in Coconut Grove. Two hours later, I fell asleep at the wheel on my way home and ran into a tree. It was only two blocks from my condominium and I had not been moving very fast. My head had busted out the windshield and my knees had broken the steering column, but I could walk.

I made it to my apartment, cleaned off the blood, changed clothes and arranged to get to my office to pick up the necessary papers and arrive at the mayor's office by quarter to eight. The mayor of Dade County signed the papers, and I returned to the closing room at my law firm.

I told no one what had happened. I did not notice that people were alarmed at my appearance. I did not know that I was as pale as a ghost and shaking like a leaf in a strong wind. I just kept smoking, drinking coffee and calling the bank in New York for confirmation that the money had been wired.

By ten-thirty the money was confirmed and the deal closed. Wall Street had bought its first publicly offered tax exempt lease out of Florida. I would render tax law and securities law opinions on over a billion dollars more in such leases bought by Wall Street out of Florida in the next ten years. But in October of 1982, I could not have guessed that. All I knew was that the deal was closed. I congratulated everyone, walked up the hall to a friend's office and asked her to drive me to the hospital. I did not tell her what had happened. She did not ask. I just said I did not feel good. It was true.

She dropped me off at the emergency room entrance. Three minutes later the law firm was notified that a man with business cards from the firm had walked into the emergency room and collapsed on the floor, unconscious. I was not in good shape.

During the next several days, almost every one of my law partners, most of my friends and even my first wife visited and begged me to stop. Stop drinking. Stop running. Stop moving. Stop.

But I am not able to stop. I do not know how to stop. In law school I could not stop. In college I could not stop. In my four years living at a seminary for high school I could not stop. It is as if a huge locomotive is constantly bearing down on me, a massive freight train of shadows relentlessly approaching me from behind. I cannot seem to step out of its way. I am bound to the rails. I cannot veer left or right and let it by. If it catches up with me, it will run over me. My only hope is to keep moving, to stay ahead of it, to not let it catch me.

Yes, Gary is right. I think. This is familiar. Every time I crash

I always assume it is because I have not run fast enough. So I keep running faster. And the crashes keep getting bigger. My personal life is a mess.

"What do you suggest?" I call out to my brother in the living room.

He seems stunned that I would ask his opinion. "What?" His face is soft but determined.

"What do you suggest?"

It's the opening he is hoping for. He walks back into my view and plants himself in the center of my gaze.

"You've tried it your way. Now try it His way. Give your life to Jesus, right now, tonight, right here. Let Him steer your life from this moment on."

I am expecting Gary to announce a ten-point plan to get my life on track, a checklist and budget. He has blindsided me. I am caught completely unawares.

Give my life to Jesus? I almost laugh out loud. I rise to my feet and walk through the empty rooms, mulling it over. *What does that mean? What will that accomplish?*

"You're afraid, aren't you?" He follows me into the kitchen, where I am trashing the empty wine bottle and meditating on the slurry of iced vodka.

How can I be afraid of something that does not mean anything to me? I slam the freezer shut, deciding that vodka will probably make me puke tonight.

"How do I do that?" I finally shrug.

"You say it. You say, 'Jesus, I give You my life. I don't want anything unless You want it for me.' And then I will lead you in a prayer, the sinner's prayer."

"We were all baptized, you know," I counter, stalling for time. "What will this do?"

"It will change everything."

His sincerity is total. He really believes it. This brother of mine, whom I have known for 25 years and have never seen excited about anything except the Detroit Tigers and the marines, has made the most enthusiastic presentation of his life. I do not know if it is all true, but I know he thinks it is true.

"Okay," I say with a nod, sweeping my hand in a gesture that takes in the empty rooms of my empty house and my empty soul. "What have I got to lose?"

Only years later will I realize that this is the moment when the thief steals into the house, that because of this moment I will lose every illusory thing I have thought important and be given everything that really matters.

4

Giving God's Way a Chance

"**What does it mean** to gives one's life to Jesus?" That is the question I ask myself many times as the days pass. Gary is demanding that I do something meaningful, like start attending a Bible study with him. In the meantime, he wants me to move from the last row to the front row in church on Sunday.

Because I try to be a good father, I always take the children to Sunday church. They sit in the second to last row, and I make sure they listen to every word the pastor says. I sit in the last row behind them and mark up documents. I bill the time to clients.

Now Gary, who is not above frequently reminding me that I have given my life to Jesus and reneging means certainty of damnation, is dragging me and the kids out of the house early enough to get the front row at church. If we were still going to my old church, we could get the front row fifteen minutes after the service has started. My old church is like the churches of my childhood: fire and brimstone, frequent sermons on low collections and so many old ladies saying their rosaries that you can barely hear the priest over the banging of the beads against the pews. I like going to the old church. I can get a lot of work done without being distracted.

But Gary will not have that. He keeps harping at me about a personal relationship with Jesus and about worship and singing. And he insists that we have to go to Sunday service at St. Louis Parish, where you have to arrive an hour early to get any seat at all, let alone the front row. I agree to try it just once. What have I got to lose?

As soon as we pull into the parking lot, I know this is a mistake. This church is not square like I think a church is supposed to be. It is round, shaped like an upside-down bowl. People are not quietly locking their cars, walking reluctantly to the building with downcast eyes and slipping into the side doors like they are supposed to. No, these people are waving at each other and running up to each other. Some of them are even hugging each other.

When this obsessively touchy-feely crowd starts in our direction, I grab my kids, shoot into the door and almost kill myself falling on the stairs. To my way of thinking, churches are supposed to be nice and flat, with real long pews so that you can quietly and mindlessly amble to your favorite spot and establish yourself. That way nobody else can get anywhere near you.

This church, if that's what it is, is built like a theater inside with half-circle rows of pews that are really short. Even if I can secure the end of the pew, there will be people all over me. The whole design of the church telescopes down, narrowing into a focus on a small white table that might be an altar. Behind that are huge walls reflecting overhead projectors with words to songs and pictures that change.

How am I going to get any work done in here?

Gary and his girlfriend lead us down to the very front row. My kids are already clapping and bouncing and smiling, behavior in church that would have landed me in the cellar as a child. I order them to stop, but they cannot hear me.

"I am out of here, man," I yell to Gary over the heads of my children. "There is no way that this is a Catholic church." It is pointless. He cannot hear me.

Then, even as I am in midsentence, a silence falls on the whole church, a bell rings, words appear on the wall and people all over the church start singing. I am too stunned to react. My children are humming. Why do they know what to do, but I don't?

Finally, a guy comes out dressed like a Catholic priest, and he starts saying prayers just like they do at a normal Roman Catholic service.

I take in the whole 270 degrees of church behind me. The aisles are full of people singing. There is absolutely no way to get from where I am to any of the doors or even a window. I am a prisoner and will have to ride this one out. Whoever that guy is down on the stage dressed like a Catholic priest, I will watch him like a hawk.

After the Gospel he steps to a microphone. Now I will find out whether he's really a priest.

"I am the pastor of this parish, and I want to welcome all the Christians to this celebration of faith."

That is bad. He sounds way too happy, like he is a phony.

"Now, if all of you would please extend your hands and pray that the Holy Spirit will give me the words to speak."

That is it, I mutter mentally. *If I am going to have to get here an hour early and put up with all this noise and frivolity, the least he could do is prepare a homily.* I look around, however, and nobody else seems to be annoyed. The entire church stretches out their hands and starts praying; at least I think that is what they are doing. Finally it stops. We can sit down.

Now, instead of going to the podium like I presume a priest should, the pastor walks toward us. He stands right in front of us and looks right at us, from two feet away, as he talks. I feel like I am going to come right out of my skin. I want to scream to him and the whole church, "Back off! Get out of my face!"

I make it through what seems like a service, but even then we cannot leave. None of these people want to go home. They are all hugging each other again and leaning against each other like they have not seen one another in twenty years. I elbow my way outside, and they are doing it there too. There are donuts and coffee in the vestibule. I am feeling claustrophobic. Donuts or no donuts, I have got to get out of here.

I have no intention of ever going back to St. Louis Parish, whatever kind of church it really is. But now the children are in on it. They love it. My brother has built an alliance of my own seed against me. To add insult to injury, he wants me to attend the parish Bible study for single and divorced people.

"Absolutely not!" I insist. "In the first place, I don't think that Roman Catholics read the Bible. Only Protestants do that. In the second place, the Catholic Church does not recognize divorce. There is no such thing as a Catholic Bible study for single and divorced."

"Shut up, meatball. You're going."

My brother the marine. He does not remember how to lose anymore, whether it's pinochle or saving my soul. Life is too short to fight this battle. I agree to go, just once. What have I got to lose?

The St. Louis Bible study for single and divorced meets on Tuesdays, a weeknight, at six-thirty. So right off the bat I know none of them have kids. I do not remember ever not having kids. I was rinsing yellow, brown and green turds out of cloth diapers in a pail when I was five. I was making meals and potty training snot-nosed siblings when I was nine. My oldest son was born when I was twenty-two. Now I'm thirty-one and have a nine-year-old son and six-year-old and three-year-old daughters. There have always been kids, and I would never schedule anything for six-thirty on a weeknight.

My law firm is downtown. Jeanette, the three-year-old, is in day care at the Presbyterian church on Brickell Avenue, two blocks from my office. Tony and Christina attend the Episcopal school near Cutler Ridge Mall and are picked up after school by an older woman who keeps them until Jeanette and I come home. It is a long-haul, everyday round trip on U.S. 1 between Caribbean Boulevard and downtown Miami. After our daily evening streak south, Jeanette and I pick up Tony and Christina. At that point my day is only half over. Going out on a Tuesday night is going to be tough.

I line up a high school girl who sits for me to watch the kids on Tuesday night. She is the children's favorite, which makes it easier to leave them after being away from them all day. She does not drive yet, so I must return from work, pick up the children, feed the children, put everybody in the car and fetch the sitter, take all of them back to the house, go to the Bible study, come home, put everybody in the car, take the sitter home, return home and put everybody to bed. This better be one heck of a Bible study.

Once I start attending, I will find out that this Bible study follows a set schedule. It starts with a social half hour. Then from seven o'clock until nine o'clock there is praise and worship, singing and sharing of Scripture. From nine until ten there is a real social hour. I cannot get there until seven, and the sitter has to be home before nine-thirty. No social time for me. This will truly be a spiritual experience and nothing else.

Gary decides to ride with me the first time. He says it is a spiritual companion thing. I know he is just making sure I show up. Gary has been going to this Bible study for almost a year. He started attending with his girlfriend.

"It is really great. You will love it."

"Yeah, I'm sure." My voice is noncommittal. "Which room at the church do they meet in?"

"We meet at people's apartments."

"The priests are willing to come to people's apartments?" I am half-amazed, half-suspicious.

"There's no priests, meathead. It's for single and divorced."

"Wait a minute. Are you telling me that you people have been getting together at each other's apartments to read the Bible for almost a year, and there are no priests with you?"

"You don't need a priest to read the Bible." By his anger and the fact that he is using our father's voice, I know he thinks I am creating a pretext for backing out of my commitment. "The Bible's been translated into English, you know. Can you read English?"

"The contracts I write are in English, but my clients and the other side want a lawyer to tell them what it means. Priests are supposed to tell you what the Bible means. Who died and left you as an expert in Scripture?"

"Don't pull your lawyer crap on me. You're going."

The group is meeting that night at the apartment of a Miami-Dade Community College student. It's a third-floor walk-up in a fourth-rate apartment complex on the west side of U.S. 1, past Cutler Ridge Mall. We walk into the assembled group of about fifteen young men and women, mostly early- to mid-twenties, just as the opening prayers have begun. Gary leads me to a seat in the corner of the living room, a gray folding chair. He sits opposite me, in the dining area, next to his girlfriend. I spend the rest of the night looking at the woman with the guitar, who is sitting on the other side of Gary's girlfriend and leads the singing.

She sings like an angel. Her features are delicate but she has a commanding presence. I figure she is about five feet, ten or eleven inches; it is hard to tell with her sitting. Her blond hair is really blond, no roots, and is tapered in an expensive cut. Her clothes are tasteful, distinctive and not off-the-rack. She pronounces her words with exquisite diction, a sharpness that says she is her own person and that she draws lines easily. She only looks my way once or twice the whole evening, smiling sweetly and making eye contact both times. Without a single word between us, I read her loud and clear—class, poise and smarts. I try to listen to all the sharing about the Bible, but my mind is elsewhere. I have got to meet this lady. Who is she? What is she doing here?

Because Gary and I arrive late and have to leave before the ending social hour, I meet no one, not even her. I know I will be back.

"So, what did you think?" Gary's voice is not subtle about how badly he wants for me to be excited. I try my best.

"It was really interesting. I'm glad you had me come." Maybe this is the time to fish for facts, while he is hoping to get me back here. "I think I might like to come back."

"Great. Great." He turns on the final landing to start down the last flight to the parking lot. "What did you like the best?"

"Oh, that's easy." I breathe deeply. It is now or never. "By the way, who's the cute blonde that was playing the guitar and sings like an angel?"

Gary stops so abruptly that I run right into his back, but not hard enough to prevent him from swinging around and planting a full-blown sucker punch soundly into my gut and up to my diaphragm.

"Listen, buster," he says to the back of my head as I hang on to the railing and suck wind from the stairs. "You're here for your soul. Don't you dare go picking up any of the girls in this group. They don't know about guys like you. You leave her alone."

"Okay, okay." I am suddenly aware that I have never before tried to speak while sucking in. "I was just curious." I still cannot straighten. I have been smoking filterless Camels since I was in the Teamsters at nineteen years old, and I have worked my way up to over four packs per day. As I wheeze into the stairs, which will not stay still, I wonder if this is what emphysema feels like.

"Did they teach you any other communication skills in the marines?" I am finally regaining my composure.

"I'm sorry," Gary responds, sounding truly apologetic, "but she's a really nice girl, and she's been through hell. She doesn't need to get mixed up with somebody like you."

"Thanks for your concern," I say out loud, thinking to myself that I'll have to find out some other way.

After two more weeks of attending the Bible study, I know no more about her or anybody else. Years later I will find out that my brother, for my own good and with my best interest at heart, has called an emergency meeting of the group (except for the blonde), and they have all committed to protect her identity from me. The fact that I cannot talk to her at the Bible study is working in their favor. But in time, their efforts and the problems of my schedule are meant to be overcome.

On the first week of May 1983, St. Louis Parish hosts a coffee-house for a pair of Christian singers. I decide to go and take the children on the chance that the blond guitar player from the Bible study might be there. I am successful in keeping my plan a secret up until the last moment, but the children rat me out to Gary and ask if he is going with us. Now I am being escorted under protective custody.

It turns out most of the Bible study group is there, including the mystery woman, who I surmise is tight with Gary's girlfriend. We are all sitting at a large, round table.

Gary's girlfriend is sitting to my right, between me and the blond guitar player. Another lady from the group is sitting to my left. My three children are sitting at the same table opposite me, with Gary positioned among them, looking back smugly and nodding at me every few minutes to let me know my jailer is paying attention. I take note that the round table puts my jailer much farther from me than the blond guitar player is. Also, it's pretty dark and pretty noisy. My advantage.

Gary's girlfriend, who I will learn is the mystery woman's college sorority sister and best friend, sits with her back to me and keeps the object of my interest talking right up until the first set starts. I survey the situation and determine that coffee will continue to be served at the booth in the rear throughout the set. I've noticed that during the Bible studies the guitar player drinks coffee. My advantage.

Gary is sitting with the kids. My advantage.

About halfway through the first set, the couple on stage stops for a breath and to sip water. Now is the time. I stand and lean forward all the way across the big round table toward my brother, almost lying across it from the waist up.

"Gary, will you stay here and keep an eye on the kids while I get some coffee?"

"Sure." He responds predictably, always the good uncle.

In one motion, as I reach halfway to standing, I turn to the blond guitar player. "Can I get you some coffee?"

She knows I am talking to her and coyly responds, "No, thank you." It is the first time she has ever spoken to me, but I sense she is just being appropriate and would really love for me to get her coffee. My brother is fuming, but he has already lost. Instinctively, I up the ante.

I stand straight and turn to another lady from the Bible study group who happens to be sitting at my left. She quickly accepts my invitation to join me for coffee. As we turn our backs to the table and walk to the coffee booth, I can barely resist turning to look back. Once at the booth, I lean against the ledge and count in my head as this new lady stands at my right and orders her drink. One, two, three . . .

"I think I would like some coffee," says the now familiar voice of the blond guitar player who is suddenly standing at my left.

"Great," I speak quickly. "What's your name?"

"Susan." That is all she can say. Gary's girlfriend is suddenly standing between us. It does not matter. I have found out the most important thing. The interest is mutual.

I still cannot be at the Bible study during the social times. But there are a lot of ways to skin a cat. As I contemplate the situation, it becomes clear that the problem is the way I have been framing the challenge. I have been approaching it as a religious thing. I need to reframe it. How would I analyze the variables and solve the problem if this were business?

Of the group of twenty or so people that comprise the St. Louis Bible Study for single and divorced, there is one doctor, one lawyer (me), one CPA (Gary) and a nurse (Gary's girlfriend). All the rest seem to be students or hardworking folks barely making ends meet. It is time to help them out a little.

At the next gathering I pass out a flyer inviting everyone to a pool party at my house that Saturday. I will provide the steaks. They just need to bring a swimsuit, their Bibles, of course, and chips. Everybody shows up, including Susan. It is a wonderful party. We share the Scriptures before the eating begins. After swimming and pool volleyball we sing beautiful praise and worship songs so gently that the next day my neighbors tell me they opened their windows so they could listen.

By all accounts, it is a great gathering. With my children running around, I have only a few opportunities to talk to Susan. Before the party breaks up, Gary and his girlfriend agree to come for dinner Monday evening. To my utter amazement, Gary's girlfriend brings Susan with her. A few weeks later I am able to ask Gary's date the obvious question, "After all those weeks of protecting Susan from meeting me, what possessed you to call her and invite her to join us for dinner?"

This very spiritual woman shrugs matter-of-factly. "The Lord told me to."

The Monday dinner with the four of us is over about eight o'clock. By ten o'clock, Gary and his date are weary of listening as Susan and I get to know each other. They excuse themselves. We end up talking until three A.M.

She is the first woman I have ever met who can listen to the technical description of a complicated financing scheme and ask incisive questions about the mechanics. We talk about our families, our jobs, our hopes and our failures. She is finishing up her doctorate in child and family psychology.

After walking her to her car in the driveway and waving as she pulls away, I find myself standing inside the foyer of my home, leaning my head against the front door. *Are You kidding? Is this for real?*

It occurs to me that maybe this is one of those things that should be out of my hands. Maybe this is one of those things that you give to Jesus when you give Jesus your life. I sit for a long while mulling that over. Finally, I decide to do it.

"Jesus," I say, just between Him and me, "I really like this lady. She is twenty-for-twenty on my list of everything I wish a partner would have. I think I really want this relationship. But I do not have a good track record, so I do not want any relationship unless You want it for me. Jesus, I am giving this to You."

Sleep finally comes at about four on Tuesday morning.

By Wednesday morning, I could kick myself all the way back to downtown Miami, at least 35 miles from the small law office where I am sitting near Andrews Avenue in downtown Fort Lauderdale. I talked with her until the middle of the night on Monday and did not ask her for her phone number, not even her work number. I do not even know how to spell her last name. Her maiden name is easy—Ward. But her married name from her first husband—what was it? She works with children at some social service agency. How many can there be in Dade County?

The operator at information is incredulous, and more than a little peeved. "You want the phone number for all the social service agencies in Dade County that work with children? Do you have any idea what you're asking for? Don't you have anything that might narrow it down, like an address or a name?"

"Well, I know it's somewhere near Kendall."

"Oh good." Her New York accent smacks with a sarcasm that says that two-thirds of Dade County is somewhere near Kendall. The helpful public servant mutters to herself about the fact that I am wasting her time and pushes unseen buttons that cause strange clicks and tones at my end of the line.

"Here's ten. Start with these." The transplanted northerner rattles off the numbers too fast to copy. "If those don't work, call back for some more." She dispenses with me, both of us well aware that if I call back, some other unfortunate lady working for minimum wage will be stuck trying to help me.

I begin dialing the eight numbers I was able to jot on my yellow pad. My question to each of the inevitable female voices that answer is the same. So is my plea.

"Good morning. I'm trying to reach a psychology intern from Nova who is working with children at your agency. Her name is Susan. Can you direct me to her?"

The responses are also consistent. "What?"

On my sixth dialing, a helpful older woman breaks ranks and provides real intel. "We got no psychologists here, mister. Try Youth 'n' Family Services."

"Where are they located?"

"Right off Kendall by 112."

"Do you have the phone number?"

As I jot down this latest number, I know that this will probably be the place where she works. She will probably be there. I will probably end up talking to her. This is not the chase anymore. This is the encounter.

Like most men of my culture, I have been prepared for a lifetime of chasing: chasing the ball, chasing the goal, chasing the fish and the squirrel, chasing the woman, chasing the job, chasing the good life, even chasing God. But I have had no preparation for the encounter.

Why is my heart pounding as I dial this new number? Is it because she might say no or because she might say yes? The line rings a third time.

"Dade County Youth and Family Services."

"Good morning. I'm trying to reach a psychology intern from Nova who is working with children at your agency. Her name is Susan. Can you direct me to her?"

"Ah, let me see. Hold, please."

A train rumbling nearby steals my thoughts, triggering a memory of an old black-and-white movie I watched as a child at my grandfather's house, something about a voice in the mirror, something about a man on skid row who is awakened from a drunken slumber by the intense light of an approaching locomotive. He stumbles to his feet, realizing that he has passed out on the tracks and is within seconds of being crushed by a train. In sheer terror, without thought, he jumps or falls out of harm's way just in time, as the cold steel flanges of the engine tear at his clothes. He stumbles home and confronts his reflection in the mirror.

"I'll transfer you now." The reverie is broken. I brace for the encounter.

"This is Susan."

I know it is her. Her voice is light and alive as she says her own name in that most unusual way, with an exaggerated accent on the first syllable, as if to say, "I'm not like any other Susan you ever met. I may have a common name, but I'm a very uncommon woman."

I stumble through. She agrees to dinner. I am to pick her up at eight-thirty. I get her address. Directions. Even her home phone number and the spelling of her last name.

Where shall I take her? The objective is to impress her permanently. There is only one place. I make another call.

"Is Max there? Great, let me talk to him. This is Mr. Recinella." The only thing that can improve things at the most exclusive, most romantic Italian restaurant in all of Miami, probably the best Italian restaurant south of New York, is a Jewish maître d' with acute attention to details and tips. Max will make sure everything is perfect.

When Susan and I arrive at Giovanni's in South Miami, Max has everything ready. My friend the senator is out of town, so we have his table. A violinist is assigned to us. Giovanni himself comes out and sings for us at our table. It is top-drawer all the way.

As we pull up to her house afterward, Susan invites me in for coffee. That is a good sign. Once inside, her preparations complete, she sets the tray down on the small table in front of the couch, turns, takes my hand in hers and looks me straight in the eye.

"Dale, six weeks before you showed up at the Bible study, your brother Gary put you on our prayer list. He said you were going through a horrible time with a divorce and all. Well, I was going through that, too, and I knew that your pain must be a lot like mine. So I started praying for you every day, by name. I never expected to meet you."

Susan pauses, as though she is about to say something very important but very vulnerable.

"This evening has been incredible. I mean, I have never been to a restaurant like that before in my life, and the music and all . . . But I know that the most important thing is for God to lead us."

She pauses again, looking at me closely as if for a sign as to whether I agree or am rebuffed.

"So, would it be okay if I say a prayer right now for both of us, to give God whatever is happening between us and to ask Him to take control of it, to take His dominion over us, so that nothing will happen between us that is not His will?"

I am speechless but able to nod in the affirmative.

After arriving home I sit out by the pool until dawn. As the sun comes up I am still wondering, *What does it mean to give God dominion over your life? Who does such a thing? How does one do that?*

Fifteen years later I will learn that, at about that same time as I am asking myself these questions, four hundred miles away in a town I have never heard of, a priest I have never met is on his knees praying for God to send a helper to minister on Florida's death row.

5

Did Jesus Mean What He Said?

BY THE END OF AUGUST 1983, my mother in Michigan has died unexpectedly from complications wrought by a childhood disease. Gary has moved back to Michigan to help our dad. Susan and I are engaged. And on New Year's Eve 1983, thanks to discussions started by movies at their Christian school, the three children gather around me for a picture of my last carton of cigarettes being crushed into the trash. By God's grace, no cigarette will ever touch my lips again.

In February of 1984 Susan and I are married in a civil ceremony at the Dade County Courthouse. We have both filed for Church annulments of our prior marriages, but that will take years. There can be no Church wedding until those annulments are granted.

Also in February, I leave my excellent law firm and make the move across Brickell Avenue to the waterside, to a prestigious "super" law firm, Greenberg Traurig, almost ten times the size of my former firm. This is the crème de la crème. I am surrounded by top professionals in every area of commercial and financial law and covered with an abundance of staff support. The windows of my top floor office overlook Biscayne Bay. Butlers in white jackets wearing gloves greet our clients and serve lunch at our desks. Our cars are detailed in the parking garage while we work. Everyone in the firm knows that we are part of something extremely important.

My new colleagues in tax are the best in the country. Those in securities law and structured financings are the attorneys who teach at professional conferences. Of all the honors of association, none is greater than being colleagues with former Florida governor Reuben Askew. After he withdraws from his bid for the U.S. presidential nomination, I find myself traveling with him throughout Florida to drum up public finance business with the far-flung municipal and county governments of the Sunshine State. There is no doubt in my mind that he is the best example of Christian principles embodied in public service. Many years later, as I teach business ethics and negotiation skills in graduate schools overseas, Governor Askew will be cited frequently in my lectures as a model and a standard for ethics in our endeavors.

By February of 1985, I am named a partner in the firm and am handling significant accounts at the state level. I must be in Tallahassee during legislative session to explain the new lease-backed financing plan that will allow the State of Florida to use bonds to build office buildings for the first time in decades. State house members and senators are champing at the bit to gain access to Wall Street's money for desperately needed regional service centers in their home districts. The financing mechanism is complex and involves creating a new state agency. I must be in the committee meetings and the sessions to explain in detail what Florida will be promising to its investors and what Florida will receive in exchange for those promises.

Susan is pregnant with our first child, which is due in May. I lay down the law with my clients. This expectant father will not be available outside Miami after March 31. The committee meetings that require my presence are set for the last two weeks of March.

It is Thursday night, March 28. After spending the week in front of Florida's lawmakers in a myriad of forums in Tallahassee, I am enjoying dinner with the director of the State Bond Finance Agency, a client that issues untold billions of dollars in bonds every year. Dessert has not yet been served when my name is paged. The voice on the phone at the maître d's station is the desk clerk from my hotel across the street. He informs me of the crisis.

"My wife? Is she all right?"

"She only said to tell you that she is on the way to the hospital with her friend the nurse, and to call the hospital when you get back to your room."

In mere minutes I am in my room at the Governor's Inn, on the phone to Baptist Hospital in Miami. There is no one who can speak to me except the doctor.

"Your wife has broken her water."

"That means," she explains patiently, in response to my dumb-founded demand for more details, "she is in labor."

"What about the baby?" I am already leafing through the yellow pages for charter air companies as she answers.

"We don't know. It's too soon to tell. But there are definite signs of distress."

As the line clicks dead, I'm already dialing the next number . . . and then the next . . . and then the next.

It is the Thursday night before Easter. Every single state legislator, senator, aide and lobbyist from outside Tallahassee is headed home tonight or in the morning for the three-day weekend. There is not a rental car to be had in the city. Every piece of charter air equipment in north Florida and south Georgia is already committed. I obtain a list of companies located in central Florida and hit pay dirt on a call to Clearwater, near Tampa.

"Yeah, I can fetch ya." The private pilot is still struggling awake as I splash him long distance with my tale of woe. "But I can't guarantee I can land. They got real bad fog up there this time of year, and them smart people up there built them an airport in a swamp."

"So, what happens if you can't land?"

"Well, to be blunt, and I am blunt, you be buying my gas to fly there and back."

"What are the conditions now?"

"Well, I been checkin' while you been jawin', and right now it's clear. But no way to know what it'll be like in an hour or so."

"What do you need to come get me?"

"Your credit card number."

"Ready to copy?"

When my taxi pulls up to the general aviation terminal at the Tallahassee airport, the fog is already moving in. The cabbie closes out his meter and makes change for me but decides to stick around. He will either pick up a return fare to the hotel or leave with a pretty good story. It is another 45 minutes before the propeller whine of an approaching single-engine craft penetrates the billowing fog.

"It's not good." The tower operator is yelling down from his open window. "We can't clear him to land."

"Could it clear? Can he circle till it clears?"

There is a moment of silence while the tower communicates with the unseen pilot circling above.

"He says he'll hold a circle as long as he can." The tower finally barks down to us. "He says it's your American Express Card. If you want, he'll circle until he has to go home or crash."

The fog never lifts. It only gets worse. Finally, after over an hour, the unseen pilot waves us off via relay through the tower and heads home.

It is four o'clock on Friday morning, March 29. There is no point in going back to the Governor's Inn. The cabbie drops me at the main terminal without even asking for a fare. I figure I must look pretty pitiful, but that is not always bad. When I was a Boy Scout in Detroit, selling Christmas wreaths door-to-door, the days with the worst weather were always the days for the best sales. The oil of human sympathy is a great lubricant for closing the deal.

There is not a single seat available on any flight to Miami until late that night. I have a seat for the evening already. What I need is a seat on the six o'clock flight run by a barely solvent Bahamian company, affectionately referred to by Florida's frequent flyers as Ghost Air. As soon as the single gate agent shows up, I am pleading for a seat. Of course there is none. So I beg for the next best thing.

As the passengers start queuing up at five, he pretends to ignore the fact that I am standing on the baggage check waving cash and yelling for someone to sell me their ticket. My offer keeps rising until I finally buy a seat for three times the price. Years later, friends will ask if that event was the inspiration for airlines to oversell their flights and then have gate agents hawk the passengers to sell the tickets back for a free flight.

All the way to Miami a single issue consumes my thoughts: *Why am I away from home when my family needs me? Why am I always on the road when there is an emergency?*

At eight-fifteen I walk into my wife's room at Baptist Hospital in Miami. She is fine. I have not slept or showered. Our new baby boy, Chris, born at three A.M., is being transported to the neonatal intensive care unit at Variety Children's Hospital. As we make the trek to his new temporary home, my wife, Susan, is stunned at my question: "What would you think of living in Tallahassee?"

"I love Tallahassee," she says without hesitation. "When I went to college there I thought it was the most wonderful city in the world." Her voice indicates that more of a response is still coming.

"But that's not really the question." She needles me because she knows I have had no sleep, and she feels great. "The real question is, What do you think of moving to Tallahassee?"

"It's time," I say with a nod. "It's way past time."

○─○─○

Such changes take time to put in place. It is a beautiful Tallahassee Saturday in late January of 1986. Here the winters usually last from mid-December through mid-January. Then the buds peek out, and the warm sun blesses the great outdoors with a scent of spring that folks north of the Mason-Dixon Line cannot even hope for before April. Florida is experiencing a net gain in population of three thousand people a week. But this January day, almost nobody is interested in looking at houses. Everyone is outside enjoying the weather.

Poor Ms. Maxine has pulled weekend duty. The Investors' Realty office on North Thomasville Road, in the upscale area of Tallahassee, has no traffic today. We are her first customers.

"Good afternoon." She smiles sweetly, welcoming us and placing her business card in my hand with one smooth motion. "How can I help you today?"

"We are looking to build our new home here," I answer. "I have just taken a position with Governor Farris Bryant's law firm, and we are moving here from Miami."

"Well." She is really smiling now. We are not going to be wasting her time. "What do you have in mind?"

"Let's assume I'm moving to Tallahassee to become the governor's chief of staff. What neighborhood would you show me?"

"Let's go." Ms. Maxine whips her purse on her shoulder. "I'll drive."

The neighborhood is called Highgrove. As Ms. Maxine corners onto Chatsworth Way, a beautiful oblong lot with stately trees slips into view. The houses surrounding us are impressive, to say the least. She senses my next question and starts rattling off the answer.

"Across the street, in the Tudor, that is the top doc at the regional hospital."

"And there?" I point kitty-corner.

"That's the chief whatever-you-call-it at that big law firm across from the State Capitol."

I recognize his name and the name of his firm immediately. "And there?" I point to the lot behind.

"He is the Mormon bishop. Great family."

"And there?" I point to the neighboring lot with a huge frame-and-glass split-level under construction.

"That is the new secretary of labor."

Susan and I pace off the property along the lot lines a few times while Ms. Maxine waits patiently by her car.

"Can the builder meet with us today?" I finally ask.

"Yes. I called him a few minutes ago. He's waiting for the word."

Ms. Maxine does not steer us wrong. Within the year, the newly elected governor will move into the Florida Governor's Mansion. His new chief of staff will move in four doors up the street from us.

○─○─○

In early March 1986 Susan and I meet with Ms. Maxine and the builder at our new property. The closing will take place on acceptance of the completed house. We have designed it ourselves through modifications to a basic plan he suggested. It is time to break ground. I hand him the fifty-thousand-dollar cashier's check required by the contract for him to start work. We are on our way in Tallahassee. We will celebrate with dinner later tonight, after attending the Saturday evening vigil service at our new parish, Good Shepherd Roman Catholic Church.

Since the change of law firms in Miami in February 1984, my work hours have exploded. The intense spiritual focus that was giving gravity to our lives in 1983 seems to have waned as the pressures of children and career have dominated our schedules and our daily resources. It could not be anything of our making that causes us to step into church on the very night of signing the contract for our dream house, only to be confronted by the Gospel reading of the rich young lawyer in Mark 10:17–25.

> As Jesus started on his way, a man ran up to him and fell on his knees before him. "Good teacher," he asked, "what must I do to inherit eternal life?"
>
> "Why do you call me good?" Jesus answered. "No one is good—except God alone. You know the commandments: 'Do not murder, do not commit adultery, do not steal, do not give false testimony, do not defraud, honor your father and mother.' "
>
> "Teacher," he declared, "all these I have kept since I was a boy."
>
> Jesus looked at him and loved him. "One thing you lack," he said. "Go, sell everything you have and give to the poor, and you will have treasure in heaven. Then come, follow me."

At this the man's face fell. He went away sad, because he had great wealth.

Jesus looked around and said to his disciples, "How hard it is for the rich to enter the kingdom of God!"

The disciples were amazed at his words. But Jesus said again, "Children, how hard it is to enter the kingdom of God! It is easier for a camel to go through the eye of a needle than for a rich man to enter the kingdom of God."

Although the story has been read at church many times before, we hear it that night for the very first time. The dinner afterward to celebrate the contract on our new house is not going as planned.

"Do you think He meant what He said?"

"Who?" Susan is not picking up my thread without some context. "The builder? Did the builder mean what he said?"

"No." I am unfairly impatient. "Not the builder . . . Jesus. Do you think Jesus meant what He said?"

"What did He say? What do you mean?"

"What He said in the Gospel reading tonight."

Susan has the thread now. She sets down her fork and looks at me intently.

"Do you think Jesus meant what He said tonight in the Gospel?" I lean forward to speak softer, intuitively aware that anyone in the restaurant who heard me ask such a question would think I am nuts.

Susan shrugs. "Does anybody think He meant that? Does anybody take it literally?"

"Well, I guess priests and nuns do," I concede in acknowledgment of the well-known assumption by Roman Catholics for centuries that the literal Gospel only applies to those called to the so-called religious life—priests, brothers and nuns. "But the guy He was talking to in the Gospel tonight was not religious. He was like me. He was like us."

"And . . . ?" Susan leaves both her words and her fork hanging midair.

"And so the question is, did Jesus mean what He said?"

"I don't know." Susan instinctively lowers her voice too. "I've never heard anyone discuss it."

"Me neither."

"Maybe we should find out."

At first we begin reading the Gospel to each other in the evening. We are so stunned at the challenge of Jesus' actual words that we decide not to even try to discuss the question for at least six months. Instead, we separately pray and study His words, searching for an answer. By the end of September 1986, weeks after moving into our spacious new Tallahassee home, it is time for us to sit down and compare notes.

"Well, I'm not sure what to do with my answer, but I have my answer." Susan leans back in her chair opposite the fireplace in the alcove that makes up a portion of our 1,200-square-foot bedroom.

"Me too." My nod and shrug in a single gesture indicate that I am stuck in the same predicament. "Who should go first?"

"I'll go first." Susan leafs through her Bible to the gospel of Matthew and finds the end of the Sermon on the Mount, Matthew 7:24–27:

> Therefore everyone who hears these words of mine and puts them into practice is like a wise man who built his house on the rock. The rain came down, the streams rose, and the winds blew and beat against that house; yet it did not fall, because it had its foundation on the rock. But everyone who

hears these words of mine and does not put them into practice is like a foolish man who built his house on sand. The rain came down, the streams rose, and the winds blew and beat against that house, and it fell with a great crash.

"I don't know what everybody else thinks." She closes the book with her finger between the pages, like a bookmark that will prevent those un-preached, un-thought-of and un-discussed words from disappearing forever if she needs to refer to them again. "But, obviously, Jesus thinks He means what He says."

"That's where I come out, too. So, what do we do with this?" My right hand sweeps outward in a gesture that symbolically takes in our monument of a house, 22 ceiling speakers and all. "And with this?" My left hand holds up the book of God's Word.

"Dale, I haven't a clue."

"Me neither."

The fire crackles loudly into a spray of sparks as the top log falls behind and rolls to the bottom.

"Sounds like we better pray, Dale. This is not going to be easy."

Susan has never spoken truer words. For weeks, in addition to prayer, we brainstorm ways to begin making ourselves available for service to God's Kingdom. The same obstacle keeps asserting itself, the unyielding limit of time. There is not enough time. All our resources of time are committed to the needs of earning and maintaining our affluent lifestyle.

It is said that the blessing of limited resources is what makes human beings moral creatures. Limited money requires us to prioritize. Limited energy requires us to choose between the greatest good and inferior goods. And limited time requires us to pick between the things of the Father and the things of the world. If money and energy and time were unlimited, no choices would be necessary.

Each one of us could do everything. But they are limited, and we must choose. We keep praying for God's direction.

○─○─○

In November of 1986 I wake with a scream from a dead sleep, pouring sweat from a profound nightmare. Susan bolts upright in the bed next to me, scared awake by my sounds of terror.

"Dale, what happened? What made you scream?"

"A dream. A horrible nightmare." The sheets and pillow on my side of the bed are soaked. I push myself up by the elbows and turn on my back to lean sitting up against the brass headboard. "It was incredibly real."

"Tell me about it." Susan sounds very clinical, with a voice that would usually irritate me, but not tonight. This dream must be shared.

"I am outside our bedroom here, on the west side of the house, raking leaves with the kids. It is late afternoon. Very pleasant. Everyone is in a good mood. I am thinking how lucky I am. Then . . ." I pause, groping for words.

"Then what happened?" Susan's hands rotate toward herself in a circular gesture as though trying to reel out the words from somewhere inside me.

"Then I hear a voice. It is more than a voice, more than music—music is not descriptive enough. It is the sweetest, most beautiful sound I have ever heard in my life. It is coming from the direction of the setting sun. Everything in me knows I must follow it. So I start walking toward it. But I can't. I can't walk toward it because something is holding me back."

"Dale, what was holding you back?" Susan speaks with a gentle sharpness that is rare for her.

"I cannot move my left leg. I look down, and there is a huge chain on it. Massive steel links in this chain running from my ankle back to the house. The chain is embedded into the bricks of the house, right into the outside of the chimney for this fireplace." I wave my hand toward the bedroom alcove that we knew was essential to our happiness.

"What did you do, Dale?"

"I try to tear off the chain. I try like a madman to break the steel links, even to break my leg to get it off, but it will not budge. And then . . ." My voice fails as the desperation and despair in the dream leeches back into my senses. "And then, the voice starts to fade. I can't get to it. The voice is going away. I am filled with terror because the voice is going away. It isn't just about wanting the chain off. It is all about the voice. It is so beautiful that I cannot imagine not running to it, not being with it.

"I try to pry the chain out of the wall. I even try to pull the whole blasted house behind me. But it is futile. As I stand there trembling and weeping, the voice fades, the sun sets and, finally, it is completely dark. The voice is gone. The cold is absolute. In the dream I know that there will be no second chance. I have lost it forever. I scream and wake up."

Susan seems oblivious to the sweat and tears that are erupting anew with the recounting of my visit to personal hell. She is holding me close and praying softly.

"Sweetheart," she finally whispers so low that I can hardly hear her. "I think God may have given us our answer. Maybe we can't have all this and His Kingdom. Maybe we have to choose."

○-○-○

It is hard to describe the interior swirl of emotions unleashed by moving from the fear that Jesus may have meant what He said in general to the shock of thinking that He may have meant it for us personally.

Our prayer and Scripture reading and studying of the lives of others who dared to think such thoughts burgeon. We find that many who have trod this path have turned in prayer to the Bible for specific guidance—praying and then opening the Holy Book for God's leading through specific passages.

That effort will take real focus and quiet time, a luxury usually unavailable to us with four children in tow. We decide that the soonest opportunity for such an undertaking is an upcoming business trip in May 1987, when we will be staying at the Opryland Hotel in Nashville, Tennessee.

As with so many other states in the mid-1980s, Tennessee is facing a crisis of an exploding prison population. The state needs thousands more beds in capacity, and it needs them last year. That is what brings us to the Tennessee Governor's Mansion on the Saturday of Mother's Day weekend. By evening, our group has adjourned to the new General Jackson paddle-wheeled showboat for a superb dinner of classic southern cuisine and a cruise of the Cumberland River. Afterward, Susan and I return to our room at the Opryland Hotel. It is time.

We hold the Bible in our joined open hands, praying intently over it for a long time, begging the Holy Spirit to lead our next steps through the passages that the Bible opens to. We need God's guidance, clarity and protection from confusion. Then we open the Bible three times to read the map of our future.

The first opening is to the Hebrew Scriptures and contains a call to prophetic living through authenticity, Isaiah 21:1–10:

> An oracle concerning the Desert by the Sea: Like whirlwinds sweeping through the southland, an invader comes from the desert, from a land of terror.
>
> A dire vision has been shown to me: The traitor betrays, the looter takes loot. Elam, attack! Media, lay siege! I will bring to an end all the groaning she caused.

At this my body is racked with pain, pangs seize me, like those of a woman in labor; I am staggered by what I hear, I am bewildered by what I see. My heart falters, fear makes me tremble; the twilight I longed for has become a horror to me.

They set the tables, they spread the rugs, they eat, they drink!

Get up, you officers, oil the shields!

This is what the Lord says to me: "Go, post a lookout and have him report what he sees. When he sees chariots with teams of horses, riders on donkeys or riders on camels, let him be alert, fully alert."

And the lookout shouted, "Day after day, my lord, I stand on the watchtower; every night I stay at my post. Look, here comes a man in a chariot, with a team of horses. And he gives back the answer: 'Babylon has fallen, has fallen! All the images of its gods lie shattered on the ground.' "

O my people, crushed on the threshing floor, I tell you what I have heard from the LORD Almighty, from the God of Israel.

The second opening is to the New Testament story of the early Church and contains the call to a life of community, Acts 2:42–45:

They devoted themselves to the apostles' teaching and to the fellowship, to the breaking of bread and to prayer. Everyone was filled with awe, and many wonders and miraculous signs were done by the apostles. All the believers were together and had everything in common. Selling their possessions and goods, they gave to anyone as he had need.

The final opening is to the gospels and sets forth the call to live a life of faith based upon the Gospel guarantee, Matthew 6:19–34:

Do not store up for yourselves treasures on earth, where moth and rust destroy, and where thieves break in and steal. But store up for yourselves treasures in heaven, where moth and rust do not destroy, and where thieves do not break in and steal. For where your treasure is, there your heart will be also.

The eye is the lamp of the body. If your eyes are good, your whole body will be full of light. But if your eyes are bad, your whole body will be full of darkness. If then the light within you is darkness, how great is that darkness!

No one can serve two masters. Either he will hate the one and love the other, or he will be devoted to the one and despise the other. You cannot serve both God and Money.

Therefore, I tell you, do not worry about your life, what you will eat or drink; or about your body, what you will wear. Is not life more important than food, and the body more important than clothes? Look at the birds of the air; they do not sow or reap or store away in barns, and yet your heavenly Father feeds them. Are you not much more valuable than they? Who of you by worrying can add a single hour to his life?

And why do you worry about clothes? See how the lilies of the field grow. They do not labor or spin. Yet I tell you that not even Solomon in all his splendor was dressed like one of these. If that is how God clothes the grass of the field, which is here today and tomorrow is thrown into the fire, will he not much more clothe you, O you of little faith? So do not worry, saying, "What shall we eat?" or "What shall we drink?" or "What shall we wear?" For the pagans run after all these things, and your heavenly Father knows that you need them.

But seek first his kingdom and his righteousness, and all these things will be given to you as well.

Therefore, do not worry about tomorrow, for tomorrow will worry about itself. Each day has enough trouble of its own.

"What do you think?" Susan asks, cocking her head slightly and breaking our prolonged silence. "Is it clear to you?"

"Yeah." I laugh, closing the Holy Book. "It's clear we need professional help from our pastor, and it's time to get it."

6

The Downward Ascent

WE FIRST MEET PASTOR MICHAEL FOLEY at our new Tallahassee parish, Good Shepherd Roman Catholic Church, in January of 1986. He is approachable, humble and kind. Even so, as I approach him to secure an appointment on the Sunday after Mother's Day, 1987, it does not occur to me that when a married couple asks for an emergency appointment with their pastor, he will steel himself for a grueling bout with the specter of divorce. Nothing could be further from our minds.

"Did you get an appointment with the pastor?" Susan has been rounding up the children and herding them into the minivan John Wayne–style while I have been in line outside the church.

"Yes." I shrug, settling into the driver's seat. "But he didn't seem very happy about it."

"Did you tell him it was important?"

"Yeah, real important. Urgent. But that didn't seem to help."

"My mom will watch the kids."

At two we present ourselves to our pastor at his church office.

"Well," Pastor Foley begins as he leads us into the small office where he sits surrounded by carefully neatened piles of articles waiting to be read and memos from church committees, above and below, awaiting response. "What's on your mind? How can we help you?"

"We have a question." My hesitancy reflects the almost painful tension in his face and his neck. He is sitting bolt upright.

He nods without appearing to move at all. "Okay, what is your question?"

"Please don't laugh." I instinctively try to inject a bit of levity because he looks like laughing is the furthest thing from his mind. "We may be making a mountain out of a molehill. . . ."

"Believe me. I have heard it all before." His hands are facing us palms out and spread apart in his effort to put us at ease.

I inhale hard and exhale harder. "Okay, then. We need to know, Did Jesus mean what He said?"

"Excuse me?" Pastor Foley finally breaks the overly long moment of awkward silence. "Pardon me?"

"That's what we need to know, Pastor. Did Jesus mean what He said?"

"That's your question?" He is stunned beyond gestures. "Is that what you want to talk about?"

"Yes." I have the fleeting thought that perhaps Susan has told him secretly that there is a different issue to be addressed, but a quick glance her way reveals she is nodding in the affirmative. She senses more than a nod is in order.

"That is our question, Pastor." Susan goes on record and jumps into the soup with me. "Did Jesus really mean what He said, or are we nuts?"

In a flash his demeanor changes completely. Gone are the tension and the rigid body language. Gone are the guarded voice and posture. He leans back in his chair while removing his jacket in a single motion that culminates in slipping his collar from around his neck and into a pocket.

"Let's see." He is all smiles and leans toward us with hands on his knees. "Catch me up."

Three hours later, we have our answers. No, we are not crazy. Yes, Jesus meant what He said, but each person is called to hear it and live it in a way that God ordains, unique to them, to their circumstances and to the grace that God provides for them. And we must go slowly, praying, discerning and staying very vigilant over how our changes impact our children.

"You are hearing Him clearly and headed in the right direction," he says in blessing us in conclusion. "Go slow, slower than you want to. Your children cannot live on your faith. They must grow their own."

○-○-○

In June 1987 we begin helping at the evening meal served in the soup kitchen across from the Florida State University campus. By August, our family purchases a downsized home in Killearn, an affluent suburban community where many of our new neighbors are striving to move up into Highgrove. When the stock market collapses in October of 1987, our big house in Highgrove still is not under contract. The listing expires as it sits empty.

On October 14, Addie is born in the middle of the night. This time I am home and present for the delivery. Later that month, Susan and I receive the annulments of our prior marriages from the Church.

Christmas week, the former Realtor shows up unexpectedly at our door and presents a cash contract for purchase of our empty big house, with closing scheduled for the first business day of the new year. Christmas Eve, our families and friends pour in from as far away as Michigan and California for the combined service at Good Shepherd Roman Catholic Church on December 26 when Addie is baptized. Susan and I also restate our vows and have our marriage blessed in the Church. Pastor Foley presides over it all. At home later, we also celebrate my 36th birthday. And on January 4, 1988, the big house is sold.

Our externals are finally in order. We have arrived where God wants us, I think. This must be the plateau from which we will work for Him for the rest of our lives.

I could not be more wrong.

○─○─○

In February of 1988 the parish announces a new weekend Scripture renewal program for the men, something called Christ Renews His Parish. Upon hearing the announcement at church, I really do not understand the significance of the focus upon the Scriptures coming alive in our daily lives. I know that my career is waning in importance, leaving a vacuum for friendship and fellowship. I decide to attend, simply to meet some men from church.

The emphasis of the March weekend retreat is Scripture. One passage, from Matthew 6:31–33, in particular catches my attention:

> So do not worry, saying, "What shall we eat?" or "What shall we drink?" or "What shall we wear?" For the pagans run after all these things, and your heavenly Father knows that you need them.
>
> But seek first his kingdom and his righteousness, and all these things will be given to you as well.

I know that Scripture. It is part of the third Scripture passage Susan and I received in prayer at the Opryland Hotel on Mother's Day weekend the previous year. Here it is again, God's phenomenal offer: If we take care of God's business, God will handle our business.

It is a gospel guarantee. If it is for real, how could anyone turn down such a deal?

I am sure there must be a catch. There must be an exclusion, an exception, or everyone would be doing this. I search the footnotes of study Bibles and concordances, call other men in the group and even check with friends who are from evangelical traditions. No one knows of any passage where Jesus took it back.

I want to pick up that deal but do not have any idea how to do so. It is time to schedule another meeting with Pastor Foley.

"How do I seek the Kingdom and God's righteousness?" My question blurts out after barely a greeting. Before he responds I have time to note that both the stacks of articles and of memos on his office desk are taller than they were a year ago.

"Well, that's really pretty easy, Dale." His mischievous Irish expression tells me it will be anything but easy. "Pray to see the world as God sees it and to see yourself as God sees you."

"That's it? That's all? Why don't they print it on milk cartons if that's all there is to it?"

So I begin to pray in earnest to see the world as God sees it and to see myself as God sees me. With even a smidgeon of spiritual sophistication, I would be terrified to pray for that. But I do not have a scintilla of understanding.

○-○-○

The second week of May 1988 finds me in Baltimore's Inner Harbor as a guest speaker at a national conference of investment bankers. It is high-minded stuff about pooling capital needs for financing by securitization on Wall Street. I arrive in Baltimore a day early and ask the hotel concierge for a walking map of the Inner Harbor and its surroundings. He hands me a guide and circles in red the areas that I should avoid.

As Thursday evening approaches, I have a full schedule. At

five-thirty I am meeting with potential clients at the lounge of the Harbor Court to discuss a financing at Kennedy Space Center, at six-thirty there is a conference cocktail party and at seven-thirty a formal dinner party followed by professional entertainment and a hosted reception.

At about five-fifteen I am walking the two blocks from my room at the Hyatt to the meeting at the Harbor Court when a derelict approaches the man about a block in front of me and asks for money. The street bum is filthy and unable to walk straight. Just laying eyes on him triggers an olfactory disgust well before the smell actually arrives. His tack in my direction tips me off that he will hit me up next.

From the Scripture retreat weekend, I know that Jesus told us, "Give to everyone who asks you," Luke 6:30. I know what God expects of me.

As the bum and I walk toward each other, I am reaching into my suit jacket pocket for my secretary billfold to give him a dollar. Then I freeze. Out of the corner of my eye I realize that two investment bankers at the conference from a major Wall Street firm are right behind me. Shame and embarrassment engulf me. They will see me giving money to this filthy derelict. I know what they will think of me. I know what they will say to other bankers about me. I will be an object of ridicule and lose the credibility that I need to woo these men as clients.

In a split second that is less decision than reflex, I stuff my billfold back into its sheath and slide by the down-and-outer without a word, looking the other way as though he is not even there.

Later, while my five-thirty business appointment drones on over drinks at the lounge in the Harbor Court, my thoughts are obsessing on that derelict and on what I had not done.

I know what Jesus told us to do. I read the Scriptures on the weekend retreat. I know God's instructions, yet I deliberately disobeyed. I am not able to get any peace and am unable to think about financings at Kennedy Space Center.

The potential clients and I wrap up late, and they head for the cocktail hour, but I slip away in the crowd and exit the Harbor Court through a back door. Everyone I know in Baltimore will be at that cocktail party. Now it is safe to look for that bum. No one will see me.

After searching through the shops and the walkways of the Inner Harbor area, I find him lying facedown behind some bushes, just off the diagonal walkway across the center green. When I turn him by his shoulder, my eyes meet open sores on his face, neck and lips. As impossible as it seems, his appearance is more revolting up close than at a distance.

"Here's your money, man." I shove a single into his hand and turn to leave, but he doubles over in pain. I help him sit up on the ground and crouch next to him.

His name is Dennis. No, he has nowhere to go. Yes, he is very sick; he feels as sick as he looks.

My instincts click into problem-solving mode. I do not dare take him into the Hyatt where I am staying. There is a huge Shriner's convention, and the mezzanine will be jammed. It simply will not be possible to slip him in or slip him out.

I maneuver Dennis to a park bench near the harbor boardwalk.

"Can you understand what I'm saying, Dennis?"

"Yeah." He is woozy and listing badly to one side.

"I want you to stay right here. I will run to my hotel, get my car and come back for you. Then we will get you someplace where you can get help."

His eyes are closing and he is almost horizontal.

"Do you promise you will wait here for me?" I maneuver him upright again by gripping both his shoulders.

"Yeah." He is already back thirty degrees toward the horizontal.

Running in a custom-made designer suit is not something I am used to. In mere seconds I dash to the Hyatt, grab an immediate elevator up and burst into my room. One hand is grabbing the phone, the other leafing through the phone book. My mind is shooting off a series of short and impassioned prayers for divine assistance.

The first few calls to rehab centers go unanswered. Someone finally answers the phone at the rectory of the inner-city church of St. Vincent de Paul. They direct me to Christopher House, a rescue mission or outreach center of some sort. They provide the secret number that rings a phone that will actually be answered.

Christopher House is full, but they direct me to the Baltimore Mission and provide the unpublished number that will actually be answered at that facility. Cradling the phone between my right ear and shoulder, I trace the directions to the Baltimore Mission with my left hand on my little map from the hotel concierge. The mission is located about six blocks into the forbidden red circle. Well, it is not dark yet, and we are driving, not walking. My mind's voice overrides my emotions. I'm sure we'll be fine.

Within minutes of when the valet produces my luxury rental car, I am idling in front of the bench where I left Dennis. He is gone.

There is nothing to do but find him. Tonight I will put the search and rescue tactics learned as a teen Boy Scout in Michigan to good use. The area around the Inner Harbor easily divides into quadrants. The empty park bench is ground zero. Methodically, I cruise the back streets and alleys in widening concentric circles, checking off the negative results, block by block.

After almost twenty minutes of widening loops around the Inner Harbor, I find Dennis. He is quite busy at that moment—busy getting rolled by two very large teenagers in an obscure alley. My reaction is totally irrational. It is definitely adrenal and not thought through. Maybe it is one of the negative effects of all the crime shows on television.

In any event, at the sight of Dennis being pummeled by two of Baltimore's almost adult delinquents, I lay on the horn and screech the car to within two feet of the underage linebackers. Then I jump out quickly, pulling my billfold from my suit pocket and flashing it like a badge while yelling some gibberish authoritatively. For all I know, I could be speaking in tongues.

The young assailants throw Dennis against the back wall of a garage and, holding their hands in the air, yell, "It's cool, man. Hey, it's cool." Then they disappear. I run around to the other side of the car and partially lift, shove and pour Dennis into the passenger seat. He is a bleeding mess. He looks at me and sighs, "They got my dollar."

When we arrive at the Baltimore Mission, a staff member escorts Dennis inside for an intake interview. I am left standing outside with the bouncer, probably the biggest guy I have ever seen in my life. In the glare of the bouncer's stare, I am extremely conscious of the clash between the impoverished area around me and my three-piece herringbone suit with monogrammed shirt, silk Countess Maria tie and "leather uppers" Bali shoes. When the mountain of a man speaks for the first time, remarking about the expensive car I have pulled up in, I nervously assure him that it was just a great deal at the rental agency, that back home in Florida I drive a very ordinary, inexpensive car. He laughs mercilessly.

Our exchange ends abruptly when Dennis stumbles back out the front door of the mission. Apparently a person can flunk the intake interview at a ghetto mission. Who knew? Dennis left detox at the mission just three weeks ago, and the minimum return time is thirty days. He is a bad penny, and he cannot stay.

My helpless gestures make no impact on the smirking bouncer and the disgusted staff member, both filled with disdain at my guilt by association.

"What am I supposed to do with him?" I yell over my shoulder while helping Dennis back into the passenger side of the car.

"Take him to Church Hospital. It's a public hospital. Maybe they'll take him there."

As I trace their directions on my little hotel concierge map, it is clear that Dennis and I will be venturing many blocks deeper into the forbidden red area that I have been warned about. I begin to feel afraid.

Forget the parking lot at Church Hospital. One glance at the landscape tells me all I need to know. It is way too far from the door. Those teenage miscreants could mug me five times between that lot and the emergency room. I pull up behind an ambulance at the entrance and use a fireman's carry–type maneuver to pry Dennis out of the car and steer his dogleg limp into the emergency room. I have never been in the emergency room of an inner-city public hospital. It is long overdue for new chairs, new floor tile, new paint and a new sense of mission. Everything about it screams "We do not care."

The city policeman at the entrance watches us with amusement, the overweight, prosperous attorney decked out for cocktails and the filthy, long-haired derelict in tatters.

The receptionist is not at all amused. She is all delivery. With nose tilted back just enough, she assesses Dennis and me in a single cursory glare and delivers her knockout punch with a sniff. "I need his insurance card."

She is not the only one with airs. My juices are starting to flow, too.

"Dennis, do you have insurance?" My voice is too loud and betrays more than a tinge of sarcasm as I yield to passive-aggressive assertiveness. He has none, of course.

I tell the receptionist and anyone else present who will listen that I will pay for his bill, whatever it is. I present three American Express gold cards and two VISA cards and a signed blank check. This is not charity. I am in a bind and willing to buy my way out.

The receptionist is delighted. She smirks through more than a whiff of gotcha. "I'm sorry, but we can't take private pay. We can only accept patients with insurance."

I know the logic without asking. Once the hospital takes Dennis as a patient, it will be responsible to fix whatever is broke—whether my money can cover it or not. So the high-priced hospital lawyers have told staff not to accept any patients unless they have insurance. That way the hospital will get paid for whatever unforeseen medical care is required.

With tail between my legs, I gather up my $150,000 in plastic available credit and throw myself on the mercy of the cop who is holding his hand over his mouth to avoid laughing out loud.

"What am I supposed to do with him?"

He has no idea. He calls dispatch and hands me his squawk box. They give me directions to North Gay Street, to an indigent detox facility.

I half-lead, half-drag Dennis back to the car. In all my worldly wanderings, I have never contemplated what kind of neighborhood an indigent detox facility is in. I do not even know what an indigent detox facility is.

After Dennis is strapped in to the front passenger seat, leaning forlornly with his head against the side window, I pull out my little hotel map and trace the new directions. The map is blank for the area we are headed into. We are going way past the forbidden red zone. We are bound for the don't-even-think-about-it zone.

I mumble an unquotable string of colorful words as I crumple up my little hotel concierge map and pitch it over my shoulder into the backseat. Dennis just looks at me and nods sympathetically, as though to say, "Yeah, I do that a lot, too."

As we work our way up Broadway, it feels like all the people standing on the curbs and sitting on their porches are staring at us.

When I make the turn at North Gay, with many blocks still to go, I know I have never been in a neighborhood like this before in my life. My teeth are banging together. This is a new depth of fear.

Dennis, even in his sickly stupor, is aware enough to be scared to death. He keeps asking for assurance that I will not leave him here on the street in this neighborhood. I assure him that he has nothing to worry about. Surely, the indigent detox facility will accept him.

They do not.

The building itself looks like a trashy prop left over from a World War II film about the bombing of someplace. It sits alone on an otherwise razed lot behind barbwire fence and a weed-ridden unpaved parking area. The upper floors are all but gone, burned or decayed into mere husks of exterior walls. The bottom floor has lights and a huge red metal door, painfully visible under a streetlight-size bulb hanging impossibly from a bracket directly above.

I stand at the detox door, turning fifteen shades of red and purple, as a lowly bureaucrat explains the process to me with a great deal of irritation.

"We cannot just accept people who show up at the door. Everybody would show up here."

"Fine. But do you have any open beds? Can I bring him back later?"

"We can't tell you that when you show up at the door. You have to call ahead of time and ask."

Unruffled by my unvarnished description of what I think of his procedures, Baltimore's civil servant continues. "And you cannot call. The person who wants the bed has to call."

I am incredulous. Dennis would have to go to a phone, call and request a bed. Then, and only then, they would tell us if a bed is available.

"Where is he going to get a phone?" I scream. "What am I supposed to do with him?" But to no avail. Mr. Indigent Detox Administrator is already disappearing behind the red door as it slams shut.

We climb back into the car and pick our way back down North Gay Street. Dennis begins to cry about his life and about what will become of him, about how he has sunk so low that no one will take him in.

I promise him I will not leave him until we find a place for him to spend the night. I remember the church I originally phoned, St. Vincent de Paul. They must have a phone.

While balancing Dennis on the edge of the broken concrete step with one arm, I lean on the rectory buzzer with the other. The pastor is not there, but the fellow who answers the door takes us to the phone.

I dial the indigent detox facility and hand the phone to Dennis. His request is barely intelligible, so when he looks up and mutters, "They said yeah," I grab the phone and ask them to confirm it to me.

It is true. They can take him but not until ten o'clock. It is only nine. I hang up the phone, wondering how to spend an hour. Dennis answers my unspoken question. He starts heaving.

The fellow from the church and I steer Dennis into the bathroom. Then the other fellow excuses himself. As I stand there holding Dennis upright over the toilet by the back belt loop of his pants, I realize how dirty and sickly he is. My mind floods with thoughts of AIDS or typhus or hepatitis or other diseases. My stomach tightens with revulsion.

In the uneven light I imagine that I can see lice or other vermin crawling in the long, stringy, filthy hair that hangs down over his shoulders and tangles into the mess that is his beard. I shake myself to reality with a shudder. But the distance between us increases with each thought, as my arm holds him farther and farther away.

During the brief interludes between business over the toilet bowl, Dennis talks about God abandoning him. I ask him if he wants to pray. He does. I help wash his face and we pass through the rectory entrance into the 150-year-old church of St. Vincent de Paul. It is absolutely dark, except for the candles in the sanctuary. We are alone.

I steer him to the front row, where we are side by side in the light of the votive candles in front of the side altar. I stand next to him with my hand on his shoulder—mostly to ensure a safe distance between us—and start to lead him through the words of the Lord's Prayer.

It is empty, flat. Our words feel void and meaningless. In my head I say, *Lord, where are You? This isn't working.*

In the next moment Dennis breaks into hysterical tears, sobbing uncontrollably and crying loudly, over and over again, "God, don't let me die like this! Please, God, don't let me die like this."

In the midst of his sobbing, he wraps his arms around me and buries his face against my shoulder and my neck. I freeze. Horror and panic fill me.

He is filthy. He is diseased. He stinks. He is drooling all over me. His tears and his saliva are running down my neck and my Countess Maria tie.

My horror deepens as I realize that I am about to pull his arms from me and shove him away hard. I do not want to do that. It is a reflex. I do not know how to not push him away. My mind is panicking. It is a moment of pure fear and crisis.

Then, in the back of my mind, I hear my own voice whisper, *Jesus, help me.*

It all vanishes in a flash, all the fear, all the panic, all the terror . . . gone. It all disappears.

Without even thinking it, my arms are holding Dennis and my hand is on his head. Just as the men on the retreat did for me, I am praying out loud for him and for his healing and crying with him.

I am too broken, too full of fear, too worried about my survival to hug Dennis. But Jesus can hug Dennis with my arms if I let Him use them. We stay together in the church praying for the rest of our time until we leave for the indigent detox facility.

I take Dennis back to the bombed-out building with the big red door at ten o'clock. It is pitch-black dark. I do not even notice.

As the big guy who opens the door is walking him down the hall, Dennis stops, turns and comes back to me.

"Thanks for caring about me." He hugs me one last time.

At 10:25 I am back in the Harbor Court Hotel. The professional entertainment, a Ronald Reagan impersonator, is just finishing, and the crowd is gravitating into the ballroom for after-dinner cocktails and cordials. Everyone is decked out nicely, and the conversation is familiar: vacations to New Zealand and Europe, best places to shop, big deals and big profits. It is all familiar to me. But tonight I feel like a stranger in a strange land.

This is the world that I have treated as reality for years, but only fifteen minutes away is Dennis. Suddenly, all this hoopla is clearly only an illusion. All these material trappings are junk, trinkets.

I realize in a flash that I have seen the world as God sees it. God sees a world full of troubled, broken and debilitated spirits who are just as sick and needy to God's eyes as Dennis's body is to mine.

As I look around at the gowns, jewelry and champagne, I hear my own voice in the back of my thoughts screaming out, *God, don't let me die like this! Please, God, don't let me die like this.*

The first half of my prayer, to see the world as God sees it, has been answered. The answer to the rest of my prayer, to see myself as God sees me, is just weeks away.

7

The Pearl of Great Price

MATTHEW 13:45–46

I ARRIVE HOME FROM BALTIMORE with a hit list of preparations for bringing Dennis to our hometown: phone calls to the indigent detox facility on North Gay Street; advance preparations with the rehab facility he will be moved to in Baltimore; research for services; housing and job possibilities in Tallahassee. Dennis is going to make it. I will see to that.

During the week after the Baltimore conference, I head to the "Space Coast" of central Florida to close a major financing for the Brevard County School Board. Even though the deal is one-on-one and not publicly offered, the negotiations are rough. Therefore, the investor and the underwriter throw a typical closing dinner, a fancy and expensive affair, to cap off the heated exchanges of negotiation with pleasant memories.

With only one investing institution involved in the financing, it is possible to close the deal in Brevard County at the school district's offices. Even so, the closing dinner for the Brevard County School Board's new mainframe computer system follows the Wall Street playbook. The restaurant is top-drawer; the room is private. The food is exquisite. Wine is flowing and hors d'oeuvres are plattered-in and stacked around the ten-seat table. My young paralegal—who will henceforth be nicknamed the "black widow" for almost killing her boss—sits to my right and is passing a plate of raw oysters on the half shell.

"Oh, my mistake." She pauses, whispering just loudly enough for me to hear, with a large half shell from the tray in her cupped left hand. "I don't like the big ones."

"I like 'em." I jump in to save any embarrassment. "I'll eat it."

"Here." She slides the shell from her hand to mine instead of recalling the platter that is now halfway down the table. "This one is for you."

As a transplanted Yankee, I have never heard the warnings against eating a raw oyster in a month without an *R* in its name. Yet the moment I bite into that raw oyster, I know something is wrong. It does not taste right. Now I have the hot potato because my concern is to not embarrass myself as I expel the clump of grayish white meat without swallowing it.

At the first moment when it appears that all the table diners are looking in a different direction, I discreetly move my napkin to my lips, spit out the offensive lump and roll my napkin tight enough to slide under the corner of my plate. Mission accomplished. No one sees it. If I were a product liability lawyer, I probably would spit it into a baggie and settle for $10 million out of court. But I am a transactional lawyer. I am only worried about being seen spitting it out. On with the dinner.

That evening, I bunk down at an Orlando airport hotel. In the morning I will be flying to Detroit to rent a car and drive to Holland, Michigan, where an investment banking client is negotiating to finance the expansion of the community hospital.

Before leaving the next morning I check in by phone with my wife, Susan.

"You do not sound good," she says.

"Man, I'm coming down with something." My answer is distracted and noncommittal. "Just feels like a head cold, maybe. Nothing to worry about."

After landing at Detroit Metro and picking up a rental car, I head to the nursing home near Five Mile Road and Outer Drive to visit my sister Jan. She is now in her thirties. The visit is short. My head is starting to pound as I leave Detroit for Holland. Also, my throat is parched.

By the time I reach my hotel in Holland, it is clear that I am succumbing to summer flu. The next morning, flu is off the table.

"Susan." I have trouble holding the phone steady enough to speak directly into the receiver. "I have a high fever, and I'm shaking." Shaking sounds less alarming than convulsions. But verbiage does not change the reality.

"They have arranged for someone to drive me to the airport nearest here." With the energy of screaming, my voice barely manages to be just above a whisper. "I need for you to meet me at the Tallahassee airport. I don't think I can drive."

Whatever this is, it is really bad. During the next four weeks, the fevers fall into a pattern, starting low and building to a very high level. Then the fever breaks for about twelve hours and the pattern starts over. Dysentery is the order of the day. Nothing will stay in or down, and nothing seems to provide any energy. Outpatient treatment accompanies an incredible number of tests and interrogations.

The tests are all negative.

Tests are performed for hepatitis and HIV and for parasites. All negative.

Meanwhile, the fevers keep getting higher, and I keep getting sicker.

"We know about one thousand things you don't have." My doctor feigns humor as he signs the order to admit me to Tallahassee Memorial Hospital, the regional facility for the Big Bend area. "We just don't know what you do have."

The obvious next sentence is left unsaid: I am dying.

The intravenous antibiotics do not even touch the progress of the disease. Finally, after several days in the hospital that follow almost six weeks of extreme illness, the doctor shows up in my room outside of rounds.

"Please sit down." He motions to Susan and slides a chair in her direction. She sits to my left and takes my hand in hers.

"And please listen carefully." Now he is speaking directly to me, as I lie in the bed with my head slightly elevated and a fever raging in the high 103s. "Are you able to hear me and understand me?"

I nod slightly, knowing that I will not want to hear him or understand his words. It is early evening, and I am beyond tired. It has never occurred to me that a person could be this sick for six weeks and still be alive. I do not want to die. But in reality, at this point, the thought brings a sense of relief.

"We cannot figure out what you have." He speaks without gestures and without affect. My intuitive sense is that he is feeling failure.

"Clearly it is bacterial." He pauses for a quick eye check that Susan is securely seated. "Whatever it is, it has won and you have lost. Your liver has stopped functioning." Another eye check at Susan. "All the major organs in your body are engaged, and they are shutting down."

The room is completely silent . . . too silent.

"Mr. Recinella . . . Dale." He clears his throat. "It's over. You cannot survive the night. You cannot live more than another ten or twelve hours. You will not see tomorrow morning."

Susan is absolutely rigid, except for the squeezing of her hands wrapped around mine. I know he is going to say it. I have not thought I would ever hear it.

"Mr. Recinella, you need to get your affairs in order."

The children have visited in the afternoon. Susan's mom is minding them at home. Our pastor comes for the last rites. Before losing consciousness I kiss Susan good-bye. She is crying. She is staying. She will be here through the end. She is on *death watch*, though we have not yet heard the term.

The fever spikes tremendously high. I cannot keep my eyes open. I want to, but am unable to. My last visual moment is Susan, sitting next to my bed, looking at me as though the strength of her gaze could hold me here. It cannot. The fever has its way. My eyes fall closed. All is darkness.

Suddenly, at some point in the night, I find myself standing in the center of a room. It is not my hospital room. It is dark except for the illumination pouring from the person in front of me. I recognize Him immediately. It is Jesus. He looks exactly like His picture that hung in my bedroom as a child. He glows with a heat that defies description, both warm and luminescent, radiating out, penetrating the whole room and even my body. He is gazing at me intently, but He is not smiling. He is deeply saddened. There are tears on His face. He is weeping softly.

"Dale." His arms stretch out toward me as His head shakes gently with sorrow and disappointment. "What have you done with My gifts?"

The lawyer in me responds by defensive instinct, "What gifts?"

As He lists my skill set He does not look angry or perturbed, just sad, very sad. I will not be able to wriggle off this hook. He details every aspect of the intellect, education, upbringing, personality and temperament that is part of my worldly success. I still do not get it. The moment does not feel like a judgment. But every response that comes into my mind is defensive. "I have worked hard. I have made sure that my children go to the best schools." Even as the words spill from my lips, it occurs to me that I am talking code for upper class and expensive.

"We live in a safe neighborhood; my family is safe." There is that sensation again. While my mouth is yet moving, in my thoughts I hear the same code being expressed.

"Our future is financially secure." There it is again, the voice in my head, code for "We have filled all our barns and are building bigger ones." Only this time the thought comes with a memory of Jesus' words in Luke 12:16–21 about fools who fill their barns.

"I have taken care of my family, just like everybody else does." The overt defensiveness of my voice makes me realize that I am arguing with somebody. Who? He is not arguing back. Who am I arguing with? Myself?

Finally, His hands drop to His sides. His expression is not one of condemnation. Rather, it is like the look of dismay of a parent who has told their teenager something a thousand times and is beyond the point of belief that the child still has not heard it. He speaks with a pleading that borders on exasperation.

"Dale, what about all My people who are suffering?"

In that moment it is as if a seven-foot-high wave suddenly and unexpectedly breaks over me on an ocean beach. I am not at a beach, and the wave is completely transparent, invisible but tangible. I can feel its substance, and it is acidic—corrosive in the extreme. I feel that my very being will be dissolved in it.

Somehow, intuitively, I know in the moment that the acid is shame, the shame of the selfishness and narcissism of my life. My family is an excuse for taking care of only me, my ego and my false sense of importance. I struggle against the sense of dissolution penetrating every cell of my being, trying to muster a coherent response.

"Please!" I summon the energy for my last plea as Jesus is still tearfully before me. "Please, I promise You. Give me another chance, and I will do it differently."

That is it. That is all. The wave is gone. He is gone. The room is dark.

It is about six-thirty when I open my eyes the following morning. Susan has been sitting next to my bed all night, waiting for me to die. I shudder at the reality of my last visual thought before the night, my mind's last picture of her in this world.

"I'm not dead, am I?" My voice betrays its surprise at hearing itself again. There is a long moment before she responds.

"Well, you look pretty awful." Susan smiles with the full irony of her very long and rough night. "Obviously, you are not dead." There is another long moment of silence.

"Uh-oh." My sigh bears the full weight of having no clue as to what I have promised Jesus I will do.

There is no more fever. The bacterium is gone. The doctor says it is truly impossible. Three years later the bacteria will be identified as vibrio vulnificus, a flesh-eating bacterium that causes deadly food poisoning and wound infections. It is overwhelmingly fatal with external exposure. I swallowed it.

Nonetheless, the second half of my prayer has been answered. I have seen myself, my choices and my life as God sees them.

After Susan and I share with each other our experiences of that night, we look for an answer to the question, "Now what?"

In July of 1988 we fly to Steubenville, Ohio, and attend a tent revival. From the physical debilitation of the oyster, I can barely stand or walk. I need to return to our room often to lie down and rest throughout the day. Stamina is coming back very slowly.

The revival is maxed out, with more than one thousand people in attendance. The summer heat is intense. Susan and I have never attended a revival before. The experience is almost overwhelming. On the second night of the three-day weekend, the leader, speaking from the stage, invites anyone who is so moved to stand and proclaim aloud that Jesus Christ is their Lord and Savior.

I am not able to stand up on my own. Susan helps me to my feet. I am half-leaning on her and half-balancing on my cane. With a deep determination that almost throws me off balance, I close my eyes and say aloud what I have never shouted out loud before.

"I accept Jesus Christ as my Lord and Savior!"

In a moment I am seated and Susan is standing. Her words seem to come more easily and sound less forced:

"I accept Jesus Christ as my Lord and Savior."

I cannot believe it. In front of so many people, we have stood up in the one-hundred-degree heat and said out loud that we accept Jesus Christ as our personal Savior.

For two upper-crust conservative cradle Roman Catholics, it is a tough step. But the proof of the pudding is in the eating. When we stand up in front of all those people and say, "Jesus Christ is my Lord and Savior," we come away knowing it is true in a different way than we knew it before.

○-○-○

Our post-oyster, near-death experience question "Now what?" is still hanging out there. After returning from Steubenville in July of 1988, for me the question seems to point in only one direction: Fix Dennis. Get Dennis down to Tallahassee and rescue him. That means making a list of actions to check off. That is something I am good at.

I am still severely debilitated at the end of July. It is not easy to get on the plane to Baltimore-Washington International Airport, or to catch the cab to the rehabilitation center where Dennis will be ready and waiting to return with me to his new home in Tallahassee. I have spoken with him on the phone several times, even last night before this trip. Everything is set.

When I arrive at the rehabilitation center, about a thirty-minute cab ride from BWI on this sunny Saturday morning, a staff member motions for me to stay in the cab. I have a sinking feeling in my gut as the staffer walks closer and motions for me to roll down my passenger window.

"He's gone," the staffer explains and shrugs with an acquired sense of helplessness. "Dennis ran away about an hour ago. He appears to have snuck out through his window. We've looked everywhere, and no one can find him."

"What do I do?" Without realizing it, my air of attorney-on-a-mission competence has evaporated, and I am mirroring his shrugs of helplessness. "What do I do? Everything is set. How can I help him if he is gone?"

"You can't. Just go home. That's all you can do."

The return rides in the cab and the plane all blend together into a prolonged sense of confusion, mixed with anger, peppered with the physical pain of having made a trip far beyond my stamina. "It's a bad joke," I mutter over and over to myself while rocking my cane from left to right. "This is all just a really bad joke."

A few days later I am sitting in a follow-up meeting at church with about thirty other men from the Scripture renewal weekend in March. They have all heard the story of my night with Dennis in Baltimore. They have endured my illness and are as shocked as I am that I am still alive and walking around. Now they are my community of grief as I struggle to comprehend what the heck God is doing.

Within the white stucco walls of our regular church meeting room, we sit in a circle of molded plastic chairs, taking turns sharing the news that updates the stories of each of our lives since the big weekend. My anger is palpable. So is my frustration. A couple of the men slide away from the orbits of my swinging cane to avoid direct impact from its punctuation as I speak.

"Why? Why all of it? Why any of it? What was the point of this whole stupid exercise?"

My questions hang in the air for a few minutes before a chuckle breaks out from one of the elders of our group, Jim Galbraith, a retired architect, a Scotsman who grew up on a ranch in the Dakotas during the Great Depression. He has that rare gift of being able to laugh so warmly that you know he is just as embarrassed as you are, but he is also as tickled as he knows you are going to be. What starts as a chuckle grows into a belly laugh. He cannot hold it back anymore.

"Don't you get it, Dale?" He is standing and has an arm around me, maybe to stop the cane. "Don't you see it?"

"Get what? See what?" I am still way out of range.

"Dale, God did not bring you into Dennis's life for you to save Dennis." Jim is laughing so hard, he can barely speak. "God brought Dennis into your life to save you."

The room erupts. Everyone is laughing to the point of tears.

"I never thought of that possibility." My lawyer self tries to salvage some dignity.

"We know!" Jim is doubling over while slapping both his knees with both hands. "That's what's so funny!"

We make another visit to Pastor Foley and also to Friar Murray, the trusted friend and spiritual advisor who redirected my life after high school. We tell both of them what has happened and ask our post-oyster question, "Now what?" They encourage us joyfully. After reminding us to go slowly with extreme vigilance for the five children who are traveling with us, they point out that today the Roman Catholic Church teaches there is a place for even married people with children who want to take Jesus at His word.

We respond, "Show us the laypeople who are doing this so we can learn from them." In answer, our spiritual advisors direct us to a foreign land to study two laypeople who lived almost a millennium ago.

In August of 1988 Susan leaves for Assisi and Rome, Italy, to spend sixteen days in prayer and study of the lives of Francis and Clare of Assisi, two laypeople who sought to live the literal Gospel in their place, in their circumstances and in their time, the early thirteenth century. Francis did not want to be ordained. Clare did not want to be secluded in a cloistered convent. At heart and in spirit, they were both laypeople who wanted to live a life that made no sense unless the gospels are true. Yet they ended up becoming "religious," the Catholic term for nuns and monks and the ordained, because there was no other way to fit them into the Church of that time.

The study-pilgrimage is a great idea. It will be a great experience for both of us, but not together. A married couple cannot take five children, ages one to fourteen, on a study-pilgrimage with forty-eight nuns and priests. Susan goes first while I tend to the children. My turn will come later. Susan returns from her study-pilgrimage filled with the desire to step out in faith. But she has to wait patiently for me to catch up.

In June of 1989 it is my turn. Susan and the children will stay at my dad's house in Detroit while I attend the study-pilgrimage in Assisi and Rome.

On my first day in Rome, the fifty attendees are all invited to spend four hours begging in the streets of Rome. The experience is an intense exercise to rip us out of our First World milieu and transport us into the mind of Francis of Assisi, the beggar. That sounds nice. I am oblivious to the fact that I am wearing $150 jeans and a $125 pair of tennis shoes.

In the course of my begging in the streets of Rome, we are hit with a major storm. We find out later that it is the worst rainstorm in Rome in at least a decade. I have no jacket, no umbrella and no money. I cannot ask anybody for help because I do not speak the language. Still decked out in my hefty-priced jeans and shoes, I resort to scavenging through the garbage barrels at a construction site near the Church of the Stigmata, looking desperately for anything to protect me from the storm. I find an old blanket and some discarded plastic. They are filthy. I do not care. The blanket is to cover my body. The plastic is for my head.

The blanket swells with rainwater, unleashing streaks of gray filth that soon cover my shirt and run down my jeans. The dirt from the plastic runs down my hair and my face. As I struggle toward the Coliseum in gale force winds, American and German tourists who have taken shelter in the arches are pointing my way. A few laugh out loud. Rage burns in me, and I think, *I could buy and sell you five times in a week.* Suddenly, I stop dead in my tracks. This is it. This is what it feels like to be poor and ridiculed in the midst of people with excess.

As the storm wanes, I work my way closer to the pensione that is our temporary home in Rome. Finally, I drop in a heap on the ground in Largo di Torre Argentina, a bus terminal near Piazza Venezia, the national monument of Italy. I really look like a derelict now. For four hours, I sit with my hand outstretched, experiencing people's feelings toward me. I learn another truth: We do not have to say a word to the poor. They know whether we are feeling compassion or derision without us even opening our mouths.

The study-pilgrimage leaves Rome and heads for Assisi, where we will stay at Papa Giovanni, a pensione just a block from the city center. In this walled medieval city, Francis and Clare heard the challenge of the gospels and stepped outside the walls, outside the protections and status afforded by their elevated social and economic life, outside to where God's people were suffering. They heard the gospel challenge of Jesus' description of the Great Judgment in Matthew 25. So, as they sought out the lame and the lepers, the poor and the strangers outside the walls, they were filled with joy at ministering to Jesus.

After Assisi we move on to Rieti, which sits at the geographic center of the Italian peninsula and whose town center features a spot known as the "belly button of Italy." More significantly, it is the locus of so many significant events in the lives of Francis and Clare that it is called Francis's second home. After almost three weeks of study, prayer and visitation of holy and historic sites in Rome and Assisi, we will pause in Rieti to pray and reflect on how the pilgrimage is challenging us.

The night before we are to begin three days of silence at the mountaintop Monastery of Michael the Archangel, high above Rieti, I am having a cappuccino at an outdoor café with one of the nuns in our group. She is a quiet, gentle lady. I am impressed with her holiness and the presence that she brings to every situation. I was rendered speechless by her quote in open discussion of the words of St. Augustine, "So long as there are people who lack necessities, a person who has more than he needs is holding the goods of another." Tonight is finally an opportunity to become better acquainted.

Our discussion turns to the Vietnam War era. I am stunned as she matter-of-factly describes her Vietnam experiences as a missionary tending to orphans in the war zones. The stereotypes I have laid on her diminutive size and self-effacing manner are demolished as she relates her experiences evacuating small children to planes and choppers under live mortar and machine gun fire during the last days of the American evacuation.

"Well . . ." I finally break the silence that punctuates the end of her story, feebly clearing my throat. "Ah . . . what do you . . . ah . . . do now?"

"I work with AIDS patients in a Brooklyn hospital." Her response is as level and unruffled as her voice relating stories about dodging bullets in Southeast Asia.

I respond with a question that is truly fearful, a question rooted in a false sense of moral self-righteousness. This little Sister Mary Rambo looks me straight in the eye and says softly, "Who of us wants to face the worst possible consequences of our smallest mistake?"

Who wants to face the worst possible consequences of their smallest mistake? What a question. There is no room for arrogance or self-righteousness in the face of that question. I know the deeper meaning of her thought: "There, but for the grace of God, go I." That is the oft-quoted statement of Francis of Assisi when asked about his fleshly opinion of those who have done wrong. It is only by God's grace, he implies, that we ourselves do not face the worst possible consequences of our smallest mistake, let alone our worst.

I know what she means, and she knows I know what she means. I stare into my diminutive Italian coffee cup for a long time, unable to look into her eyes for the rest of the evening.

During the next two days of silence, we enjoy hours of prayer and Scripture reading in the small chapel of the mountaintop monastery.

On the final day of the pilgrimage, the leaders of the retreat ask me to read the closing Gospel selection. I agree and then can barely get through John 20:10–16:

> Then the disciples went back to their homes, but Mary stood outside the tomb crying. As she wept, she bent over to look into the tomb and saw two angels in white, seated where Jesus' body had been, one at the head and the other at the foot.
>
> They asked her, "Woman, why are you crying?"
>
> "They have taken my Lord away," she said, "and I don't know where they have put him." At this, she turned around and saw Jesus standing there, but she did not realize that it was Jesus.

"Woman," he said, "why are you crying? Who is it you are looking for?"

Thinking he was the gardener, she said, "Sir, if you have carried him away, tell me where you have put him, and I will get him."

Jesus said to her, "Mary."

She turned toward him and cried out in Aramaic, "Rabboni!" (which means Teacher).

The challenge is clear. If Jesus is the Teacher, as well as God become man, then how can I call myself His follower and not do what He said?

The flight from Rome to America takes eleven hours. The drive back to Florida from my dad's house in Detroit takes two days. But it may as well be a thousand years. Our old life is over.

8

Who Am I without a Desk
and a Phone?

BY THE TIME I RETURN from Rome and Assisi to Tallahassee
in August of 1989, the Lord has put it on my heart to minister to
people dying of AIDS. Susan has a strong desire to use her professional skills in working with their caregivers. I propose to support
our family and use my secular skills by developing housing projects
for the rural working poor in the areas around Quincy, Florida, near
Tallahassee. Based on our upbringing as cradle Catholics, we assume
God must want us to perform these services under the auspices of
the Church.

We prepare a full-blown package, like an investor prospectus,
and send it to our bishop in Pensacola, Florida. The attachments,
which are tabbed and indexed, detail our skills, our journey and
our call. The cover letter asks for an appointment for a meeting in
Pensacola at the chancery, the official name for a Roman Catholic

bishop's offices, to structure a way for us to live out Jesus' words in service to our Church. The Federal Express package elicits a brief telephone response from a clerical secretary at the chancery. We have a date and a morning appointment.

"How long do you think you will need?" Her voice grates like burnt toast. For a moment I wonder if she has misunderstood and thinks we are making a sales call.

"Well, we want to discuss with His Excellency how to structure our service for the Church. It should take a couple of hours, at least."

"Uh-huh. I'll put you down for thirty minutes."

No matter. We are ecstatic. This is it. We pray and fast and pour with new energy into reading Scripture and singing praise and worship. The big day comes. It is a Friday.

Susan's mom, who will stay with the children while we make the four-hour drive to Pensacola, meet with the bishop and then drive home, waves hesitantly as we back out of the driveway before dawn. We wave back enthusiastically.

The chancery building looks like any other southern frame church building. Our feet are barely touching the ground as we whisk from the parking lot to the reception desk. We are ten minutes early. Not late. Not too early. Perfect. I am sure that will create a good first impression.

"Good morning." My greeting fails to bring any cheer to the diocesan receptionist whose "thank God it's Friday" demeanor is now being interrupted before she finishes her first coffee. "We are the couple from Tallahassee, the Recinellas, here to meet with Bishop Symons."

"Oh yeah." Her tone, accented by accompanying rim shot, speaks volumes. My lawyer gut tells me this may not be what we think it is. I decide to ignore my business sense. After all, this is church, not business.

"Have a seat." She motions to a set of four identical chairs around a low-slung coffee table. "His assistant will be right with you."

My reaction is a nonverbal expression that says, "His assistant? We have an appointment with Bishop Symons."

Her nonverbal response to mine is a smirk that says, "You'll see."

When the young priest appears about twenty minutes later, we assume he will take us to the bishop. Instead he simply turns around with his back to us and closes the two doors that slide into the wall. Our waiting room is now a parlor of sorts. The coffee table is between us as he flops into one of the two remaining chairs, clearly annoyed at all of this.

"What can we do for you?" He speaks as though we are nameless vagabonds who have shown up from the street without notice to ask for money.

"My name is Dale Recinella, and this is my wife, Susan." I put my best foot forward. If this is going to be a cold call, then I'll handle it as a cold call.

He nods absentmindedly, as though our names are an inconvenience. With growing discomfort I note that he looks barely old enough to shave, hardly old enough to hold a driver's license. It occurs to me that this must be the newest seminary graduate, who serves as the bishop's driver and gofer. The sense that we are in a bad episode of *The Twilight Zone* edges into my spleen.

"And we sent Bishop Symons a Federal Express package two weeks ago, asking to meet with him to discuss—"

"Excuse me." He lifts an outward palm to me indicating it is time to stop talking. "The bishop has asked me to meet with you for him. There is really only one question here. Do you have children?"

"Why, yes." New energy comes to my words. At least he is interested in something. "Yes, five. We have their pictures here."

"No need." This time he is shutting Susan down as she reaches for the photos. "This is really very simple."

As much as we would like to hear something simple, my sense is that this simple news will not be good.

"You are laypeople with children." His tone is dismissive and condescending, as though we had shown up without identification and asked him to tell us who we are. "But you are trying to act like priests and nuns. You are suffering from excessive zeal."

"But . . ." I try to derail his canned delivery. This is worse than *The Twilight Zone*. Does he know that we are not kooks? Does he know that we are both accomplished professionals who are making an informed and well-thought-out choice for the Kingdom? Did anybody even read our blasted package? "Excuse me—"

"Go home." He will not allow me to speak. "Leave the work of the religious to the priests and the nuns. Go home and be good laypeople. Be an usher in your parish and teach in your Sunday school."

I want to respond that we are already doing those good things, yet we feel called to do more. But there is no chance for me to speak because this meeting is over. He stands abruptly, as if to avoid entertaining another word, and opens the doors. He motions for us to leave. As we step in front of him toward the exit, he speaks without extending his hand. "The bishop and I will have you in our prayers."

Susan is only able to hold back her tears until we are in the parking lot. I help her into the car and then vow that the stone cold receptionist inside the window over the lot will not have the enjoyment of seeing me cry. Even so, I am barely able to hold my pain until we are out of sight of the chancery building. We pull off to the side of the road and weep bitterly.

"Did we screw up?" I speak into the steering wheel, but Susan knows I am talking out loud to God. She always says it is an Italian thing, and instinctively leans away from me to avoid the lightning bolt if God is not part Italian. "Did we misunderstand about coming to Pensacola this morning? Did we discern this trip properly or not? What are You doing?"

"That's a thought, honey." She is still wiping tears and mascara from her face, but willing to recover quickly if God gives a sign. "Obviously Bishop Symons is not going to see us, but is there something else to see in Pensacola today?"

We pause and pray and think and keep wiping tears and sniffing into our hankies.

"There was a flyer at church last week. One of the guys from my men's weekend was passing them out. Something called a school for lay evangelization?"

"Is it here?"

"I think so."

"Is it open?"

"I have no idea."

"Well, dear, we have the whole morning and no place to go. Let's find it and check it out."

The School of Lay Evangelization is easier to find than we would have guessed. The Waffle House staff is able to give us dead-on directions. As we pull up to the brown-brick building, it strikes me as a recycled Catholic school. The building is surrounded by cars.

"Looks like something is going on here today." I open Susan's door, and we walk, hand in hand, up the concrete stairs and into the vacuous foyer. I turn and point toward where a man's voice is booming from behind doors that look like they might give access to a gym or an auditorium at an old school. "Whatever is going on is in there."

"Can I help you?" A greeter surprises us from behind. She sounds like she really wants to help if she can.

"Uh . . . who is speaking?" I nod my head toward the booming echoes rolling like thunder out of the auditorium.

"That is David Stewart. He is one of our teachers." She pauses sweetly and then helps us out with the obvious. "He is teaching right now."

"David Stewart? From Tallahassee?"

"Yes, is that where you're from?"

"I've heard of him. Is it possible to meet with him?"

"Not until after he finishes this class. Do you want to sit in on the rest of it?"

A furtive glance from Susan confirms what I am feeling: A large crowd is the last thing we need this morning. "It would be better if we could just sit someplace quiet until he is done."

"Sure. No problem."

Our greeter leads us to the end of the hall and opens two old metal swinging doors that bear a hundred coats of repainting but still cannot hide their rust. I am thinking that this looks just like a locker room door in high school. Then we step through it and realize that we are in an old locker room. The walls and vents have been barely retouched before removing the benches and sliding in gray metal desks for an administrative office.

It seems like ages before the doors swing open again. When they do, they swing wide in front of the warm smile and broad shoulders of a man who saunters with the gait of a farm boy. His arm is fully stretched out, palm open, ready to greet.

"Hey. I'm David Stewart," he begins, sounding pleased to meet us, "and I'm glad you're here this morning."

"We're glad you're here this morning," I rejoin before introducing Susan and myself. I notice that his eyes glint with a spark like fire. He is alive and intense. And he is joyful, really joyful. He really is glad we are here today.

"You all are a long way from home." He pulls himself up to the closest desk and sits atop it, facing us both from barely two feet away. "How can I help you folks?"

We share with him a brief recap of our journey from the High-grove house to the morning meeting at the chancery and our non-meeting with the bishop. He pauses before responding, looking at us and then down at his hands several times. Finally, he looks us dead in the eye and speaks the way a loving father speaks to his children.

"Don't be upset with anybody. It's not their fault. Nobody knows what to do with people like us." His smile spreads a little wider as he notices that I have picked up on his use of the word *us*.

"It wasn't too long ago, I was exactly where you are right now. I know exactly what you are going through, and I think I know just what you need." He is even more animated and excited, as though he is about to give us a free supply of our favorite ice cream for the rest of the year.

"I'm all ears," I say and nod with sincere interest. "We've got nowhere else to go."

"I run a street ministry in Tallahassee, in Frenchtown."

"That's it." I almost jump up from my desktop. "I knew I'd heard your name before. Frenchtown is the worst ghetto in Tallahassee."

"Yup." He nods without elaboration. "I want you to come down and help me minister to the people who live on the streets there, to learn how to love people who are different from you, different from any people you have ever known before."

"Wow. That's quite a proposal."

"I'll tell you what. . . ." His voice and expression have all the energy of the dealmaker about to spring the trap. "Seeing as how you've been a lawyer for fifteen years, I'll give you a desk and a phone until you know who you are without a desk and a phone."

"And an office window?" I cannot resist bargaining with this guy.

"Yeah, we have one of those. And even an office window."

The following Monday I take an extra-long lunch break in order to be orientated for volunteer service at Good News Ministries in

Frenchtown. There is no shortage of parking spaces in the twenty-foot-wide area between the porch and Georgia Street. All the patrons are on foot. Many of them are stretched out full length on the disintegrating asphalt, napping in the hot August sun before the lunch meal is announced. After working my car and then my steps around the obstacle course of sweaty bodies, I navigate the cockeyed angle of the three front stairs, push open the metal-cased glass door and find a greeting committee.

David is first, welcoming me with that whole body smile. Next to him a former Fortune 500 executive, wearing close-cropped hair and a shirt with sharp creases, grasps my palm in a business handshake, promising unlimited assistance with anything I might need. Claude, a Cheshire-grinning Cajun who arrived just weeks earlier to cook in the soup kitchen, smacks me smartly on the back with the force of his gratitude at not being the newest guy anymore. Randomly strewn around the lobby floor are piles of old clothes and chewed-up people.

David was not kidding. My mind sums up the new experience. This will be different, all right.

"Where's my desk and my phone?" I laugh over Claude's shoulder to David standing behind him. "With a window, don't forget."

"It's here." David is reassuring without sounding too committal. "But first we have to do lunch. How about helping Claude in the kitchen."

Another fellow already in the kitchen helping Claude has an MBA and seems exceedingly proud of his ability to wear a goatee now that he has escaped the confines of the corporate world. Both of the corporate refugees found their way here via the same route as Claude. They heard David preach about a different way to live, a different way to understand the gospels, a way that assumes Jesus meant what He said. When David said, "Come and see," they came to Frenchtown. They saw, and they stayed. As my eyes and my nose

struggle to identify—or in some cases, to avoid identifying—the assault of unfamiliar sights and scents, it is not at all clear to me that I will be staying.

"You are the newest guy, so you have door duty." Claude seems too happy with this delegation.

"What is door duty?" My blank expression telegraphs more naïveté than they could imagine.

"It is really very simple." At his answer, a cringe of acknowledgment rolls through me like shocks following a major temblor. *That is always the introductory clause for bad news,* I am thinking as he shoves a little pink pad and a pencil into my hand. What he is not telling me is that most new volunteers either quit or become permanent after just one or two days of door duty. It is the front line of this soup kitchen ministry.

"You just stand outside the back door and make sure that all the patrons line up and wait their turn." Claude has the understated tone of giving directions on how to flip a light switch on and off. "As people show up to get in line, you write a number on the next pink sheet and give it to them. Then, when we start the lunch, you call out the numbers in groups for seating. First to come, first to get a number, first to be served. It's really very simple."

"I'm sure it is. How many can come in at a time?"

"Oh, about ten to fifteen."

"And how many are usually lined up?"

"Sometimes forty or fifty. Sometimes more."

"Isn't it over one hundred degrees with ninety-nine percent humidity outside right now?" The question shadows my real thoughts. *Don't police go to school in riot control to learn how to do this?*

"It's really very simple. . . ." He purses his lips, indicating that this discussion is over, as he slides a solid steel strong bar out of its braces and swings open the reinforced door.

"We will be ready to sit the first wave in about ten minutes."

As with any ideal system that should be simple, there are a few glitches. The primary one is that almost everyone in line is determined either to beat the system or to make sure no one else beats the system. Another glitch is that the mere fact that one is assigned to door duty tells the street patrons that he is green. It is always open season on the new door guy.

It is not at all clear to me whether I have stepped out onto the concrete back porch or simply slid there when pushed by the door closing behind me. The clang of the heavy security bar being shoved back into position on the kitchen side of the door leaves a sinking feeling in the pit of my stomach, triggering the thought of one of my pet rules of life: Every job is simple until you have to do it yourself.

The sudden appearance of a hefty man in a three-piece charcoal gray pinstripe suit with flaming red silk tie and highly polished wing-tip shoes induces a stunned silence on the chatty, sweaty throng. My pupils are still adjusting to the transition from under-lit kitchen to blinding sunlight when the trouble starts.

Forty people? Fifty people? It seems to me that there are about a hundred people in line, if one can call it a line. It is more like a smear, meandering wildly to and fro from the back porch toward an old white cross mounted in the yard. Just short of that cross, it abandons any attempt at definition and spills off the remnants of pavement onto the remnants of grass. As my eyes focus, the blur of skin and sweat resolves into faces and glares and anger.

"What in blazes are you supposed to be?" yells an angry thirty-something midway between me and the cross. "Are you a cop?"

"No. Can't be," screams a lady of the street, barely covered at all against the August heat. "He's too fat to be a cop."

The mass of hungry people immediately disintegrates into raucous random debate about being fat in general and fat cops in particular. The words and the logic elude me because I am focusing

on the fact that the smear that was almost a line is morphing into a pulsating oblong pear shape and pressing in toward me. My back is pushing against the door, but it is not opening. This is it. There is going to be a riot.

"I see what the problem is here." An unfamiliar voice with just enough resonance projects itself from the far back of the mass. His pause has the timing of a stand-up comic. The shouts and raised fists subside instantly as everyone cranes against the sun to see who the new player is. As far back as he can stand away from me and still be on the property, a craggy, old, bone-thin black man, leathered by years of street life, is energetically pumping his pointed finger at me over the heads of all those between us.

"What?" A disembodied voice that might be mine responds from the porch where I stand between the locked door and the hungry, sweaty street people of Tallahassee.

"I see what the problem is here." He looks both angry and determined. He is moving my way, heading directly up the short side of the crowd, pointing relentlessly at me, working the audience up like a piston building a head of steam. He knows he has me. The whole crowd from the street knows he has me. I am the only one who does not yet know that he has me.

"What?" I am a little more forceful. The din of hysteria has vanished into the new focal point of everyone's attention. There is dead silence except for his accusing finger and my breathing. "What's the problem here?"

"I see what the problem is here!" He arrives at the steps to the porch as the front line of the mob falls back and yields the stage. With obvious difficulty and some help from the crowd, he lifts his rickety frame onto the porch and right in my face. He pauses for effect, baiting my response.

"What? What is the problem here?"

"The problem . . ." He turns and speaks to the crowd while

repeatedly driving his bony finger into the cotton vest sheathing my girth. "The problem is that you have been eating our food!"

Total pandemonium explodes like a thunderclap. Catcalls. Amens. And almost musical chants of "You tell him, brother."

The heavy metal bar screeches out of its sleeve and the door behind me opens. Claude steps out onto the porch bristling to my rescue with his full few weeks of authority, waving a wooden spoon high over his head and chastising the snickering patrons for abusing the volunteers. He calls them to order and prays a short blessing for the lunch meal.

"They were not in very much of a line," Claude sniffs disapprovingly to me with a sideways glance as he leads the first wave inside, "but I'm sure you'll get better."

I finish my first tour of door duty amid sneers and hiccups of "Hotshot Mista Lawya gotta have Momma Claude protect him" and "Big man, big suit, big whatever."

After the lunch David directs me to a room that is to be my new office. As soon as I clean it out, I can move in an old desk (which is standing on its side in the hallway) and plug in the phone, which is on the floor in the washroom. Since the phone is composed of parts that are three different colors, I assume it is a product of three broken phones.

In any event, as I clean out my new office, maggots are pouring out of holes in the paneling. After all the visible critters have been scooped into plastic trash bags and deposited into the rusted brown Dumpster in front of the building, I know that if I see one more maggot I will puke. I return to the little room only to find swarms of maggots—more than before—still pouring out of the wall. Three garbage bags of junk, rot and maggots later, I decide that my stomach is stronger than I thought.

By Wednesday, the office with a desk and a phone has been emptied of over forty years' worth of stored trash from the original owners and cleared of maggots and cockroach feces. The office does indeed have a window—with an unimpeded view of the posterior side of the Dumpster.

Susan picks out drapes for me. I am totally flexible on color as long as the liners are solid enough for me to pretend that Biscayne Bay is outside my window. After we hang them and set up a small table with a lamp, we pause for a moment to take in this new environment.

"In Miami I had a prestigious fourteenth-floor penthouse office overlooking Biscayne Bay with over twenty thousand dollars' worth of cherrywood furniture."

"Yeah," Susan responds with a laugh as she tries to get comfortable in one of the two Good News Ministries chairs that now appoint my street office. "I remember. I was there. I helped you pick out that furniture."

"Up the street, here in Tallahassee, my penthouse law office boasts a prestigious downtown address and an exquisite view of Tallahassee's Park Avenue, the Capitol and Florida State University."

"Yeah," she says, still laughing, "but you must admit, you've never had a view like this."

○─○─○

With habit, even exceptional activities can become routine. The daily lunch hours at Good New Ministries, from eleven until one-thirty, become the axis of every busy day in my week. My regular Good News Ministries assignment is door duty. It turns out that I am pretty good at it. I enjoy standing at the back door, chatting with the street people who are waiting to eat. By the end of the first week, they know I am not there to arrest, interrogate or investigate them. I am there only to learn how to serve them, so that I may serve my Lord by serving His least.

As summer merges into early fall of 1989, Susan and I spend

many long nights discussing our pilgrimage experiences of the walls that surrounded Assisi in the time of Francis and Clare. Those walls separated the comfortable people from the uncomfortable people, the insiders from the outsiders. We ask ourselves, "Where are those walls today?"

Through our experiences at Good News Ministries and our new relationships with the people who have never been to our suburbs, we learn that the invisible walls are there and are still very powerful in keeping us apart.

"How can the people we are getting to know at Good News present their needs to us?" Susan asks rhetorically after another prayerful rereading of the Great Judgment in Matthew 25. "They can't. They do not even have a phone to call us."

I am flustered as well. "Honey, they cannot move here. The only way we can be available to them is for us to move closer to them, close enough for them to walk to us without getting picked up by the police."

She nods and then smiles softly. "It's true, but the children have to be safe and be happy with the change."

"Absolutely, and if we can find the right rental, that could free us up to live on a lot less to boot." I reach for the brass ring. "I might even be able to work part-time."

In October of 1989 we sell our smaller suburban home and move into a center-city apartment, eight blocks from the soup kitchen at Good News Ministries. It is on the east side of Monroe Street, far enough away from the crack dealing to be safe for our children but close enough for our new friends on the streets to walk to our house and present their needs. We move ourselves with the help of a 28-foot truck and all our friends from Good News and our suburban church.

On Thanksgiving weekend, 1989, a few weeks after we move to the center city, we open our apartment for a potluck celebration of thanks to all of the friends who have helped us relocate our stuff. It is right out of the gospels. Engineers, university professors, government agency heads, lawyers and doctors sit, eat and talk with recovering drug addicts and former prostitutes and the homeless.

Starting with that weekend, every Thanksgiving and Christmas that we are in Tallahassee we host an open table at our home for anyone who wants to celebrate with us. We set the table, but dinner is whatever everyone brings to share. The experience is incredible. The street people come. They comply with our rule that they must be clean and sober. People from the wealthier neighborhoods come too. So do the elderly. Some are transported by friends because they are wheelchair-bound or using a walker with oxygen. Every time, right before beginning the meal, we all join hands—sometimes as many as thirty or forty of us—and praise God and bless His food.

The Gospel is breaking down the invisible walls in our lives, but there are still walls that are quite visible. Walls stand that we have not yet seen or crossed.

9

Which Master Do We Serve?

MATTHEW 6:24

How much money does a family need? That is the question on the table week after week as Susan, the children and I evaluate the possibility that I might work part-time. The upside is that I would be able to spend half my time in volunteer ministry and be able to stop traveling for business. The downside is that I will make a lot less money. Peter Cowdrey, a friend from the men's Scripture renewal weekend, is both educator and historian by profession. He finds our family's questions about Jesus and what Jesus said fascinating enough to join me at least once every week for prayer, Scripture and discussion.

"I don't know, Dale." Peter strokes his beard before placing his hands together in a prayer-like gesture. "I read the same gospels you're reading, and I understand what you're saying, but I don't think people do this."

"Peter, doesn't it really come down to the level of lifestyle that it is my duty to provide for my wife and children?"

"Well, yeah." He chuckles and leans back with his hands still joined in the supplicant gesture. "Everybody thinks it's a father's duty to make as much money as he can for his family—legally of course. I mean, why wouldn't you?"

"I wouldn't if my part-time income is sufficient for my family's needs, and the extra time will be available to relieve human suffering."

"I understand what you are saying, but again, I don't think people do that."

"That is not the question, is it? The fact that people don't do that really doesn't matter, does it?" My intensity causes Peter to laugh and roll his eyes a bit.

He recovers his serious composure in a flash. "I think, Dale, that it all comes down to this: If God has called you and Susan and the kids to this step, then you cannot not do it. You'd better be sure, though, and it had better be soundly based on Scripture."

"Doesn't it come down to the question of which master we are serving?"

"How do you figure?"

"I figure based on Matthew 6, verse 24." He opens his Bible as I thumb mine to the right page. "No one can serve two masters. Either he will hate the one and love the other, or he will be devoted to the one and despise the other. You cannot serve both God and Money."

"Yup." Peter laughs so softly that he does not seem to be laughing at all. "That's a scary one, all right."

"Well, I can tell you what it does not say."

"Fine, Dale." He leans back with a handover gesture, letting me have the floor. "What does it not say?"

"It does not say that if we pray hard enough, we can serve both

God and money. Or that if we go to church enough, we can serve both. Or if we are in the Word enough, we can serve both."

"You're right. It does not say that."

"But isn't that what most of us are pretending it says?"

"How so?"

"By making our decisions based on money and not on Jesus' instructions. Then we act like if we pray enough and go to church enough and read the Bible enough, it will still come out right."

"Careful," he needles me, refusing to concede, "or I'll tell the bishop you're getting overzealous again."

○-○-○

Wall Street is not favorable to part-time commitment. After the near-death experience with the oyster, I inform my firm and my clients that I will not work on Sundays anymore because of God's command not to work on the Sabbath. Competitors rev up potential clients with the fear that Recinella is now a Jesus freak, and if your deal needs a Sunday meeting or negotiation session, he will not be there for you.

Now I am proposing to reduce my availability to part-time. That will really throw a wrench in the works. The firm that welcomed me to Tallahassee in 1986 is too small to handle a part-time arrangement. That means my first step is to move to the Tallahassee office of a major firm. All my cards are on the table. I am offering twenty hours per week. Also, I am clear about how the rest of my time will be spent and why.

The Fort Lauderdale–based statewide firm Ruden McCloskey has the depth on the bench and the breadth of specialties to accommodate such an arrangement. They offer a strong Tallahassee office, headed up by a remarkable man of strong Christian faith, James Harold Thompson, former speaker of Florida's House of Representatives.

They promise the flexibility to accommodate my goals. In exchange I will supervise and train younger lawyers in public finance.

By January of 1990, we have lived for three months in the center-city apartment, affectionately referred to by friends, family and ourselves as the white house. My law firm work commitment is scaled back to twenty hours per week. Susan is working twenty hours per week in her post-doctoral residency at Eastside Psychiatric Hospital in northeast Tallahassee. She is accumulating valuable experience, working with the severely mentally ill. Meanwhile, I am earning my spurs learning how to serve the mentally ill on the streets.

We are astounded at how many of the street people patronizing the soup kitchen at Good News Ministries suffer from mental illness. The permutations in narrative are endless. What they all have in common is a lack of community services. The immediate need on the streets is for someone to be approved by the local office of the Social Security Administration to receive their monthly disability checks, deposit them in trust accounts and disburse their money to them three times a week. In a matter of days I am the payee for almost a dozen mentally ill on the streets.

By the beginning of 1990, Susan and I have both completed our training at Big Bend Cares, Tallahassee's nonprofit regional service provider for people with AIDS. Susan is trained to provide support for the caregivers. I am trained in death and dying in order to be a buddy.

No sooner have I completed the training than Big Bend Cares makes its first call to me for help. Less than a half hour later, I am inside the tilt wall–constructed office and cubicles of Tallahassee's regional AIDS service provider. The carpet, chairs and desks all smack of state government surplus, vintage 1970s.

"Thank you for getting here so quickly." The director is a young woman in her late-twenties, with highly polished skills for both gentle one-on-one support to the dying and the gladiator skirmishes over funding in the legislature. "I have the feeling that this new client is really going to need your spiritual guidance."

"In what way?"

"He showed up here yesterday, somewhat distraught. Then he said, 'I'm a veteran; I have AIDS and a gun, and if you don't give me a friend, I will kill myself.' I immediately thought of you as the best person to care for him."

"Really?" Hopefully, my thin mock question is masking the surge of outright panic.

"Absolutely." She sounds very confident for me. "He needs spirituality more than anything. We can make sure he has medicine and social services, but he needs spirituality."

"Because . . . ?" I invite her to finish the sequence.

"Because his spirit is dying from loneliness. I don't think he has a single friend in the world, only his mother."

"And you want me to be his friend?"

"That's why you're here." She makes a hint of a shrug at the obvious. "He is going to be a challenge, and I think you are the best one to handle him."

His apartment is on the first floor in a low-end project. A freshly painted brown wheelchair ramp has been hastily installed in anticipation of the inevitable. My banging on the door triggers a less-than-enthusiastic response.

"Who is it?" His question is peppered with profanity.

"I'm here from Big Bend Cares. They said you need a friend."

"So get in here already."

The unlocked door opens to a disheveled efficiency. The kitchen area to the left is piled high with dirty dishes and reeks from an abundance of trash avalanching from a plastic can that has long since given up the fight. The single bathroom is visible straight ahead. To the right, where one would expect a sofa, is a hospital-type bed with my new friend sitting upright toward a television, mindlessly surfing channels.

"So, how much are they paying you to be my friend?"

"I'm a volunteer. No pay."

"Well, aren't you special."

"No, just a volunteer."

"What do you know how to do, Mister Volunteer?"

"What do you need?"

The strange young man on the hospital bed lets the remote drop to his lap and stares into space.

"I don't know," he says without looking at me. "I don't know what I need."

"Then let's start by getting you out of this place for a while. Can you walk?"

"Yeah, I'm not dead yet."

"That's a good sign. Let's go to Lake Ella and feed the ducks. You know, the beautiful lake with a fountain surrounded by a walking path just north of downtown Tallahassee? There's a ton of ducks there."

"Why would I wanna feed ducks?" he grouses, sprinkling his words with curses as though they were punctuation marks.

"I've always found that, no matter what is bothering me, feeding ducks makes me feel better."

"If I call that stupid Big Bend office and tell them I fired you, will they give me someone else?"

"Nope. I'm your only shot."

"You and the friggin' ducks!" He lets go with a blue streak of protest as I drag him against his will into the car and to Lake Ella, where I retrieve several bags of expired bread from the trunk.

"What are you, a baker?" His cynicism is unreserved.

"No. It's expired bread from the soup kitchen, too old to use for people."

"So you give spoiled bread to the ducks? What kind of a person are you?"

"The kind of person who is sitting here with you."

We go to movies, attend FSU baseball games and feed ducks. As his ability to walk begins to falter, we take a wheelchair. Soon, even that is barely feasible.

To the extent any cleaning has been done in his apartment, it has been done by his mother. Her husband, a stepfather to her son, has been the heavy lifter, literally. A navy vet himself, he is the one who has helped bathe and lift her son. This stepfather is all man, and all compassion. I cannot help but wonder if Joseph, the earthly stepfather of Jesus, was not cut from the same cloth.

As for the mother, I consider the woman an absolute gem for Jesus. She is a solid Christian, a Southern Baptist with generations of religious roots. Her boy went off in the military and came back addicted to heroin and a victim of AIDS. Since returning from overseas, he has refused any interest in God or faith. She never complains and never condemns what God has allowed. She keeps her Bible close and her Savior closer. She keeps praying.

As the disease progresses, my friend is becoming bedridden. My assistance is now as much practical as spiritual. A male nurse is frequently on duty, as diapers must be changed and medications monitored. It is a late-summer afternoon. I am standing at the kitchen sink in his apartment, washing dishes and compressing trash. The odor of bleach hand wipes and latex gloves is so prevalent we no longer notice it. He is too debilitated to speak much. So I am shocked when he summons the energy to yell out to me from his station in the hospital bed in the living room.

"I want to go to church."

"I don't believe you. Is this a ploy to get something from me?"

"Blast you. I mean it. I want to go to church." The words are laced with his customary profanity.

"Great. I'll call your mom, and she will be very happy to take you."

"Not her church." There is the profanity again. "I want to go to your church."

"My church? You do not even know what faith I am. Why would you want to go to my church?"

"Because I want to understand why you would come here."

I pause to turn off the water before shaking my hands off over the sink. "Well, we know it's not for the money."

I refuse to take him to church without his mother's approval. I will not allow him to use me as a weapon against her by feigning a new zeal for God. When I give her the news, she breaks down crying over the phone.

"Please, by all means. I've been praying for this for years. Get him to your church. Bring him to the Lord before it's too late."

Getting my friend to church will not be a small feat. He is diapered, wheelchair bound with an IV bag and only weeks from the end. I cannot just wheel him into a packed Sunday service. There is no way to know how people will react. Moreover, I will need the help of his nurse.

There are two options for a weekday morning service. One is at eight-thirty nearby at our new center-city parish. The other is nine o'clock at our prior suburban parish. The earlier one should be less attended and easier to arrange access to.

I contact our new shepherd, Pastor John O'Sullivan. He is totally supportive and welcomes my friend's attendance. He even arranges for some folks to be there as greeters to welcome him.

When the special day for my friend's church visit finally arrives, the nurse and I clean him, change him and struggle to maneuver him into his chair, out of his apartment and into my car. No sooner is he buckled in than his bowels let loose. Now we do it all again in reverse.

By the time we are pulling out with him in the car, we have lost the opportunity for eight-thirty. There is no choice. We head to the suburban parish for the nine o'clock service. It will be a just-in-time arrival, unannounced and unexpected.

As we wheel into the chapel, there are about fifty attendees standing in song to open the service. The priest immediately assesses the situation and responds with more grace than one could have dared to ask for.

"We have a special guest this morning," he announces, motioning the folks in the front row to slide toward the end and remove two of the foldable seats on the aisle. "Please, come right up here in front."

Then, as we settle into the front row, the priest comes to my friend, bends over his chair and hugs him warmly.

"Welcome," he says loudly enough for all fifty to hear. "Jesus has been waiting for you to get here."

At the handshake of peace, just before Communion, every single person in the chapel comes to my friend and hugs him. Everyone is smiling, and there is not a dry eye in the place.

After the service the nurse and I are wheeling my friend to the parking lot when three older ladies approach him.

"Here." They shove a fistful of beautiful color prints into his hands. "These are pictures of the gospel stories. You can look at them while you pray."

"Thank you," I mumble on his behalf, not wanting to seem overly grateful to these ladies, whom I have always considered to be a bit over the edge.

The youngest of the three grabs my arm. "Oh, you should know this. It's miraculous that we are here. We always go to the service at eight-thirty in town, but our car broke down. The only service our ride could get us to was this one."

Those pictures hang over my friend's bed from that day until the moment he dies. They are the only Gospel he reads; legible to his eyes that can no longer focus on print. When he is unable to speak without extreme difficulty, his eyes lock on those pictures for hours at a time. Often, he points to Jesus in the pictures and smiles.

Before he dies he indeed comes to the Lord. As he breathes his last, his head and shoulders are in my arms, his mother and stepfather are holding their arms around him from the other side of the bed and the nurse is standing at the foot of his bed. All of us are praying aloud together the Lord's Prayer.

As his soul is leaving his body behind, I find myself reflecting on that special day when my friend came to church. The priest and the people surrounded him with love and acceptance, and the women who were not supposed to be there showed up with the Gospel pictures he needed to understand God's love and accept salvation. *How far God will go to save us*, I think in a moment of profound gratitude. *Use me, Lord, for Your saving work.*

O-O-O

As the weeks and months pass, there are more buddies to meet and to say good-bye to. In the meantime my Good News office is becoming a sacred place for prayer with men who are in need of Gospel healing for their memories, their emotions and their thoughts. These are not just men from the streets, but even men from my prior life—former clients, colleagues and fellow parishioners. Word is getting around that I have had some kind of a drastic life change. Some call it a breakdown. Others call it a conversion. Still others call it insanity. Be that as it may, I find a fairly steady procession of old acquaintances venturing down to Georgia Street to find out for themselves.

One former client who visits is concerned that I may have misunderstood what Jesus meant. He sits pensively in the chair opposite mine, with a panoramic view of the Dumpster and the street life outside my window. A prostitute is hawking for tricks across the street. A wobbly fellow without shoes is chasing someone down the center of the street while waving a baseball bat over his head.

"I used to have curtains that closed, but someone stole them," I say, smiling weakly, noting that the reflection of my apology in his eyes seems to prove his point.

"This is not the best use of your talents, Dale."

"Yes, I know, the gospel passage in Matthew 25, verses 14 to 30." I cut to the chase. "But we think that Jesus is talking about something other than money in that parable, especially because it comes right before His description of the judgment of the nations. Their apathy in the face of relievable human suffering appears to merit eternal condemnation."

He is unconvinced. "Tell you what. Give me your phone number so my dad can call you. He is a minister. You can talk to him about it."

A few days later, when one of our children answers the home phone and tells me that it is a minister guy, I take the call in my favorite chair. That way I can at least sit comfortably for another bout of the talents speech. We get the lecture so often now that we have given it that nickname. It started after our move from the suburbs to the center city and the reduction of my lawyer hours to part-time in order to be freed up for uncompensated ministry. Before that almost no one ever spoke to us about Matthew 25:14–30. Since that, we hear about it more than once a week.

The lectures are well-intentioned and are from folks who genuinely believe that in Matthew 25 Jesus was talking about the ability to make a lot of money. Understood that way, the parable stands as ironclad proof that, at worst, Susan and I are apostates. If given the benefit of the doubt, we are suffering from excessive zeal and acting like uppity laypeople who think they are priests and nuns.

The problem that no one seems to address is that, if Jesus is talking about making money in Matthew 25:14–30, then no layperson is in His Father's will unless he gives his whole heart, whole mind, whole soul and whole strength to making money. We know that cannot be what Jesus meant. I know that intellectually and experientially. I remember what my life was like and what I was like when all my time, mind and resources were poured into making money. Life was so barren and my soul so dead that I needed the constant medication of nicotine and alcohol and disastrous relationships just to keep putting one foot in front of the other. We are convinced that the making of money cannot be the use of our gifts that Jesus is talking about in Matthew 25. However, we lovingly allow others to try to do us well by telling us otherwise.

"This is Dale Recinella." I slip into my lawyer phone voice without thought.

"Good evening." The voice on the other end is gentle and melodic. "I am so glad to meet you, even if just by phone. My son has told me all about your work with people with AIDS down at Good News Ministries in Tallahassee. God bless you for your wonderful work."

"Well, thank you, Reverend," I respond, sincerely thinking, *Never heard this approach before. This guy could sell ice to Eskimos.*

"That is why I want to talk to you tonight."

"I'm ready, sir." Susan hands me a cup of coffee as I get comfortable in my chair, readying myself for the lecture. "What's on your mind?"

"I am the senior chaplain of a two-thousand-man prison in the Panhandle of Florida."

"Uh-huh." I almost spill my coffee by sitting forward too quickly. This is not the right script.

"Our medical staff has told me that a large percentage of our inmates are HIV positive. Why, I have men going into the final stage of AIDS. . . ."

"Uh-huh." Now my coffee is spilling. This is not the talents speech. Get on task—the talents speech.

"I cannot get any Christians to come into the prison and minister to them. Everyone is afraid."

"Uh-huh." No, no, no. *God, don't ask me to do this.*

"But you already are ministering to people with AIDS. You are not afraid."

Susan rushes over to me and takes the coffee cup. She has no idea what is wrong, but she is sure that I look like I would if I were having a seizure or a stroke.

"So I'm asking you, Brother Dale, will you come to my prison and pray with the inmates with AIDS?"

"Chaplain," I finally break the silence that has extended far too long. "I'm overwhelmed at your request." It is easy to sound sincere, especially knowing that he has no idea how overwhelmed I am. "I promise you I will pray about it." That also sounds sincere because I will pray, and I am certain that God could not even think of asking me to do this.

"Thank you, Brother Dale, and we will pray for you to hear God clearly."

Susan is as surprised as I at the request, but she is not as certain that God is out of the mix. The apartment is too small to allow for private discussions in the living room. In a matter of minutes the discussion expands to a family round table. Someone in the room suggests that this would be a good subject for a family meeting.

Since leaving the path most traveled, our family makes all our decisions by family discernment. That has included the three older children from my first marriage, who live with us, and the two younger children born to Susan and me. By now, my eldest son has moved on up north where he will go into business with a friend. But Christina and Jeanette are still here. They and Chris and Addie participate in discernment of all issues that affect our daily life as a family. That is part of our new Gospel life. Anyone in our family, even the three-year-old, can call a family meeting over their concerns. Everyone in the family has covenanted to hear them out and to take the concern seriously.

The family meetings are a reflection of the mechanisms Susan and I use for joint discernment. We have covenants with each other that we will not take a step unless both of us are called. That makes it possible to fearlessly allow each other to dream out loud about what God might be calling us to do. We trust and rely on each other's integrity, in and with God, to refrain from any stepping out until God calls us both. And we are on solid scriptural ground because, before God, we are a unity, a unity that God will not tear asunder.

This restructuring of our family relationships is a major part of my effort to learn how to be a servant leader. I have known how to be a top-down power leader, a do-it-or-else leader. But a servant leader? That is coming slowly with grace and the often humbling and difficult effort to overrule my ego by surrendering to mutual spousal and family discernment. Prison, however, seems like a whole different kettle of fish. I am not at all convinced that my going to prison is a proper subject for a family meeting. Everyone else disagrees.

After a few days for Susan, the children and me to separately read Scripture and pray for God's leading, our family meeting on Dad's issue of prison ministry is convened around the dining room table. We start with an opening prayer and a Scripture. Everybody but me already has their Bible open to the same place, Matthew 25:36: "I was in prison and you came to visit me."

Obviously, some caucusing has been taking place outside my presence.

"There is no doubt that Jesus wants us to visit people in prison in general," I lead off with my best defense. "The question is whether He is asking *me* to do it."

Susan speaks as though explaining the obvious to the oblivious. "Honey, you would never have come up with this on your own, not in a thousand years. You get claustrophobia in a stairwell or elevator. This has to be from God."

"Yeah, Dad." Christina, now a high schooler, feels entitled by life stage to be principled about my principles. "And you always say that Jesus meant what He said. Well, He said this."

"And," adds Jeanette brightly, refusing to be in anyone's shadow just because she is a middle schooler, "Jesus says He's going to be really mad at the people who don't do it. See?" Her little finger is tapping at the first line of verse 41: "Depart from me, you who are cursed, into the eternal fire prepared for the devil and his angels."

"Doesn't sound good, Dad," Chris goes on record. Addie, who cannot yet read, still looks exceedingly solemn as she shakes her head in agreement that it sounds pretty bad.

The vote is five to zero with one abstention, mine.

The only way to trump that vote is to go over their heads. I make an appointment to see Pastor Michael Foley. He greets me with a combination of genuine warmth and the apprehension borne from knowing that God only knows what I will ask him.

"What's on your mind? How can I help you?"

"Prison . . ." I recap the whole story and end with the punch line, "So, what do you say?"

"Have you ever been in prison?"

"Not really. I have financed prisons and jails, but I have never been in one except in law school, and that didn't go so well."

He is smiling too much. My blood starts to chill. "Well, Dale, Susan and the kids are right. You would never have come up with this."

"And . . ." I am not sure that he is headed in the right direction.

"If you did not come up with this, then who did?"

"Could it be from the evil one?"

"Not likely, since it's exactly what Jesus asked us to do and remarkably what God has prepared you to do."

"Is 'not likely' the same as no?"

"Dale, I think this one is from God. He will give you what you need to do it."

Wrong answer. I repeatedly clench the steering wheel down Thomasville Road on the way home. What trumps a wife, four kids and a pastor?

"This is Friar Murray." The voice on the other end of the line is reassuringly familiar. My spiritual director from high school is still at the same phone number after all these years.

"Yes, Friar. This is Dale Recinella." We exchange pleasantries, catch him up on the developments since Susan and I were each with him on our Assisi pilgrimages and then turn to the task at hand.

I repeat the story from the chaplain's call until my meeting with Pastor Foley earlier this evening. "So, Friar, I need to know if you think this is God's will for me."

"That will take some prayer and reflection, Dale. How soon do you need an answer from me?"

We agree on a week. He calls exactly one week later to the day. Susan and the children pile around my chair as I brace to take the phone.

"Yes, Friar?"

"Well, Dale, I'm not sure you're going to like my answer."

"It is what it is, Friar. What did you discern?"

"I rarely experience an answer in such dramatic terms."

"Okay, Friar, I can handle it."

"I think that if you say no to this, you will be turning away from God's plan for your life."

It is not possible for me to say anything more, except "Thank you" and "Good-bye."

Susan can read my face. Christina and Jeanette grasp my affect. Chris inhales their understanding. Addie is left a bit in the dark.

"What happened?" she asks, reminding us that she is barely three.

"Dad's going to prison," someone explains. The other children nod with satisfaction.

"Yes." My nod is neither energetic nor determined, just quietly relenting. "That's exactly right. Dad is going to prison."

10

Going inside the Walls

MATTHEW 25:36

APALACHEE CORRECTIONAL INSTITUTION, called ACI, is a large prison just fifty miles west of Tallahassee, near the town of Sneads. It sits on the far side of the Apalachicola River, well into the rolling hills of Panhandle Florida, barely into the central time zone. The prison is divided into two camps, a west unit and an east unit. I will be serving in the west unit, which has its own beautiful chapel building. The chaplain of ACI West meets me in the parking lot with a warm hug and, by an arm around the back, steers me to the control room gate.

From the parking lot most of the prison is barely visible. It is a collection of white and yellow one-story buildings, mostly dorms and work areas, dispersed around a central yard that is ringed with double- and triple-razor-wire-topped fences that are at least twelve feet high. Huge gates sporting massive padlocks stand as the portals from each section to the next. Off to my right, behind layers of fences, sits the little chapel of ACI West. If it were not for all the fences and razor wire, it might pass for any ordinary Bible Belt church. It even has a tad of a steeple. But there is nothing ordinary about this situation and no way to pretend the fences, razor wire and locks are not there.

The control room is housed inside an ivory white mini-building that serves as the entrance to the prison. The exterior grounds are immaculate, trimmed and manicured to a degree that is unique to prisons, military bases and monasteries, which have an unlimited supply of young male laborers who are not allowed to refuse work orders. The loud, grinding metallic shrieks that emanate from the opening gate are jarring.

As I step through the portal from outside to inside, my instincts for self-preservation impel me to walk as close as possible to the chaplain, who suddenly feels like my new best friend. He does not appear to be aware of my closer proximity as he introduces me to uniformed officers and plainclothes staff with the offhanded casualness of bringing a new guest into a party in process at his home.

"This is our new volunteer chaplain." He is all smiles as he leans forward, speaking into a muffled porthole in the bulletproof glass of the control room. "Brother Dale will be coming every week to be a prayer partner with our inmates."

The faces on the other side of the glass appear noncommittal. The white-shirted female lieutenant, the brown-shirted sergeant and numerous correctional officers, called COs, all sport a "We'll see" expression as I wave numbly from the narrow beige sally port.

"You'll need to go through security here." The chaplain points to a metal arch of a machine that stands between two very tall, very gruff-looking COs. He is completely unruffled. As I empty my pockets and strip off shoes, glasses, belt and watch to pass the metal detector, he calmly narrates the history of the camp, as though giving a tour at Disney World.

"This was a farm for the mental health system when that was under the Department of Corrections. Then a few years ago, it became part of ACI. It's a good camp, and the staff is happy you are here."

Before I have time to complete the thought that they do not look very happy, his narrative is suddenly interrupted by a sharp bang in the wall behind us. I jump at least a foot straight into the air.

"No worries." He smiles with a hand on my shoulder to keep me back on the ground. "That's just the electric bolts snapping back into place. It's for security."

We clear control and enter an outside passageway that is flanked on both sides by triple rows of the high fences topped with razor wire. I must look a bit peaked because the chaplain's hand is on my shoulder again.

"It's for security."

From our narrow fenced path I can observe the main yard. Hundreds of men dressed in prison blue are lined up in rows for count. As the COs grunt and call out numbers, the prisoners seem to be taking a break from their monotony by checking me out. Hundreds of eyes size me up. I feel naked and vulnerable. Without realizing it, I am walking so close to the chaplain that he almost trips as his heels hit the front of my shoes.

"That's your flock." His grin is imbued with wonderment, pointing toward the assembled masses of blue. "It's a mission field. Many of the guys in this camp are lifers and have nothing to lose but their souls."

Before reaching the chapel, we must traverse two more gates. They are padlocked and can only be opened by a guard in the yard.

Each time we wait, I check to see if the mission field is still checking me out. They are.

"I know. It's for security," I quip. My smile is too lame and my voice is lamer, as a yard officer unlocks the last gate.

The chaplain unbolts the white wood chapel doors and ushers me into a rustic sanctuary. The wood of the ceiling and pews mates evenly with the light brown brick walls, marshaling a solemnity that surprises me. I find it inspiring, an oasis of heaven in the midst of barbed wire and massive electric dead bolts.

"We will do your training this morning." The chaplain steers me through the small kitchen, past the card room that will be used for my prayer counseling and into his office. "Then I will show you how to get your keys when you come in. Next week, you can start."

So far, so good. I have not had a panic attack or fainted. Surveying the kitchen and the card room, I note approvingly that this place is clean enough to eat off the floors. No maggots or cockroach feces or Dumpsters or baseball bat–wielding wild men. Maybe this won't be so bad after all.

The card room that will serve as my base of operations for prayer ministry is about four feet wide and ten feet deep. It is ringed with shelves six layers high and serves as the storage closet for Christmas cards, Mother's Day cards, Father's Day cards, greeting cards, birthday cards, thank-you cards, get well cards and bereavement cards. Every possible kind of card that the inmates might need are all sorted, counted, labeled and filed in neat piles on the shelves.

"We will make it clear that none of your prayer partners are allowed to ask you for cards." The chaplain speaks with a seriousness I do not yet comprehend. "The inmates are not allowed to have money, but cards are a commodity that can be traded like money. If the inmates think by coming in to see you, they can get cards from you, well . . ." His voice trails off. "We just cannot allow that to happen."

"Security?" I attempt to change the subject by pointing to the small shatterproof glass window that has been inserted into the otherwise solid fire door of the card room.

"In more ways than one." He shakes his head sadly. "Of course, we never want an inmate to think he has you alone out of everyone's sight. That is not a good idea. A lot of these guys have problems."

"Sounds like there is more to it," I prompt without being sure that I really want to know more.

"Well, some of the guys might find out that you're a lawyer, and they might think you have money. So if you were behind a closed solid door with them for twenty or thirty minutes, they could claim that you made sexual advances on them."

"In order to shake me down for money?"

"Yeah, it could happen." He is waving off the thought as though it is as remote a possibility as the earth colliding with Mars tomorrow. "It's not to be expected."

"But that is why every single door in this building, even to the bathrooms, has a window?" I am mentally reassessing how likely a planetary collision must be in light of all the precautions.

"Yes." He nods and defaults to his warm southern grin. "It's just security."

We spend the next four hours in his office as he orients me to the world inside the fences. Finally, he strolls to my side of his desk, engaging my sweaty palm in a long warm clasp.

"Brother Dale, welcome to ACI West. You are going to really serve the Lord here. I can feel it."

"Thank you, chaplain." I am praying inside that some of his confidence in me will rub off on me. "Are we done?"

"Just one more thing. On the way out we have to stop in classification so you can sign some release papers."

"What kind of release papers?" the lawyer in me asks reflexively.

"You know, the usual bureaucratic stuff. The department is not liable if anything happens to you." He pauses to let me digest that before finishing. "If you are taken hostage, they will not negotiate for your release or for your life. You're a lawyer. You know how all that paper work stuff goes."

By the time I am finally sitting back in my car in the prison parking lot, I pause to re-collect my stamina for the hour's drive home. Before turning the ignition key, I am filled with a sense of relief that visual inspection confirms my bladder has not voided on me.

○─○─○

Our regular life is filling with ministry. There are the street people for daily lunch at Good News Ministries. Then there are the mentally ill payees who need their money three times a week—at least three times a week. My payees have grown into a small mob. The thrice-weekly money handouts frequently are accompanied with lectures about proper behavior and leaving the police alone. There are the AIDS victims on the streets and in their apartments. Just a few years ago, Susan and I had asked, "Where are the people who are suffering?" Now we are fairly drowning in them.

How does one fit this new prison ministry work into such a schedule? The obvious answer is Saturday. The children are busy with activities. Susan is busy with weekend errands and grocery shopping. The payees are not expecting money. I do not have to be at the law firm. Saturday is the day, and from eight A.M. until two P.M. is the time.

On the Saturday of my first actual week of ministry inside the walls, I am comforted that the chaplain will be there. He believes it is best for him to stay around for a few Saturdays until I have found my prison feet. After being processed through security and finding my way to the chapel, I am stunned to find the inside swarming with blue-clad inmates.

"Good morning, sir." A stocky fellow just a tad shorter than me but built like an armored tank meets me immediately inside the door. "I am Kenny, the chaplain's clerk." He does not extend his hand first, but waits for me to do so and then responds. That tells me he has been raised in the South, probably Georgia or north Florida.

"The chaplain wants to see you before you get started, sir."

"What are all these guys doing here? Is there a program this morning?"

"Uh, no, sir, not really." He is clearly afraid of spilling too many beans before the boss weighs in, but my look demands more information. "They're kind of here to see you."

"Ah, Brother Dale." The chaplain stands immediately as we enter his office. "So glad to see you here today."

"Quite a crowd."

He motions for his clerk to step out and close the door. "Yeah, we need to talk about that."

"Okay."

"You know, after you were here last week, I met with the administration and with security and classification, and we realized that we could not put up a sign in the dorms that mentions HIV or AIDS."

"I'm not sure I follow."

"It's really very simple." There is that phrase again. I wince as the chaplain continues, speaking very deliberately. "If anyone knew that you were here to minister to men with HIV or AIDS, then every man who came to see you would be revealing his condition."

"I presume that would be a bad thing." I lapse into the Italian gesture of rolling my hands, trying to reel his words out into the open.

"Well, they would probably get killed."

"I beg your pardon."

"Brother Dale." He leans back in his chair, with hands clasped in an entreating posture that will become very familiar to me over the years. "Movies and television try to make it look like all the guys in prison are on the same side, that they all look out for each other. It is not true. . . .

"If anything, it is dog-eat-dog," he continues after a pause to lean forward and place his elbows on the desk. "These men feel outcast and condemned, so if there is a reason to think that some of them are worse than the others, they'll grab it and act on it."

"For instance?"

"For instance, if someone's crime involves children, that can never be made public inside or it's a death warrant."

"Really?"

"Or if someone has HIV or AIDS, there are others on the compound who will kill them for that."

"You're kidding."

"No. Sadly it is true."

"So why are all these men here, and why am I here?"

The chaplain smiles triumphantly. "We sent out a posting to all the dorms that you were coming to be a prayer partner for men who are dealing with difficulties."

"Difficulties? Like physical difficulties?"

"We didn't limit it—physical, emotional, spiritual. Any difficulties."

"How many men are there in the camp?"

"About fifteen hundred."

"How many aren't here for prayer?"

"That's the spirit." The chaplain misapprehends my thrust as a plea for 100-percent participation. "It is a mission field. Let's go reap the harvest."

The chapel kitchen hall cannot hold the forty to fifty men waiting for prayer. We assemble them in the chapel itself so I can explain that only ten to twelve can be seen in a day. Everyone is cooperative and agrees to accept assigned time slots over the next four weeks in the order in which they signed in. Kenny, the chaplain's clerk, creates the roster, confirms the order and prepares to usher the men into the card room, one at a time.

"Will you be breaking for lunch, sir?"

"Do we have lunch? I did not bring anything with me."

"Yes, sir. Either the chaplain can take you to the mess hall, or we can prepare something here."

"Eating here sounds faster. What do we have here?"

"What would you like, sir?"

"Surprise me."

Six prayer appointments later, the chaplain and I sit down in the chapel banquet area to an incredibly tasty meal. It turns out that one of the chapel regulars is an inmate from Miami whose culinary skills border on those of a master chef.

The day closes after six more prayer appointments. The twenty- to thirty-minute meetings settle into a rhythm, and the card room becomes a sanctuary of sorts. One after another, a new face appears in the chair facing me. We open with prayer for guidance from the Holy Spirit and with Scripture. Then I ask each new face the same question: "What would you like Jesus to do for you today?"

During the brief interlude after one leaves and before the next comes in, I pray, "Lord Jesus, give me Your words for this man today. Give me Your eyes to see him as You do, Your heart to love him as You do and Your Spirit to lead him ever closer to You."

It is only a matter of time before one of the men mentions that he is in full-blown AIDS and is starting to have severe problems physically. Although he was in church as a child, rebellion took him far away from God in his teens. Now he is barely twenty-eight and probably will not see thirty. Even as we start our regular prayer appointments in the card room, his remaining prison term is much longer than his life expectancy. He knows *of* Jesus, but he does not know Jesus. He has no one in life except his elderly mother.

I struggle during our prayer times not to think about the fact that, in addition to being in prison, with all the losses that involves, he will die of AIDS alone, shackled to his bed in a prison hospital.

Which of us wants to face the worst possible consequences of our smallest mistake—let alone our worst!

As the weeks and months wear by, he and I meet in the card room often for our time with God. The mountain is not moving, or if it is, the movement is imperceptible from the outside. Sometimes the appointments are arduous, even forced.

"Nothing is happening," he tells me often. "I don't feel any different."

"Faith is not a feeling," I assure him, "and faith tells us that prayer is the work. What we are doing here is having an effect, even if we do not yet know how to see it."

He leans back in his chair against the card room door. His hair is jet-black with a youth that will not be allowed to ripen. "Man, Brother Dale, I hope you're right, 'cuz I'm running out of time."

As his physical condition deteriorates, we have several prayer visits in the prison infirmary. The destruction of his immune system is allowing a plague of viruses to attack his eyes, lungs and brain. He is deteriorating quickly.

Regular prisons cannot afford to maintain a level of medical resources that can handle all conceivable conditions. That means that, as men with specific serious or fatal conditions become sicker, they are moved to prisons with higher levels of skilled medical staff and to medical facilities. In some cases, when prisons are out in the boondocks, the prison will contract for secure wings or wards at nearby hospitals.

As my prayer partner contracts various raging, opportunistic infections, he is moved to the county hospital in Marianna. That arrangement is under the control of ACI, so I can visit him there as his spiritual advisor. Once the infections are brought under control, he is returned to the prison infirmary at ACI, where I can see him as usual. After months of shuttling back and forth between Marianna and ACI, his case is deemed in terminal stage. He is moved to the prison medical center at Lake Butler, Florida, 135 miles east of Tallahassee, almost to Gainesville. He is now outside the control of ACI. I seek visitation approval immediately.

Fortunately, the family's and friends' visiting privileges with an inmate automatically transfer to whatever prison the inmate is assigned. However, volunteers are handled differently. Before we see an inmate as spiritual advisor at a different prison, each visit must be approved in advance. This can be difficult if a man's condition is deteriorating faster than the approvals can be obtained.

Before the approvals come through for visitation at Lake Butler, he is moved to the Department of Corrections wing of a major hospital in Jacksonville. The admitting chaplain helps obtain clearance for my visit within a couple of days.

It is late on a Saturday morning when I arrive. Something is fouled up. There is no paper work on my visit at the guard station when I show up from Tallahassee. The young officer on duty can only suggest that I wait until someone more senior comes on duty. I have my Bible and my prayers. This is a spiritual battle. I will not leave without seeing my prayer partner.

I have been praying in the hospital hall outside the guard station for about 45 minutes when a sergeant comes in. The officer hears my sad story, reaches his superior at home and waits for the call back after his boss reaches the chaplain at home. Signed faxes must be exchanged. Nobody approves access at this facility without signatures in hand. Phone responses are not sufficient.

About an hour and a half after taking up my station in prayer outside the control room, the sergeant motions for me to enter the corridor.

"But there are some conditions," he asserts almost gently, in subtle recognition of my patience. "You have to wear the mask because the patient is in isolation on a ventilator with respiratory herpes."

"No problem, sir." My automated response confirms that I am not new to the ways of the world behind the walls.

He hands me the blue mask, waits for me to don it and instructs me on how to pinch the corners to seal my breathing from infection. He then leads me down a corridor of open doors, doors to rooms with very sick men in them. I notice that every single man in those rooms is shackled by chains around his feet to the frame of his bed. Despite the resistance from the filters in the mask, I involuntarily take a deep breath, bracing for the scene in the room with the closed door. The sergeant pulls back the bolts that secure the door. In one motion he swings it open and steps sideways to allow me in.

"You are on camera," he reminds me, again gently, "but you're not on audio monitoring. Whatever you and he say will be just between the two of you, chaplain."

Between the two of us and God, I think, stepping across the plane of the door.

As soon as I lay eyes on him, I know that this young man is near the end and deeply troubled. It is more than just the hoarse breathing through the ventilator or the fungible green prison gown or even the leg chains shackling him to the bed. It is something in his eyes, something so heavy that it is virtually flattening his heart.

He looks as though a mountain of pressure is crushing him into the bed. It is not just spiritual; it is also physical. This is not the time to be breezy and cheery. The water is already fathoms deep. I can do him no good if I am not willing to jump in.

"You look like you need to cry," I offer after exchanging difficult greetings.

"You know I can't cry." He shakes his head, as though the subject is beyond reprieve.

"Why?" I know I am on thin ice, and I am praying every word. "Are you afraid it would hurt too much?"

In silent confirmation his head turns away from me toward the far wall. I slide down in my chair as a rage wells up inside me. I cannot be certain whether it is my rage or my perception of his rage. Is it the pain of his abandonment by his own father at a young age? Is it the pain of facing his crimes? Is it the pain of this way of ending life? I am not sure that it matters. What I do know is this is a depth of pain and suffering that I do not want to touch.

Dear God, this boy is in horrible pain, I scream in my thoughts. *Where is his father?*

The Lord deals with me immediately. Even though, under different circumstances, my question and my anger might be appropriate, even laudable, under these circumstances, both are rooted in fear. I am scared that I am not up to this. If this boy's father were here for him, I would not have to deal with this.

Suddenly, I remember Dennis and standing with him in that church in Baltimore, knowing that the moment was far beyond my strength. I remember the prayer to say, *Jesus, help me.*

God comes into the moment and gives me the right question,

the loving question that will lead to a loving answer. How can I be a father to this young man right here, right now? As I beg in mental prayer for Jesus' help, He brings to mind exactly what I would do if my son was in this much pain.

"Come here." I kneel on the floor next to his bed and stretch out my arms. "Let me hold you, and we'll cry together."

He turns toward me, hesitantly at first, and then melts into my arms. First with tears and then with sobs, he lays out his deepest pains and shames. We place them before the cross of our Savior for forgiveness and for His healing and the healing of those he has harmed. In his own words, he accepts both the forgiveness and the healing, first in remorse and then in joy. It is impossible to know which tears are his and which are mine.

The mask and ventilator both fall away from our faces, victims to the miracle that is unfolding. And then, as our tears subtly phase from release through relief and into joy, the door bolts pop and the door swings open. The sergeant is standing in the doorway, looking puzzled and a little concerned, while holding a mask over his face with his free hand.

"What's going on in here, chaplain? Is everything all right?"

"Yes, sergeant!" We both start laughing so hard that I can barely speak. "Everything's great!"

The sergeant signals that it is time for me to wrap up. The door slowly shuts, and we are alone for just a moment more.

"I feel like a thousand pounds has been lifted off of me," the young man says as he hugs me good-bye.

"No," I correct him, "it was a million pounds, and neither you nor I could have budged it."

"Please call my mom. Tell her I made it."

Less than 72 hours later, he goes home to the Lord in total peace. I was the last person to visit him.

○─○─○

By the winter of 1991, my prison prayer appointments have overflowed Saturday and swelled into my weekday mornings. In March I am struggling through a miserable rainy morning. The recently ended Gulf War has left interest rates in the public capital markets in turmoil. My part-time law work is reverting to full time and a half. I arrive in my law office at four A.M. to clear documents for an $80 million financing that is going to be offered on Wall Street that day.

At eight-thirty I stuff the hand-marked changed pages into a fax machine and rush out for prayer appointments at ACI West. There is no way I can make the fifty-mile drive to Sneads in time for my nine o'clock chapel appointment. As I push my luck toward the speed limit on a wet, slippery Interstate 10 west, the haunting voices of friends and relatives creep into my thoughts, vocalizing all the incarnations of the talents speech that we have heard so many times over the past few years.

This is nuts trying to live in both worlds. My thoughts are taking the other side against myself. Maybe we are delusional. Maybe we are suffering from excessive zeal. Maybe we are trying to live outside our proper station as good laypeople. Maybe our critical friends and relatives are right.

Their angst was bad enough when I cut back from eighty- and hundred-hour workweeks to normal sixty-hour lawyer workweeks. Then I cut back to part-time so that I could spend time during the week visiting and praying with men in prison. From that point on the same question always follows the talents speech: "What good are you doing, killing time with some murderer who's never going to get out of prison anyway?"

My first prayer appointment today is with a murderer. His diminutive size and young age place him near the bottom of the prison pecking order, a miserable place to be. From the first time he hugged me after praying together, he nicknamed me his fat little buddy. The avalanche of criticisms playing in my head takes on my own voice as I near the exit for the prison. What good am I doing killing time with some murderer who is never going to get out of prison anyway?

As I steer into the prison parking lot, sure that my morning appointment will be canceled because my prayer partner will have given up on me and crawled back into his bed in the dorm, my thoughts are adding ammunition to the side of our critical friends and relatives. Hasn't this criminal survived just fine before I showed up? If I went back to spending all my time on business, couldn't I make hundreds of thousands of dollars a year and give some—even a lot—to charity? Wouldn't that be a greater good?

Once through the control station and the narrow fenced corridor to the yard, I arrive at the chapel yard gate forty minutes late. A damp pile of blue is sitting on the ground, soaking wet in the rain. Only when he looks up do I realize that he is crying.

"Mr. Dale! Mr. Dale!" He jumps up and hugs my neck. "I was scared to death you weren't going to come. I just couldn't've made it another week without a hug from my fat little buddy."

As the murderer in blue is hanging on my neck, hugging me, his fat little buddy, a mental voice more authoritative than those of friends and relatives invades my thoughts. *How many big deals won't close on Wall Street without you, Dale?*

I know the answer to that question. They will all close. America's best and brightest lawyers are killing each other to get and keep that lucrative business. If I drop dead right now, Wall Street would not miss a beat. The zinger follows: *Who would be here hugging this man right now if you weren't here?*

I know that answer too. Before I met him, how long had it been since my little prayer partner had been hugged? A long time, a very long time.

As the two of us enter the chapel door and put on the pot for coffee for our prayer session, I have my permanent answer to the talents speeches about the gospel parable.

God will use my gifts where they are needed most, even if God's work pays nothing at all.

11

Whole Heart, Soul, Mind and Strength

MARK 12:30

THE MEN AT THE PRISON gradually become more than names on blue uniforms. As our prayer partnering continues over time, real people emerge with real stories and real lives. One elderly man is called Pops.

He is imprisoned for alleged complicity in the murder of a relative. The actual murderer cut a deal with the State to finger Pops and his wife in exchange for a life sentence instead of death. The alleged motive for the killing was insurance money.

By the time it was discovered that there was no such insurance, the murder-for-hire story had appeared in worldwide media. The elderly spouses, who had lived as model citizens before retiring to sunny Florida, were isolated from each other in separate cells at the local jail for two years. Finally, the State produced a jailhouse snitch, a drug addict with a career crime record. The snitch agreed to testify that the elderly woman had confessed to her in jail. The prosecutors threatened to throw away the key on the wife if the husband did not plead guilty to something.

I sit with him and the other inmates in the prison chapel as he reads poems he wrote for his wife for their fiftieth wedding anniversary. I pray with him and listen to his exploits as a decorated World War II veteran who landed at Omaha Beach in the ninth wave. We anguish as his mental acuity begins to wane before he finally will return home to his loyal, loving wife of 54 years.

They have written each other every single day of his and her incarceration. There is no home to return to. The family home was sold by his lawyer to pay for the six-figure legal fees that never even resulted in a trial. They will end their days in a small walk-up behind a strip shopping center. Susan and I will visit them in their apartment after his release. Strong Christians to the end, they never once curse God or what He has allowed.

Over and over Pops tells me, "God knows more than I do. We never know what He is protecting us from."

"Susan, this is not what I expected," I say in anguish at home.

"Did you think there would not be any innocent people in prison?"

"Well, that's a small part of it." I know my face is reddening with the memory of years past, when my frequent denunciations against inmate claims of innocence were well-known to all my friends. "It's more complicated than that. I never expected the faith that I'm finding in prison."

Another man who stands out is Kenny, the chaplain's clerk. His prayers in our sessions are not the typical "Lord, let me out" supplications that one expects and wearies of in prison ministry. His dramatically different attitude reveals itself in lunch discussions in the chapel.

It is another Saturday at ACI West. The chapel crew has prepared a fabulous lunch for our break after the morning prayer appointments. About nine men in blue are seated with me around the gray folding table, dining off of plastic foam plates with plastic utensils and paper cups.

"So, what's the deal with the fence?" I ask plaintively. The fence is a constant issue in prayer appointments. It is deeply resented, even hated. I am stirring the pot, hoping to understand at a deeper level its significance to the men inside it.

Everyone has something to say. It makes them feel like animals. They want to knock it down. Finally it is Kenny's turn.

"You may not like what I'm gonna say." He addresses his brothers in blue while looking into his plate. "I see that fence as being for my benefit."

The uproar is immediate and loud. Finally, he motions for quiet and continues. "I do not know what any of your crimes are, but I am here because I killed somebody. I was on drugs. I did not mean to kill him, but I did."

The silence is deafening. No one in prison talks about their own crimes, at least not honestly.

"That man I killed was someone's son; maybe he had kids, brothers and sisters. I don't know. What I do know is that, because of what I did, there are people out there who would want to really do me in if they could get their hands on me. I look at that fence as a protection for me, to keep them from getting to me to give me what I deserve.

"Oh yeah," he adds as an afterthought while everyone is still too stunned to reply. "So, when I pray about the fence, I say a prayer of gratitude to God for it being there."

The summation is evidently too much.

"You better eat that food before you be wearing it, man." A grizzled brother in blue almost spits out the words, to a round of support from seven other inmates.

"So, how about the Seminoles?" I quickly jump in to derail the discussion by injecting Florida State's upcoming game against the Miami

Hurricanes. Within ten seconds the typical football barbs are flying, especially from the Gator fans at the table, who have no dog in the fight. Nonetheless, I am well aware that this Kenny guy has just put his life on the line to defend the Christian principle of justice and punishment. I will keep my eye on him. He may be someone special.

○–○–○

As 1991 rolls on into spring, the wake of the recently ended Gulf War is frustrating my attempt to practice public finance law part-time. My strategy is to commit to only one deal per quarter. That means a closing every three months and should allow me to control my billable hours as a lawyer. That is the plan. The problem is that the plan only works if the markets are stable. Sudden disruptions in the public capital markets can wreak havoc on such a plan. A jump in interest rates of just 1 percent on a thirty-year, $100 million school board financing means additional costs that will wipe out a whole slate of teachers' salaries for three decades.

In the face of an uncertain and rising interest rate market, every deal becomes a crisis that must be closed immediately. My part-time work has suddenly exploded back to eighty- and ninety-hour work-weeks for over a month. I am back on airplanes shuttling between Florida and New York in March and April of 1991. That is when my two eldest daughters ask for a family meeting.

We all gather around the dining room table after Sunday church. I lead the family in shared prayer and Scripture. Then we open the meeting. This time there has been no caucusing that Susan is aware of. We are both dumbfounded as Jeanette, now in sixth grade, sets forth her request.

"Dad, when you were gone all the time, you were just gone." She flips the curl of her shoulder-length hair off of her neck with her left hand, a telltale gesture that she is dead serious. "It didn't matter. You were just not part of our life every day. But now you've been here all the time. We've gotten used to you being here. Now when you're gone like this, it hurts too much. I can't take it. I want you to quit being a lawyer."

"I appreciate your sentiments. Wow, what a compliment. Thank you." I begin after too long a moment of dead silence around the table. My glance toward Susan confirms my understanding that this ground must be tread very lightly. "There are realities that must be dealt with. Surely Christina can help you weigh those."

"We've already discussed those, Dad." Our ninth grader, Christina, is in on the plot. Instead of talking sense into her younger sister, she is a coconspirator. There will be no dash to my rescue from her corner. "It's all just about money. We don't care. We don't want you traveling out of town and being away from us anymore. We want you home."

"Look, honey." My remarks are addressed toward Susan while speaking to both of my daughters indirectly. "I take these sentiments in their best light, a sweet compliment, but what you are asking for is just not possible. Susan is only just starting her career as a clinical psychologist. You don't comprehend the reality. Moving from my part-time income to Susan's full-time income would mean living on a fraction, a small fraction, of our current cash flow."

"We think we do understand that reality." Both daughters roll their eyes at my mischaracterization of their youth. "Besides, you promised to prayerfully consider whatever we ask in a family meeting."

"That's true, but you also have promised to prayerfully consider my concerns."

It feels like a deadlock. Susan stands to fetch coffee and then deftly makes her quick football time-out gesture from behind both daughters. Unfortunately, right behind me and opposite them is a large framed picture with reflective glass.

"We saw that, Susan." Christina sighs forward till her nose touches the table in an exacerbation that says "We are not kids anymore." Then she looks toward her sister and speaks for both of them. "Why would a time-out help?"

"I think it would give us time to put the facts down on paper and make a more deliberative decision," Susan says.

"We don't need that." Christina throws her hands up in the air to confirm that there is not much more to learn in life after age fifteen. "But if that will help you, sure, we can do that."

Jeanette tilts her head in an expression that says "Dad, why do you have to make everything so complicated?"

"Life is complicated," I respond to her unspoken thought.

"What about us?" Chris raises his hand in mock deference to his older sisters. "What about our opinion?"

"What is your and Addie's opinion?" My intonation on the word *your* betrays a hope that there may be a rescue from the youngest voices of our clan.

"We want you home too," Chris says in a matter-of-fact tone that places their views on the record. Addie, who is sitting up on her knees in order to rest her chin and folded arms on the table, nods emphatically, sending her long brown curls dancing in parallel waves.

"Okay. Let's close." I move the family toward a wrap-up prayer. "It sounds like we have a lot of work to do."

Over the next two weeks we put it all down on paper for the children to contemplate. The economic consequences of my letting go of my part-time work are stiff, to say the least. They would have to pay for their own clothes, car, gas, insurance, yearbooks, prom, college, trips, even most of their own wedding costs. College will be out of the question unless financed with scholarships, loans and part-time work. It does not seem to matter. My daughters want me home. I am not sure it is a good idea. Our prayer and discussion continue for a year.

By the end of May 1992, I am still in turmoil. To make less

money is one thing. To make no money is something else. Susan says I should look at it from a different standpoint. She thinks that, before God, because we are a unity in marriage, it does not matter which of us is making the money. The only question is whether we are using the money for God's will.

Susan suggests that I might benefit from the opinion of a woman we know who is highly respected and is an outstanding professional. A few days later I am in the law office of this female colleague. She has a law degree with a post-doctoral master's in law and a doctorate in a separate field. Her perfectly appointed office focuses upon a huge penthouse window that overlooks the State Capitol Complex and Florida State University. As I sit opposite her, facing her desk and her window, I cannot avoid the thought that I am looking out upon all the kingdoms of the world. I explain to her my daughters' request and explain my turmoil.

She swivels around in her chair so that her back is facing me, as if she is collecting her thoughts to give me a professional answer. Her gaze out the window goes on so long that I am concerned I have unintentionally offended her. That's when I realize that she is crying.

"Are you all right? Did I say something wrong?"

"No, I'm okay, Dale." She turns back around in her chair to face me with tears streaming down her cheeks. The sun setting behind her infuses her wet eyes and tears with an illusion of fire, like a visibly burning pain. "I'm okay. I just don't know if you're going to understand my answer."

"I'll try."

She wipes her tears with both hands and then smoothes her navy blue pinstripe business suit from the waist down to her knees in a single gesture, as though rebooting herself after a shocking jolt. Finally her folded hands are resting across her lap, and she looks me straight in the eye.

"Dale, I would give anything in the world . . . anything at all . . . to have someone want me more than my paycheck."

My six-month notice of resignation is in the fax machine to the Fort Lauderdale office the next morning. The end of December 1992 will be the end of my career in Wall Street finance. At the firm's request, I agree to an "of counsel" arrangement. My name will still be connected with them, but with no salary or benefits.

○─○─○

As the summer of 1992 merges into fall, our family is making preparation for the end of my income. That includes Susan nailing down a position in her profession. The huge Florida State Hospital for the mentally ill in Chattahoochee, right across the river from the prison where I minister, looks very likely. By early fall she has an offer to be a staff psychologist there. She accepts. We will have several months of overlapping income to build a buffer for the coming year. The thought makes us comfortable.

Then a statewide freeze on hiring is imposed. We are moving steadily toward the end of my income, without a start date for Susan's. Some friends and members of our Scripture study groups suggest that God is giving us an opportunity to bail from a horrendous decision. We discern that this is not the case, although December is looming just weeks away.

Our new center-city church, which is just a few blocks from our apartment, launches its own Scripture study weekends for men and for women. Susan and I are each heavily involved in organizing and leading the programs. Pastor John O'Sullivan supports and encourages our commitment to the road we have chosen. In addition to the folks to whom we minister and the spiritual friends from the suburbs, we now have a whole new cabal of spiritual brothers and sisters. We lean on them all for prayer as the first week of December comes with no thaw in the hiring freeze at Florida State Hospital.

Finally, the second week of December, Susan is notified that she can begin work in Chattahoochee. Based on her start date the first business day of 1992, her first paycheck will be January 15. My last check will be December 31. There is no gap and no overlap. In time we will learn that this is a sure sign of God's hand. We have everything we need to do His work, but no extra.

As part of winding up my legal practice, it is necessary to ship all my closing reports to the main office in Fort Lauderdale, where they can be stored. In the kind of law I practiced, each financing involves hundreds of pages of documents. After the closing the documents are bound together in duplicate sets like books, with bindings lettered in gold print that identify the transaction and the lawyer responsible for the closing.

By the time I am winding out of my practice to begin full-time volunteer ministry, I have hundreds of these bound volumes. They are lined up on shelves in the law firm library. Whenever clients come in for a meeting or a conference, they see a whole wall of volumes of bound closing reports, some as thick as six or seven inches. Some are marked as volumes I, II or III. All have my name on them and titles like:

$475,000,000
State of Florida Consolidated Financing Program
(State of Florida Comptroller Consolidated Equipment Pool)

Or:

$125,000,000
Dade County Industrial Development Authority
Tax Exempt and Taxable Industrial Development Bonds
(Miami Dolphins Stadium Project)

NOW I WALK ON DEATH ROW

I have closed billions of dollars in such financings. Each of the books representing all those financings has my name at the bottom.

Career-wise, that wall of closing reports identifies who I am. The day after all the volumes have been shipped to the main office, I am sitting in the library and staring at the empty wall. It feels like I have disappeared, like I have ceased to exist.

I am thinking to myself, *Who am I now?* when a senior member of the office walks in. My face must betray the pain because she asks what is wrong.

"This is much harder than I thought it was going to be."

"Then why are you doing it?" she asks.

I stay silent, but answer in my own thoughts. All change is difficult, even good change. The fact that something is difficult does not mean it is not God's will.

o-o-o

On the first business day of January 1992, I am ready to jump into my new life in full-time volunteer ministry. By six-thirty Susan has left for her first day on the new job at Florida State Hospital, fifty miles away in the Panhandle. Words cannot describe my shock that first morning as Christina, now a tenth grader, wakes up crying.

"Dad, I am itching all over. It's horrible."

"Hold on. Let's get the light on and take a look."

The light confirms my worst fears. Chicken pox everywhere. The pediatrician's nurse is not used to giving instructions to fathers over the phone.

"She needs to take frequent oatmeal baths; that will help with the itching."

"Oatmeal baths?"

"And this is really important." She runs right by my question. "Make sure she does not scratch herself. Scratching will leave permanent scars and she will hate you for it later."

Vague memories of pox in my childhood suggest taping cotton athletic sox over my daughter's hands. It works, but that will be my last success. While she lies moaning and wailing in her room, I draw a tub full of hot bathwater and empty in a small box of Quaker Oats. A disgusting film slowly spreads across the surface of the tub water, and huge clumps congeal on the bottom. I know something has been lost in the translation.

The doctor's nurse, who grows less friendly with each of my successive frantic calls, suggests that it will be ten full days before Christina can return to school. That puts me on house arrest for almost two full weeks. All my prison callouts for the first two weeks of January 1992 are canceled. I steal away the time for school drop-offs and pickups for the other children and squeeze the mentally ill payees at Good News Ministries in as well. However, I cannot be an hour away with my daughter suffering at home. At least it will only be ten days.

The morning of Christina's emancipation from the house finally arrives. Ten days on the nose. She is pox free and jubilant. My callouts at the prison have been rescheduled to start the next day. By adding an extra day at the prison and running through lunch, I can make up the two lost weeks in just one week. Then, right after Christina leaves for school, Chris shows up in the living room.

"Jeanette's not getting up."

"Don't be silly. Jeanette is always on time for school."

"I think she doesn't feel so good."

A quick inspection reveals another ten days of chicken pox, followed by another ten days for Chris, followed by another ten days for Addie. Six solid weeks of house arrest, as all four children come down with pox. Not one day of overlap and no breaks in between. Forty unbroken days of fevers, oatmeal baths and bedside companionship. By the end of the forty days, I am facing a spiritual crisis.

When I return to my prayer ministry at the prison, it is the third week of February. Why is God allowing my time to be wasted? What is the point of freeing myself up for ministry, only to be sitting bedside for my children for six weeks? That question, with different specifics, comes back again and again over the next four years. God is breaking through my denial.

When I was in my career, my weekly Sunday night/Monday morning ritual commenced with a cab ride from home to the airport. At the last minute I would scurry about making sure that everything I needed was packed. I would stick my itinerary on the refrigerator door, where it silently announced to the family that "Dad is gone again this week, doing more important things than sitting at home with you." My eyes would finally meet Susan's. In the sincerity begotten of total denial, I would lovingly assure her of my belief that what she was doing that week was much more important than anything I was doing. Now, through my new stay-at-home experiences, God is confronting me with the fact that, even though it was true, when I said it, I did not really believe it.

Without realizing, I had become totally invested in the dollar as the currency of self-worth. I boarded planes and flew all over the country because people needed me to come to them and tell them how to solve their problems. They paid my airfare, bought my meals and provided my lodging because I was important enough for them to do it. I deserved it. I was worth it.

God is not allowing me to continue that façade on His clock. My wings are clipped. I am grounded. I must transport kids, keep house and make dinner. Except for rare, carefully discerned and elaborately planned exceptions, weekday travel is out of the question. Ministry time is from school drop-offs at seven-thirty in the morning until school pickups at quarter to three in the afternoon and on Saturdays. So where is the meaning in this service at home? Who am I now without the fans?

Jesus must know that I am useless to Him for uncompensated

ministry work so long as I need money and applause to know that my work is worthwhile. Perhaps that is why He brings me into four years of boot camp. During the span from January of 1992 until spring of 1996, first in the white house and then in a rented home in Eastgate on Tallahassee's inner-northwest side, I start to understand.

After a day of ministry and school drop-offs and pickups, four-thirty usually finds me standing at the kitchen sink with my ear in a phone, my hands in a tub full of dirty dishes and a half-prepared meal in or on the stove. The doorbell rings furiously because a four-year-old is thirsty. I kick the oven shut with my right foot and rinse suds off my hands while the Brownie mother on the phone finishes detailing the treats Addie must bring for the next meeting. I am beginning to understand something about the nature of God and the nature of us that no theology course could ever teach me.

I begin to understand that there are two ways to live. I have spent my adult years so far in the other way. This is the new way. This new way is to live in union with the life cycles and processes that supply and provide the basic things that are essential for my family and me. The life that walks in the essentials of day-to-day needs inside my home is adorned with service.

I am learning that something in me wants to share these dirty dishes, wants to share the errands and the cooking and the mop and the vacuum. Sometimes a friend will drop in for advice or consolation and will sit at the kitchen table talking as I stand at the sink peeling potatoes. I know without asking that he has never peeled potatoes for his family because, if he had, he would offer to help. It isn't that peeling potatoes is objectionable. I love to get out every last little eye and blemish without wasting a sliver of white pulp. An obsessive lawyer who craves perfectly crafted documents makes for an obsessive potato peeler who craves perfectly peeled potatoes. I have no desire to hoard my piece of this action or to exclude others from participation.

For my whole adult life I have claimed that this kind of thankless service is important, that it is the most important service even though it pays nothing. But if I really believe that, this new situation would not feel like a demotion.

Who am I now without the applause? Who am I now without the closing dinners? Who am I now without the W-2?

It does not take long to figure out that children playing outside in the Florida heat are thirsty quickly and often. My lawyer skills tell me to take control of such situations early on and minimize the interruptions to my schedule. As the neighborhood kids and my own posterity choke down blue-colored drinks, I announce that there will be no more going in and out every five minutes. A thirty-minute rule applies. No one is to come in or get thirsty in less than thirty minutes. The smug air of self-satisfaction that hovers over the computer and me as I prepare for thirty minutes of uninterrupted writing time is short-lived.

No less than eight times in the next thirty minutes, the very same little dears ring the doorbell, asking if the thirty minutes is up yet. The doorbell routine is becoming an unbearable resentment. The Lord answers my prayers for help. He brings to mind the same Scripture that He gave me when my mentally ill payees on the street made outrageous and constant demands on my time, James 2:3–4 and 9:

> If you show special attention to the man wearing fine clothes and say, "Here's a good seat for you," but say to the poor man, "You stand there" or "Sit on the floor by my feet," have you not discriminated among yourselves and become judges with evil thoughts? . . . If you show favoritism, you sin.

The passage reminds me how many times I have all but killed myself serving governors, legislators, county commissioners, airport and seaport directors, NFL and baseball team owners and hosts of other powerful and influential people. Were my street people asking any more of me than those people had? God confronted me with the real question: Is Dale willing to work as hard to relieve the suffering of the poor as Dale was willing to work to finance Joe Robbie's stadium for the Miami Dolphins? The answer from Scripture is that he'd better be.

These kids at my door are no different. Is there anybody more helpless than a hot, dirty, smelly, sweaty, thirsty kid on your porch in August in Tallahassee, Florida? How many times would I gladly fetch a drink for the president or the governor or my pastor or my bishop? More to the point, how many hours have I spent in the last two decades sitting in bars buying drinks for the rich and powerful?

In order for me to fetch drinks for these kids on demand without resentment, the Lord has to show me that the ringing of the doorbell signals Jesus coming to me in the freckled face of a thirsty kid, as in Matthew 25:35 and 40: "I was thirsty and you gave me something to drink. . . . Whatever you did for one of the least of these brothers of mine, you did for me." My fleshly eyes want to pick and choose between different kinds of service to the least of His brothers, to decide which service is valuable based on what the world holds to be valuable. God will not allow it.

He is teaching me that I need to peel potatoes, wash dishes and launder clothes in order to live a surrendered life. It has to do with living as a created being serving a sovereign God. It has to do with everything, because nobody and nothing ever looks the same after one has seen life from the laundry room and the kitchen sink.

Whether I am in prison, on the streets or at home, I must be rooted in the fertile soil of service to my family and others. I must be careful to never slip into the trap of resentment by forgetting who it is that I serve. It is always Jesus in disguise.

12

They Shared All Things in Common

ACTS 2:42-45

IN EARLY 1994 THE INVESTORS who own the white house inform us that our lease cannot be renewed. After more than four years of calling it home, we must either purchase the building or vacate. We are sure that God does not want to anchor us with a burden of ownership at this time. We find a rental home that suits our family needs in the Tallahassee subdivision called Eastgate, just off of Capital Circle on the city's northwest side, a quarter-mile south of the interstate.

This time our move requires only a small truck that is quickly overwhelmed by the number of assisting hands. There are men and women from Good News Ministries, friends from Big Bend Cares, men and women from our Scripture renewal weekends at the suburban and center-city churches and even some professional peers. Most of the non-furniture items are off-loaded at the street and then passed hand to hand through a serpentine line of helpers, from one to the next, like a New England bucket brigade that winds its way into the house.

We are satisfied that God has us in the palm of His hand, but there is still a piece missing in our search to live out the three Scriptures from Mother's Day 1987 at the Opryland Hotel: Isaiah 21:1–10, Matthew 6:19–34 and Acts 2:42–45. To the best of our ability, by God's grace, we are immersed in the life of prophetic choices based upon believing that Jesus meant what He said. We are living that life fully on the assurances of the Gospel guarantee. But where is the third leg of the stool, our call to a life of community, as in Acts 2:42–45?

> They devoted themselves to the apostles' teaching and to the fellowship, to the breaking of bread and to prayer. Everyone was filled with awe, and many wonders and miraculous signs were done by the apostles. All the believers were together and had everything in common. Selling their possessions and goods, they gave to anyone as he had need.

We have not yet found a life of structured community. We have a community of ministry, even a community of worship. But our family still lives like an island in a culture of rugged individualism.

That reality from our children's point of view is driven home to us by a tearful Jeanette, just a few weeks after our move to Eastgate. Loaded down like a pack mule by her eighth-grade backpack, she pauses and turns to us inside the front door before leaving for her carpool ride. Jeanette leans against the inside knob of the door to let it hold up her books while she says, "Don't get me wrong. I'm really on board with everything our family is doing."

"Thank you." I lean against the oak panels of the living room opposite Jeanette with Susan standing in the arch to the dining room.

We shoot each other a parental look that silently asks, "Where is this going?"

"No, I mean it." She catches our looks and dismisses them. "I believe we have got it right, and I'm glad."

"Thank you." I am trying hard not to have any look at all and not to look at Susan.

"But you need to understand." Now there is pain in our eighth grader's voice and eyes. "Once I step outside this door, there is nobody in my world who believes what we believe in this house."

"Nobody?" My attempt to keep her talking is not as subtle as I hope. "Not anywhere?"

"Nobody." Her hands move in a horizontal cutting motion that dislodges her backpack from its support on the doorknob. She jerks it back up without missing a breath. "Nobody at school. Nobody at church. Nobody in my confirmation class. Nobody anywhere in my life outside this house believes that Jesus meant what He said."

"Do you believe it?" I ask, noting that Susan's barely perceptible nod confirms my voice is as gentle as I hope this time. "Do you believe it, Jeanette?"

"Well, yeah. That's why I'm here with you, Dad. But it is still really hard."

Within just a matter of days, another lightning bolt from the blue accentuates the urgency of our moving toward intentional community. My daily routine involves picking Chris and Addie up from their church school each afternoon. I have long since become accustomed to being the only father present and standing alone at a respectful distance from the throng of moms. On this particular day, I am delighted to see another man step out of his car. He is an acquaintance from church and business.

"Hey!" I wave while striding in his direction. "Good to see you."

His expression is not one of greeting. He looks extremely apprehensive and begins scanning the area, as though he may have been followed by an assassin.

"Hey, man." My hand is out to shake his. "It is good to see you. Is everything okay?"

He is actually perspiring nervously. "Don't take this wrong, Dale, but I cannot talk to you here."

"I beg your pardon?" I am clueless. He always greets me warmly at his place of business.

"If any of these moms tell my wife that they saw me talking to you, there will be big-time trouble to pay at home. You know what I mean?"

"No, I'm not sure that I do."

"These mothers are all afraid that you will infect us guys if we associate with you."

"Infect you with what?"

"Your crazy ideas."

"What?"

"Sorry, man." He jumps back into his car, locks the door and turns the radio up loud.

As he freezes his gaze in an opposite direction, I realize that this accomplished businessman with an MBA from a national university is scared to death of the wrath of the school moms and his wife if he talks to me in public.

That evening, Susan and I discuss the reality of what our children must be bearing up to from their peers if this level of animosity is being vocalized by those children's parents in their homes.

"How do we protect our children from the consequences of our Gospel choices?"

"Dale, I don't think we can. But maybe the purpose of Christian community is to buffer them from that animosity by at least having a group larger than their own family that agrees on the same basic principles."

"You mean like the principle that Jesus meant what He said?" My laugh is more sardonic than light.

"That would be a great place to start." Susan pauses and then asks, "Where do we start?"

"I think we do two things at once." The problem-solving lawyer in me jumps to the fore. "We need to accelerate our search for a Christian community that believes what we believe, and we also start making one here."

The living room and dining room in our rented Eastgate home are large enough to consider hosting a weekly gathering for prayer, Scripture and shared meals. In April of 1994 a letter goes out from us to alumni of the scriptural renewal programs at both our parishes and to volunteers whom we know through shared ministry. In the letter we announce:

> We are starting a four-and-a-half-year commitment to open our home every Saturday night for a potluck, singing, praise and worship, prayer, Scripture and sharing. . . . It's open to anyone. We hope it will lead to a discernment of what we are being called to do to live as a witness to the gospels here in Tallahassee. . . . We don't know if anyone will come. But even if they don't, Susan and I will be here and we will meet. Whatever happens, at the end of four and a half years [July 31, 1998], when our lease is up and Jeanette goes off to college, we will know what we are to do.

The first Saturday more than thirty people show up. Whatever is brought to share for dinner is put on the table. The Gospel reading for the weekend's Sunday service is the Scripture for the night. After dinner, prayer and praise, we sit in the living room and, after each of three readings of the Gospel passage, we take turns answering three questions: (1) What word or phrase in this Gospel passage jumps out at me? (2) What does this Gospel passage have to do with our life in this place and time? and (3) What does this Gospel passage challenge me personally to change in my life?

○—○—○

Even as the Saturday evening group revs into being and gains momentum, Susan and I accelerate a parallel search for a Christian community that believes Jesus meant what He said, a community that will provide a buffer of protection for our children's faith while they grow and mature. A few years earlier, we had become acquainted with an Anabaptist group that is a denominational cousin to the Amish and the Mennonites. The group is in unity with the Hutterites, a group dating back to the 1520s, the earliest days of the Reformation. Their goal is to live a structured communal life based upon the belief that Jesus meant what He said. We think we can learn a great deal from them.

In April of 1994, Klaus and Heidi, a retired couple who have lived in the Anabaptist community all their lives, join us at our home to meet and share with our Saturday night group. They also go with me to ACI West for a Saturday of sharing with the inmates at the chapel. After lunch in the chapel banquet area, most of the men retire to their dorms to rest or watch television. My Saturday core group of prisoners sticks around for further discussion. In a small circle of five inmates and the visitors, I hear Kenny's full story for the first time.

"In March of 1983 I faced the death penalty from seven men and five women. They would decide my fate: life in prison or the Florida electric chair."

I take a quick visual inventory of those present. The other inmates, Kenny's closest friends at ACI, are all sitting back, relaxed, as if they have heard this tale before. Klaus is leaning forward, round spectacles high on his nose and one hand holding the end of his Amish-type beard. In his plain black trousers and long-sleeved flannel shirt, his body language is attentive and receptive. Heidi leans forward with her cheeks and the sides of her kerchief-covered hair firmly in both her hands. With elbows on the knees of her ankle-length jumper, her eyes penetrate Kenny like a purifying fire. She is not just listening. She is absorbing him into her spirit. Later, he will tell me that it felt as if she was reading his soul, understanding all the things he could not say because he did not want to break down in tears.

"A buddy and I robbed a gas station. We were on drugs and into drugs. No one was supposed to get hurt. We had a gun. The guy gave us the money. We were backing out of the store to leave. And this crazy dog came shooting out of the back room, jumped on us, and the gun went off." Kenny pauses for a moment to shove down a welling up of tears.

Kenny is looking at the ceiling while holding the sides of his chair with both hands. "The gun went off, and the guy was dead. Right there, he was dead."

The room is silent except for the gentle rustle of Heidi's hanky as she wipes the tears from her eyes. Something in me knows that she is crying Kenny's tears.

"I can remember the day of my conviction, March 17, 1983. It was my third wedding anniversary. That is the day I was actually convicted of murder." Kenny continues looking at everyone except Heidi. "A longtime pastor friend came to me in the holding cell and was telling me, 'Jesus loves you and wants to save you.' *Save me?* I thought. *Save me from the conviction I have just been found guilty of?* I wasn't very nice to him. I was a very bitter young man of twenty. Even though I was guilty of my crime, I still blamed everyone else, not myself."

"Then what happened?" Klaus, encouraging without being pushy, reveals an unspoken hope that there is a conversion story coming on the heels of this drug-fueled tragedy.

"The penalty phase of my trial came the next day. That is when the jury decides life or death, and I remember just how scared I was. The time seemed to drag by. Finally I got on the stand and said I was sorry. In truth, back then I wasn't sorry for my crime, only sorry that I had gotten caught.

"The jury recommended life in prison to the judge. I was told later that the critical testimony came from a cop, the investigating detective, who told the jury that I could be salvaged, that I could live a worthwhile life if given the chance." Kenny looks at the floor now and shakes his head. "I thought he was crazy, but I was relieved. April 28, 1983, my divorce from the mother of my two kids was finalized, and I was even more bitter than ever before. Then on April 29, 1983, the judge sentenced me to life with a minimum of twenty-five years before eligibility for parole. I was relieved. It felt crazy, both things happening right together."

"And then something else happened, didn't it, Kenny?" As Heidi speaks for the first time since his story began, the sounds of male voices and friendly taunts are wafting into the room from the prison yard outside the chapel. "The most important thing happened, didn't it, Kenny? When did that happen?"

"I hate to tell you this, but it's the truth." Kenny's eyes are welling up beyond holding the tears. He is wiping them with his blue sleeve as he speaks. "I came to prison like a wild animal, to the Rock at UCI, the prison where death row is now. That place called the Rock was one of the most violent prison buildings in the whole country at that time. My motto was, 'I will survive; touch me and you die.' "

Heidi's eyes will not let him go. "And, Kenny, the other thing that happened. When did it happen?"

"They put me in a six-man cell with this guy called Ken Cooper, and he started telling me all the same stuff that the pastor had told me at the county jail. Only for some reason, this time I could hear it. Right there, in a prison cell in that hellhole of a place, Jesus gave me eternal life on March 3, 1986, when I surrendered my life to Him."

"And what do you say now, Kenny, all these years later?" Heidi's smile is one of gentle victory.

"I praise and thank the Lord for this life sentence. It's been eight and a half years of blessing others' lives. God has allowed me to lead others to Him, to plant seeds and to water the seeds that others have planted." He pauses and folds his hands on his lap, as though about to give the summation of his life. "I no longer have a life sentence spiritually. Instead, I have the gift of eternal life."

I leave the prison that day with three items added to my mental checklist: First, I need to explore the spiritual life that makes Heidi such a profound vehicle of God's immediate presence. Second, I need to meet this Cooper guy, through whom Jesus worked such a profound transformation in Kenny's life. Third, I need to make time in my schedule for Kenny. This is a guy worth getting to know better.

○─○─○

By fall of 1995 many things are now becoming routine. The ministry work, including the payee services to the mentally ill, continues in the streets outside Good News Ministries. The ministry to people with AIDS continues inside and outside of prison. The prison ministry work as a prayer partner is growing and blossoming.

Marcus Hepburn from the Scripture renewal program at the suburban church and Michael Savage from the same program at the center-city church are both joining me for Saturdays at ACI West. While I minister to prayer partners in the card room, the two new volunteers are running Bible studies in the chapel banquet area. Even the Saturday evening gatherings at our home have become part of the normal schedule. Attendance ranges from three to thirty or more. Out-of-town guests, arranged through us or others, are frequent.

We all seem to be asking the right questions. However, structured community for us and our children is nowhere in sight.

Then, almost out of the blue, Klaus and Heidi call to tell us that their community members in Germany have met a group that is just like them, except that this group is Roman Catholic. They are approved by the Vatican, and they are eager to meet us. Needless to say we are eager to meet them.

In August of 1994 Christina had moved on to college in Kentucky. The week before Easter of 1996, Susan and I, with Jeanette, Chris and Addie, fly to Munich. We have spent months putting our questions together. We have analyzed everything about this group that we can get our hands on. We have obtained copies of the books written by their community's theologians. We have even sent them exhaustive summaries of our steps in faith and our professional work. We meet them in person, for the first time, at the Munich airport. After a drive of less than an hour, we arrive at the community houses in the Bavarian Alps near Lake Walchensee, one of the largest and deepest Alpine lakes in Germany.

The scenery is breathtaking. The people are warm and welcoming. We spend virtually every moment getting to know each other and asking each other questions. The community's theologians are among the most famous in the world. They make themselves available to us to answer our questions. The community has existed since 1968 and is fully approved by the Church. On the second to last day of our visit, the founder asks us if we would like to come and begin the process of getting to know the community, a process not unlike that of a novitiate in a religious order of priests or nuns.

Our family has been meeting and praying together every night of this visit. We believe that this may be the way of life God was calling us to way back in May of 1987, the piece that has been missing. We are ready to come.

The last day of our visit is spent sorting out the details. We will join the new community house in Rome, Italy, just five blocks from the Vatican. The children will need to work out school arrangements before September. Susan will need to complete her notice period for resignation from her work and will join us in Rome in October. I must obtain a release from our Tallahassee lease on the house and come to Rome in June and find employment in order to support my family. The community, after all, is Roman Catholic. Laypeople must support themselves.

Among our friends in Tallahassee, there is an excitement in the air, an electric sensation that something new and really big is about to unfold. There is no excitement at the prison. Marcus and Mike have both pledged to continue the Saturday ministry in my absence. They are good for their word. But the men I have grown close to doubt they will ever see me again. Of them all, the pain is deepest for Kenny.

Through our years as weekly prayer partners, Kenny and I have become like brothers. I will be in Rome looking for a job when Luther Rice Seminary awards him his bachelor's degree in biblical studies. After that, who knows how long we will be overseas. I promise to continue correspondence. He believes me, as hard as any inmate can believe that someone will not forget him after all the people who have promised and forgotten. Years later he will describe our move overseas as a trauma like the death of a close family member.

Rome can be quite hot in June. The more advance work that I can do in my job search from here in Tallahassee, the better off I will be overseas in June. By the end of May, I have two full five-inch binders of leads. On Monday morning of week four in Rome, I am hired to work in the Rome office of the world's largest law firm, Baker & McKenzie, out of Chicago, Illinois. I will be teaching young European lawyers how to conduct, negotiate and document international project finance and trade in English.

Our family decides to travel very light. Each member of the

family will take clothes, books and things that are absolutely essential. Everything else is going out the door. Even our car will be sold by our Christian mechanic after we have left the country. While I am in Rome looking for a job, the rest of the family does their work well. Between yard sales and donations, by the time I return, the house is empty.

The first week of July 1996, the movers show up to pack a single container of our stuff. We expect to be overseas as long as ten years. We have packed our professional certifications, our essential clothes and our books that sustain us in our faith. All told, it is less than a single full container.

Mike Savage and I spend a weekend repainting the rented house inside and shampooing the carpets, while his wife, Shawnice, helps Susan and Jeanette clean the appliances to a good-as-new sheen.

"What did you ship overseas?" Mike asks casually over the roar of the rug shampooer.

"Only what we absolutely cannot live without."

"Really? Then what happens if the container sinks?" he asks in a mystified voice.

By November, when our container still has not arrived in Rome from the States, we will know the answer. Stuff is just stuff. There is nothing in our worldly possessions that we cannot live without. Only God is absolutely essential to our life.

Our suburban church hosts a farewell dinner for us, inviting all who are interested in hearing about what is taking us overseas and what we hope to bring back to Tallahassee. More than 120 supportive friends turn out. A week later, many of them also attend the special church service at our center-city church, at which we are blessed and anointed for the journey.

On August 22, 1996, the children and I fly Alitalia out of Orlando. Mike and Shawnice deliver us to the airport with Susan in tow. She will ride back with them to Tallahassee and join us in

Italy in October. Twenty hours after kissing Susan good-bye, we are in Leonardo da Vinci-Fiumicino Airport in Rome, Italy, clearing customs and joining our new friends in the community.

Our first stop is Villa Cavalletti, a palatial seventeenth-century estate in Grottaferrata, on the hilly outskirts of Rome. This will be our home for two weeks of intensive language instruction and orientation before moving into the community apartment in Rome.

It is a crystal clear, dark summer evening in early September 1996. From the roof of Villa Cavalletti, the children and I are able to see the entire valley that is Rome. Tomorrow we will move into our new home, a fourth-floor apartment five blocks from the Vatican. The lights in the valley are twinkling almost as much as the thousands of stars overhead. Chris and Jeanette are sitting beside me, and Addie is on my left knee.

All three huddle close to me, close enough to get my arms around them at one time, as I say aloud a prayer for our new life and for Susan, who will join us soon.

The next day, we move down into the sprawling city of Rome. Jeanette is attending Marymount, the American high school in Rome on the other side of the city. Her commute requires transfers on three public buses each way. Chris and Addie attend Santa Lucia, dead in the heart of the imperial section of Rome, just blocks from the Piazza Venezia national monument and about six blocks from the Roman Coliseum. The school is a long bus commute from our Roman neighborhood on the other side of the Tiber River. It is just a few blocks past Largo di Torre Argentina, the square where I begged in 1989.

In October Susan arrives. She is handling the household and school matters. My daytime efforts are focused on my work. Actually, the Rome office of Baker & McKenzie is more like family than work. My supervisors, the international partners, GianFranco Macconi, Aurelio Giovannelli and Fabio Brembati, seem like brothers who are delighted at the skills and enthusiasm my presence can add to their office. The younger local partners and associates are bright, hardworking and anxious to learn. In a very short time I feel like I am shepherding a large flock of two dozen competent and dear colleagues.

○─○─○

On December 19, the most popular newspaper in Rome runs a long article on the last strongholds of capital punishment in the world. The impetus for the report is the plea for clemency by Pope John Paul II in the case of a man from Virginia. The article features China and my home country. I never expect to discuss the death penalty at my job in Rome. The Rome office handles the world's largest banks and multinational corporations. The values and the conversations are conservative with a capital C. So I am blindsided when the local litigation partner, Guido Brocchieri, politely enters my office, newspaper in hand.

"Dale, did you see this?" he asks, spreading the two-page article in front of me. I nod and shrug, choosing not to let the legal office be the place where I divulge my own misgivings about the American death penalty.

"How can this be in America?" he continues. "The death penalty, it's so . . . so barbaric."

"It's what the people want." I struggle for words. "In America the majority gets what they want."

"But the American Christians, surely they could put a stop to this."

"You don't understand," I say cautiously. "In America it is the Christians who are demanding capital punishment."

"No!" Guido stands straight up out of the chair. "Surely you are making a joke on me. It's not possible."

"I'm not joking. It's true. Many of the Christians in America believe the death penalty is God's will."

There is a long, uncomfortable silence. Then this three-piece-suited corporate lawyer, complete with club tie, looks at me sadly, shaking his head and his hand in a Roman gesture that I have come to know. Index finger and thumb point out at a ninety-degree angle, twisting back and forth on the wrist. *"Non va . . . non va,"* literally meaning, "It is broken; it does not work."

○─○─○

Novitiates with religious orders and lay communities are very much in a situation like courtship before a marriage. The goal is to find out if the match has the ingredients for lasting a lifetime. By July of 1997, we and the community know that our lifework is in different areas. We part as friends.

The Recinella family in Rome moves to their own eighth-floor apartment upstairs from a Blockbuster video store on Via Francesco Satolli. We are in Piazza Pio Undicesimo, about one mile farther out from the Vatican.

Our daughter Christina, a senior majoring in education at a college in Kentucky, arranges to do her fall semester of student teaching at Marymount in Rome. Now that we are no longer in the community, Jeanette decides to enhance her college acceptances by taking her senior year of high school back in the States while living with family. Those present and voting in our family meetings in the new apartment frequently gather on our new rooftop terrace to enjoy the balmy Roman breezes of late August and early September. The question on our lips with each discussion is, "Now what?"

"Maybe this is Pensacola 1989 all over again," Susan suggests. "Maybe we thought we were coming to Rome to bring a community movement home to the U.S., but God has other plans."

"Sure, that's possible," I agree, with the children all nodding. "But this is a little different from Pensacola. We're here, and everybody we know and everything we used to own is sixty-five hundred miles away."

"And there's, like, an ocean in between," Christopher emphatically adds, just in case we forgot. The other children are all nodding.

"So, what happens now, Dad?"

13

"Go to the Land I Will Show You"

GENESIS 12:1

A GERMAN FRIEND who is also a theologian has taught us the biblically and historically proven approach for God's people to discern where they are going. We must look at where we have been. If we have been faithful to God's hand through our history, then by looking back at where God has taken us, we will in fact find the direction in which we are to head. That is how I respond to my children's question: "So, what happens now, Dad?"

I answer, "I think we get on the buses and the subways and go out into Rome and find the people who are doing what we were doing in the States before we came to Rome."

That is exactly what we do. God is faithful. We find them, a huge Catholic community of laypeople, many of whom have spouses and children, who are using a third or a half of their time to relieve suffering at their own cost and without compensation. The group, known as Sant'Egidio, provides more services to the impoverished in Rome than the local and national governments combined. They do not share common housing and do not work within the community to support themselves. They do not share personal finances; everyone must be self-supporting. The members share ministry and daily prayer every night in the churches throughout Rome. Since the 1960s, they have been growing in numbers and in geographic scope with the spiritual and practical focus of relieving human suffering because Jesus told us to do so.

The mother church of this incredible group is the minor basilica of Santa Maria in Trastevere, one of the oldest churches in the city. Evening prayers are daily at seven o'clock. So our new daily routine includes early dinner for the children; then Susan and I head to evening prayers with Sant'Egidio at Santa Maria in Trastevere.

By the end of September 1997, one of the elders calls me at my law office with an invitation to participate in a conference sponsored by Sant'Egidio. After a family meeting on the proposal at dinner that night, it is decided that Chris and I will attend. This is a large conference with thousands of people and dignitaries from every continent. Many languages are spoken. I find myself thinking of the first Christian Pentecost as we file into each session and don our headsets, turning to channel 3 for English.

On the morning of the second day, we attend a program on the words of Jesus and the poor. The room is huge. There are about six hundred people from all over the world sitting in folding chairs for this breakout session. The panel is excellent. To my delight, the chairperson of the panel is an esteemed member of the American Catholic Church. At the conclusion of the program, he says incredible things about our duty as Christians to go outside our comfort zone in relieving human suffering. He speaks eloquently about our duty as Christians to live in relationship with those who are poor in so many different ways and places. Then he opens the microphone to questions.

I am so excited I can hardly stay in my seat. I have a question all right. But I hesitate. Of the six hundred people in the room from all over the world, it appears that only four of us are American. I wait and tell God that if the moderator asks twice more for questions and no one else rises to ask one, I will go forward. He asks for questions twice more. No one stands or approaches the dais. I step to the microphone in the front of the room. It is a once-in-a-lifetime event for me.

I begin. "The things you are saying about our gospel duty to go beyond our comfort zone, our gospel duty to live in relationship with the poor, our gospel duty to make management decisions in multinational companies based on criteria other than just profit, these things are tremendous. But I have been an American Catholic all my life and have regularly attended church in wealthy suburban parishes for the last twenty years. I have never heard this from the pulpits of an affluent American church. When will we hear these words from the pulpit of our American churches?"

I replace the microphone into its holder. The only sound in the room is the din of the translators' voices from the translation booths along the side where my question is being reformulated into Arabic, German, Russian, French and Italian.

By the time he leans forward to speak, I am so filled with anticipation that I am not aware of anyone else in the room. The man whose job it is in that moment to address my question to my church locks his eyes on mine and speaks succinctly and directly, straight to me. "Don't wait to hear it from the pulpit," he says emphatically while gesturing toward me in a personal way. "Jesus said it. You read it. Go do it."

That is the answer to our question. That is the answer to the bishop's assistant in Pensacola, Florida. That is the answer to the moms at the church school who are fearful of our contagion to their husbands and families. That is the answer to those who are afraid that we are overzealous and misguided.

"Jesus said it. You read it. Go do it."

We have come to Rome looking for a community that could support our faith and stand as an independent authority to shore up the faith of our children. Instead we are given our marching orders succinctly and unambiguously.

Jesus meant what He said. It is time to let go of the need for anyone else to agree. It is time to just do it.

◦—◦—◦

We land back in America on New Year's Eve, 1997, at 11:15 P.M. Where is God calling us to begin? We will need time to discern the place and the specifics of our next step. What about the meantime?

Our friends in the Anabaptist community invite us to stay with them in the mountains of southwestern Pennsylvania at their Spring Valley group while we discern our next step. We think it will take a few months. It turns out to be seven months, as we ask the tough questions of each other and of God: "Did we misunderstand? Did we let You down? What do we do now?"

Sitting together in prayer on the couch in our little room, we are able to see a towering tree outside our window. The harsh winter has stripped off all the leaves except one. Way up near the top of the majestic branches is a single brown leaf, hanging on for dear life amid the winter winds.

"That's us." I point over Susan's shoulder out the window to the trembling, barely alive leaf. "That's us hanging on to God."

Every morning, as we sit down to coffee and Scripture, I check the tree outside for our little leaf, like the famed old man who reads the daily obituaries in the newspaper to see if he has died.

"We're still hanging on," I announce to Susan after verifying that our leaf is still there. "We're not dead yet."

Prayer, Scripture and spiritual counseling provide a path for us to follow in seeking God's next step. We determine that we are not looking for a *position*. This is not a job search. Rather, we are looking for a *need* where our particular experience and gifts can be applied to relieve suffering and build bridges while seeking to live as people of community. We are looking for the place where God is ready to allow us to make a life commitment in service and authenticity. As regards community, we are now aware that for us, community is not meant to be something that we join. Rather it is to be a way for us to live and think about our world and our resources. We must live as though our stuff, our money, our gifts and our talents are not just ours. They must be at the service of all in need. We must stay constantly aware that those in need have a claim on us. This is the call on Dale and Susan to the community life of Acts 2:42–45.

Because we still have two children in tow, Chris and Addie must be part of the discernment for this next step. Their joint input is clear and unambiguous: No more moves after this one until they are both out of high school.

In our first six weeks back in the States, we receive more than fifty suggestions on possible leads. Our discernment process causes us to ask of each proposal, "Will this be a consistent next step in our journey with God?"

Our deal with God is that we will only list and apply for possibilities consistent with our discernment. Once a possibility is on the list, we will pursue it with all our gusto. Then, God is responsible to pick the place where He is calling us by only allowing the right possibility to become the first genuine offer. The first possibility that ripens to a genuine offer is the one we will accept. It is God's job to prevent any of the wrong doors from opening before the right door opens.

Based upon this prayerful and reflective process, we whittle the list down to eight possibilities, ranging from inner-city ministry to the poor, to organizational work to overcome poverty, to part-time teaching accompanied by volunteer street ministry, to legal work representing the poor, to spiritual work directing a retreat center, to full-time work in an outreach mission. The geography ranges over the entire country. The possible income varies from nothing except a place to live and food to eat to enough to live on.

In the midst of all this, Susan notes that the *APA Monitor*, the trade journal of her profession, has an advertisement for a position in a place outside Jacksonville, Florida. The ad is for a staff position at a State mental hospital located in the city of Macclenny. We have never heard of that town but assume that it must be a suburban bedroom community to the huge city of Jacksonville.

"I think we should put it on our list, Dale. I've prayed about it, and I'm pretty sure we should be considering it."

"No way!" I disagree with vehemence. "Why on earth would God take us halfway around the world, just to bring us back to a suburban lifestyle that we could have moved to straight from Tallahassee?"

"I think we should put it on our list, Dale." Susan is gentle but unrelenting. "If God is leading this, and we believe He is, then what will it hurt to put Macclenny on the list?"

"Fine," I acquiesce, knowing full well that it is a wasted effort. "Put it on the list."

o-o-o

In early May, after my interviews with a nonprofit law firm in Tallahassee, we shoot east on Interstate 10 for Susan's interview at Northeast Florida State Hospital. This Macclenny facility accepts the mentally ill in the northern half of Florida. The town is no bedroom community to the big city of Jacksonville. Rather, it is a proud, quiet, southern town of 3,900 people with deep roots and traditions, just three miles south of the Florida-Georgia border.

The staff and directors at the mental hospital are impressed with Susan. Her experience working with the mentally ill in Chattahoochee, Florida, before we moved to Rome is icing on the cake. But since the staff position was advertised, the entire State agency has been placed under a hiring freeze. No offer can be made to Susan at this time.

As we drive back to Pennsylvania, I feel a bit smug at God's apparent confirmation that Macclenny is not in the cards. Within a few weeks, it seems as if nothing is in the cards. One by one, the doors begin to slam shut.

After weeks of phone interviews, exchanges of information and a one-week on-site interview, the founder of a Bible-based movement to end poverty looks at me and says, "I'm sorry, Dale. You have all the skills we need, but we are hoping for a black female minister." Slam.

The founder of a nonprofit law firm that exists to represent the needs and concerns of the urban poor as communities redevelop is ecstatic about the possibility of having me on board. She confides to me that in her wildest dreams she never imagined having someone with my capabilities as part of her team. Her grant sources are not ecstatic. "Why would we fund our money to hire a middle-aged white male?" Slam.

A long-established ministry in Shreveport is the core of local revival, with outreach to those on the streets and encouragement to those living in the neighborhood. It is exactly what we were doing in the streets of Tallahassee as volunteers through Good News Ministries during the seven years before we went to Rome. The nun who founded the ministry and ran it for thirty years has died of cancer. We are asked to apply to move into her former house and continue the operation of the ministry. The chairman of her nonprofit board is a

Catholic priest, who directs his secretary to call me. "He said to tell you that laypeople with children cannot do ministry." Click. Slam.

And so it goes. Susan has been in contact with the State hospital in Macclenny several times. She is still their first choice. But the hiring freeze is still in place. Meanwhile, every one of the other possibilities is a closed door except one.

A Catholic college has an MBA program. They want a professor with graduate-level teaching experience to supervise the thesis requirement for their MBA candidates. In order to avoid conflicts of interest with the corporate sponsors of their program, the college requires that the thesis be a genuine real-world application of business solutions to the needs of local nonprofits. The position has a small salary and is part-time. While we lived in Rome, I taught law and business classes at the graduate level as an adjunct professor at Temple University and at St. John's University. I am sure that the position at the college, the last one on my list, is custom-made for me, especially because the low class load will allow me time for significant volunteer ministry.

Susan and I arrive at the college by car for a full day of interviews. I start with the college president, then the dean of students and finally, just before lunch, the deans of the business school and the graduate school. Everything is humming along beautifully. By the time I finish one-on-ones with each of the business school faculty, it is about four o'clock. That is when the dean of the business school, with faculty present, broaches the subject of the low salary. I can tell from their body language and his tone that they want me and are afraid I will try to hold them up for more money.

"The low salary should not really be a problem," the dean assures me with the others nodding energetically. "All of us are committed to only a part-time load because that allows us to make up additional money by consulting with the hundreds of businesses and corporations in the area. We will make sure you have a full plate of consulting possibilities all the time."

"That is not necessary," I assure them. "I see the reduced hours as a major benefit that will allow me to spend significant time working as a volunteer with the Franciscans in the inner city. My wife and I will make this work based on the salary and her professional work without the need for me to do consulting."

A difficult exchange follows as they try to clarify what they are sure must be a misunderstanding. Then the dean asks me to step out for a moment. When I am invited back into the room, the atmosphere is tense, almost hostile.

"The position you are interviewing for now carries extra responsibilities for class load. Here is the list of classes you will need to teach in addition to thesis supervision."

In a split second I realize that the business faculty of this Catholic college has decided that if I am stupid enough to give away my time to solve problems for the poor, they will take that time for themselves. They are dumping additional classes on me so that they can have more time to make more money consulting for corporations.

"I'm sorry, but that is not the job I came here to interview for." I try not to sound as bitterly disappointed as I am in each of them as human beings.

"The job you came for does not exist anymore." The dean is adamant. "This is the only job on the table. Take it or leave it."

"I cannot take it, but I have a counterproposal." My hope is that a cooling-off period will allow them to break out of the groupthink and come to their senses. "We are staying over tonight before driving back to Pennsylvania. I will call at nine o'clock in the morning to see if the original job has become available again."

The next morning the dean does not even take my call. His

secretary fields the question. "He said to tell you that nothing has changed from yesterday afternoon. Take it or leave it."

Susan sits quietly beside me for almost two hundred miles as we drive back to Pennsylvania. There is no gloating or "I told you so" in her voice when she asks the inevitable question at about three-thirty in the afternoon. "Honey, every possibility on our list other than Macclenny has come to a closed door. Maybe we should stop and call Macclenny."

About ten minutes later we pull up to a Holiday Inn. Susan heads for the pay phone inside and is only gone about ten minutes before she slides back into the passenger seat of the car.

"You couldn't get them on the phone?" I ask, ready for more bad news.

"Oh no. I got the head of the psychology department on the first ring."

"And . . . ?"

"He said that he has been trying to reach me all day at our Pennsylvania phone number. The hiring freeze has been lifted. If he did not hear from me before four o'clock, he was going to have to call their second choice and offer the job to them."

"Did he offer you the job?"

"Yes."

"Did you take it?"

"Yes. I said, 'I accept it,' and then I asked him what the final salary is."

We sit in the parking lot of the Holiday Inn in absolute silence for a while. Finally, we need to pray and to talk. We pray first.

"Dale, God let every single other thing on the list crash before He opened this door." Susan is speaking with deliberate emphasis, but picking her words very cautiously. "Why do you think God did that?"

"It is obvious." Even my grieving over my eight dead ideal opportunities cannot blind me to God's way. "He wanted us to know—strike that—He wanted *me* to know with absolute certainty that He wants us in Macclenny."

Within minutes we are back on the highway toward southwestern Pennsylvania. Tears well up at the corners of my eyes as we turn east again.

"Susan?"

"Yes, Dale?"

"What in heaven's name am I going to do in Macclenny?"

Susan takes my free hand in both of hers. "Well, I don't think we are going to know that until we get there."

Within 48 hours, while Chris is with friends on a lengthy camping trip in the mountains, Susan, Addie and I are driving to Florida, where we check into the Macclenny EconoLodge on Sunday, July 19. Susan will be starting work on July 24. We need to find a place to live and to find our new church. Our new church is easier to find than our new house. St. Mary's of Macclenny is the only Roman Catholic church between Jacksonville to the east and Lake City to the west, a stretch of 75 miles. Straight south of Macclenny, in Union County, there is not a Catholic church to be had.

When we pull up to the short paved parking area outside St. Mary's on Highway 90, there is a single car. The insignia on the dash informs us that the car belongs to a clergyman. Obviously he is inside the church.

"Hello? Hello?" I knock respectfully but firmly on the metal surrounding the glass of the locked front doors, hoping that he will hear me from his station inside. "Hello. We need to see the pastor."

In just ten seconds a short, slight man appears inside the doors.

"I will be with you in one minute." He smiles broadly and nods in a partial bow toward us. He is obviously Asian, probably Indian, based on his manners and his accent. "Please, one minute."

He disappears and then, as quickly as promised, reappears, keys in hand, opens the lock and steps out to greet us.

"I am Pastor Joe." His left hand is warmly grasping mine at the same time that his right hand is taking Susan's. "I am the pastor here. What can I do for you?"

"We are moving here from Rome, Italy." I speak in a level, matter-of-fact tone, trying not to react to his raised eyebrows at the mention of our last home city. "This will be our church. We wanted to meet you."

"And why are you moving to Macclenny?" His voice has a litheness that should tip us off as to how unusual such a move is, but we are clueless.

"I will be a senior psychologist on staff at the mental hospital," Susan explains.

"That's wonderful," our new pastor says, literally beaming. "I am the Catholic chaplain there. I am there every week."

"I will be the senior psychologist of the women's admissions ward," Susan explains, beaming back, realizing that in Pastor Joe she has an unusual audience that actually understands with some depth the nature of her new work.

"Marvelous. Marvelous." He pats her shoulder with his free hand while still holding mine in the other. Then he looks directly at me. "And what will you do in Macclenny?"

"I have no idea." My answer and shrug catch him off guard, causing him to release my hand and step back a pace.

"Well." He struggles to recover his grin. "What have you done before?"

"Before we moved to Rome, I was in prison ministry out of Tallahassee. I did that in the Panhandle for six years."

For a split second he is frozen, mouth dropping open, hands

immobile and eyes growing as big as saucers. Then suddenly, without warning, he moves close enough to grab both my shoulders.

"I have been praying for fifteen years for you to get here!" He is almost crying it out, without actually screaming, while shaking me back and forth by the shoulders. "For fifteen years. What took you so long?"

Our stunned silence demands some explanation for his outburst. He obliges us with a quick recovery of his warm grin, while tears are tugging at his eyes.

"I am the Catholic priest for death row and solitary confinement. Those prisons are just a few miles from here. For fifteen years I have been going cell to cell in those prisons alone. And for fifteen years I have been praying for God to send you." He pauses and then smiles again, but this time with a boyish grin and his arm around my shoulder in half of a hug. "What took you so long?"

Now Susan's arm is around my waist from the other side. My mouth will not move, even though I am trying to speak. My brain has no idea what to say. Finally, I hear my words eke out.

"I guess we took the long way."

Originally, our intention is to rent a house in Macclenny, but there is nothing available for rent except in Jacksonville, 45 minutes away. Our only vehicle is an aging van that was given to us by my brother Gary and his wife. One hundred miles a day of commuting is not in the cards for the foreseeable future. We must buy a place to live in Macclenny.

The Realtor we meet on Monday morning, July 20, informs us that in all of Baker County, with its population of barely 20,000, including the 3,900 residents in town, there are only six houses for sale that meet our threshold requirement for three bedrooms and a purchase price under $80,000. By late Tuesday morning we have seen all six. Only one of the houses will work for us. It is in town and has 1,100 square feet with three bedrooms and two baths. This is the house we will offer to buy.

Assuming that our offer is accepted, I will need to return to Pennsylvania with Addie to retrieve Chris and our meager possessions. The Anabaptist community is graciously providing us with the basics to get restarted on our own, including beds, a table, chairs, blankets, towels, kitchen and eating utensils and a used computer. But all of our motel, rental car and other travel expenses for interviews around the country for the last seven months have been put on plastic. Even if our offer on the house is accepted, we cannot afford for Susan to spend three weeks in a motel while we wait to take occupancy. Also, we need to move in before the second week of August because the children must start school. This will be a very unusual offer.

We submit the offer on Wednesday, July 22, with the incredible request that the seller, a single woman who is still living in the house, allow Susan to move into the empty bedroom before the seller moves out. We also ask for early occupancy on August 8, weeks before it will be possible to close on the purchase. Our Realtor shakes her head with the discomfort that flows from certainty of failure, but she honors her legal obligation to submit the offer.

It turns out that the seller is also a psychologist and is the very woman who left the job that Susan is taking at the hospital. She agrees to allow Susan to move in pending turnover of occupancy to us and to vacate completely by August 8, even though the actual sale will not be closed by that time.

There are a few reasonable conditions from the seller's end, however, like preapproval for our mortgage. The process of obtaining mortgage approval presents some interesting issues. My tax returns for the years 1996 and 1997 are in Italian and denominated in Italian lira. The application form also has a lot of little boxes to fill in, such as occupation and current job. The mortgage application will be in Susan's name only.

Thanks to the cooperation of our new banker, we are able to obtain the mortgage preapproval by Monday, July 27. We close on the contract of purchase at one that afternoon. By the time Addie and I pick up Susan from work that afternoon, we have all the utilities set up to be transferred over on the seventh of August. Before dinner we move Susan, some suitcases and boxes and a new Walmart air mattress into the empty bedroom in our new house. Then Addie and I leave for the long drive to Pennsylvania.

On July 31, in the midst of our preparations to leave Pennsylvania, I send out a letter from Susan and me to all our friends who have been staying close to us during our sojourn. In it we remind them of our letter of April 1994, in which they were invited to join us for the weekly Saturday evening gatherings at our Tallahassee home. That letter said, "Whatever happens, at the end of four and a half years [July 31, 1998], when our lease is up and Jeanette goes off to college, we will know what we are to do."

It is July 31, 1998. Susan is in her second week of working with mentally ill women in the State hospital in Macclenny. As soon as we move into the new house, I will be accompanying the Catholic priest in ministry to those on death row and in solitary confinement at the prisons nearby. We know what we are to do.

14

Into the Valley of the Shadow of Death

PSALM 23:4

CHRIS, ADDIE AND I ARRIVE in Macclenny in the moving truck from Pennsylvania at 12:45 Saturday morning on August 8. They will sleep on the floor in the living room of our new home. Jeanette, who drove up from Palm Beach after work yesterday, will sleep on the air mattress in the back bedroom where Susan has been sleeping for the last eleven days, since July 28. The seller lived up to her contractual commitments and moved out yesterday. So here we are, ready to begin.

The children and I drove here today from Roanoke, Virginia. That is where we broke down yesterday. At first we did not expect to make it all the way to Macclenny tonight. As we left the Virginia repair shop with our repaired rental truck, we turned onto a torn-up access road. An orange triangular sign greeted us with the warning "ROUGH ROAD AHEAD." I smirked sardonically, asking myself whether that warning meant the access road, the rest of the drive, our new life in Macclenny—or maybe all three? By the time I spread out on a sleeping bag on the tile floor in the writing office of our new home, the only room in the house without rugs that have been collecting cat hair for years, I am too tired to care. Rough road or not, this is where we are. This is where God has brought us. End of discussion.

Later that morning, Michael and Shawnice Savage arrive with their family. We and they will spend the afternoon and evening at the Macclenny EconoLodge. All the children will enjoy swimming at the motel pool under their mothers' watchful eyes while Michael and I shampoo the rugs in our new house. The prior owner had three long-haired cats and smoked cigarettes. I am allergic to cats, and Addie and I are both allergic to cigarette smoke. We still do not own any tools or a vacuum cleaner or a rug shampooing machine. Michael and Shawnice have driven over 140 miles to bring all the equipment to handle our problems. The rugs dry overnight. By the time church is over on Sunday morning, August 9, the shampooed rugs have dried. Michael and I unload the truck.

All our new neighbors are strong Christians and they prove willing to take us at face value. Just two weeks after moving in, our van refuses to start and is sitting dead in the driveway in the severe August heat. We are in danger of missing our Sunday church service. Our family decides to do what we have done in Rome in August. We start walking the two miles to church.

"Hey, neighbor," an unknown male voice interrupts my mental dialogue with God about heat, humidity and car batteries. "Where you all going?"

"Good morning," Susan and I respond together, turning to find a car filled with the family from two houses down the street, all dressed for church. "Our van has decided to take a day of rest, and we are hoofing it to our church for Sunday service."

"That is not a good idea in this heat." He smiles and tosses me a set of keys. "Take my truck, in the driveway right there. Bring it back after church."

I am too shocked to answer immediately. Susan quickly thanks them before the family we have not yet met drives off. The truck is brand-new, less than a month old. I do not even know the man's name.

"Wow." Addie speaks for all of us after we climb inside and the cab's air-conditioning starts blowing relief inside the jet-black pickup. "This is going to be a nice place to live."

One week after the children start school, Pastor Joe picks me up to ride with him to Union Correctional Institution, usually referred to by its abbreviation, *UCI*. We head south on State Road 121, past Interstate 10, past the hospital where Susan works, past the southern boundary of Baker County and into Union County. When we arrive at the intersection from the east of State Road 16, we turn left for two miles to the entrance of UCI. If we had continued south for another mile on State Road 121, we would have come to a flashing caution light in front of a Stop-and-Go gas station/convenience store. That is the town of Raiford, Florida. Because it is the closest town to UCI, the prison is nicknamed *Raiford*.

Situated between UCI and the most infamous prison in the state, Florida State Prison, is a creek called New River. That creek is the boundary between Union County and Bradford County. On the west side of the creek is UCI. On the east side, in Bradford County, is Florida State Prison. The nearest town in Bradford County is Starke, Florida, an actual city with a population of about 25,000. So Florida State Prison is referred to by both its abbreviation, *FSP*, and by its nickname, *Starke*.

UCI houses the main death row building, P-Dorm, where more

than 330 men are in death row cells. FSP houses the electric chair and the death house, the actual place of executions. It also contains the overflow death row wing, which holds the excess capacity over the death row building across New River.

Today, Pastor Joe and I are headed to UCI, which is itself a prison complex unique in the State of Florida because it houses every level of security and classification of inmates in the state: death row, disciplinary solitary confinement, protective custody, medical hospital, close custody, general population, even psychiatric solitary confinement. The prisoners and staff together total almost the population of my new city. When the planned construction of dorms U and V replaces the infamous Rock, with new cells for additional psychiatric confinement, UCI will be larger than my city.

The first thing we must do upon our arrival at UCI is clear security at the main entrance. Control officers behind bulletproof glass verify our IDs and confirm that we are on the day's gate pass. The pass is prepared by the chaplain and approved by the warden. Pastor Joe indicates that it is taking longer than usual. I note that several phone calls are being made by officers behind the glass, who are spelling out my unpronounceable name. Finally the steel-barred white gate slides open sideways on its track. We step inside, wait for the first one to shut and then for the next one to open.

When we step through this second gate, all we have done is make it to the security station where we will be searched. Our pockets are emptied and belts and shoes removed for wanding with the handheld metal detector. Because we are going to death row, this is followed by a pat-down search. The access sergeant makes a call and nods approval. After we re-collect our belongings, the large steel-barred metal gate, gate 5, screeches open, allowing us to step inside the perimeter fence of the UCI compound.

We walk into the compound and approach another electronically controlled gate. Somewhere in an unseen station, a button is pushed that pops the locks and allows us to step into a completely fenced walkway. Even overhead the fence is enclosed. I feel a bit claustrophobic walking down the long outdoor passageway with metal fencing to the left, right and above, and concrete below.

To our left, just outside the immediate fencing of the tunnel, three rows of high, razor wire–topped fences stand between us and the parking lot. To the right spreads the large UCI prison complex, partially obstructed by the skeletal remains of the infamously violent Rock. The sight of it triggers memories of my prayer partner from the Panhandle, who has stayed in touch with me through correspondence during our overseas sojourn. That is the building where Kenny came to Jesus in a six-man cell. That is where he found salvation in the bowels of hell.

When we come to a 45-degree angle in the path of the fence tunnel, we are now walking parallel to the exterior wall of the death row building. Halfway across the face of the building, the tunnel delivers us to a locked gate. Cameras hang from overhead above a sign bearing the metal embossed black letters that read, "Push Buzzer to Open." Scrawled underneath in black marker are the handwritten words in all caps, "DON'T HOLD IT IN!"

I surmise that on the other end of the closed circuit camera above us is a control room of officers who have grown weary of button-holder-inners who refuse to release the buzzer until the gate opens. Pastor Joe obliges with a quick press. Immediately the gate clicks open electronically, as if they have been watching us all along. I find out later that they have been. Gate 5 alerted them, as soon as we arrived, with a warning: A new guy is in the tunnel. The entire building is on stepped-up alert until they know for sure who I am and what I am there to do.

Now we progress through the brown front doors of the building into another guard station with double steel-barred doors that can only be opened from inside the entrance security room. The huge, heavy metal doors, which open sideways by sliding on a track, cannot both be open at the same time. Once we are inside the first, it grinds shut behind us. Then the second grinds open, though not right away. We will cool our heels, locked in between the two gates, while security officers inside the control room are on their phones confirming my identity with unseen authorities and meticulously recording on their logs the names of those who will be responsible for my access if anything goes wrong.

A metal drawer shoots out of the wall of the security office, surprising me with a smart smack to my right hip. Inside there are two metal boxes, each with a white panic button and a belt clip. The female officer inside the control room motions for me to put one on my belt and speaks through the baffled speaking hole in the bulletproof glass, "It will sound an alarm if you fall to a horizontal position."

Pastor Joe snaps his box on his belt and waves away my expression of concern with his other hand. "It's just for security. It's no big deal."

The interior barred gate slides open, allowing us to step into the death row building's main corridor. The main corridor is air-conditioned. Everything is painted yellow except the flat brown metal surfaces. Cameras protrude everywhere, giving depth to the warning sign at the building entrance that the entire building is under constant audio/video surveillance.

Immediately to our right, on both sides of the hallway, are small rooms with locked metal doors and large security glass windows. I will learn that these rooms are used for attorney callouts, when the men are brought from their cells in shackles, waist chains and black box handcuffs. On black box handcuffs, a plastic cover protects the key-locking mechanism so that the cuffs are tamper-proof. I will use the rooms for pastoral counseling with men in one-on-one appointments. Immediately to our left, on both sides of the hallway, are small rooms with locked metal doors that have small security glass windows in the doors themselves. I will learn that these rooms are for death row inmates to have noncontact visits and to obtain legal research on developments that affect their cases.

At both ends of the main corridor are steel-barred metal gates. Officers are everywhere. Pastor Joe hand-signals to the hall sergeant that we will be going to our left and up, meaning that we will begin our rounds on the north side, upstairs. The sergeant grunts and nods, which I will learn means "Roger," and writes something down in his log. We walk past the noncontact visiting rooms and law library to the stairwell that leads upstairs.

As Pastor Joe moves to the stairwell, I point at the elevator right next to it.

"Oh no." He shakes his head solemnly and wags his finger with a degree of emphasis that is unusual for him. "Never. Never. Very bad trouble."

There is an elevator at each end of the corridor, but people are not allowed on either, not even officers. Only carts carrying food, canteen supplies and laundry can be pushed onto and pulled off the elevators. Even then, there is no button to make them go up or down. That is controlled from the security office at the front of the building.

When we arrive at the gate for north side upstairs, we are standing in front of another access control guard station. Inside are the consoles that control all the security devices and wing and cell doors on the entire north side upstairs. The officer inside the bulletproof security glass station takes our IDs through the narrow slot in the glass and writes down our names. Then she gets on the phone and makes several calls. Now she is entering in her log the names of the people who will be responsible if I cause any problems.

The narrow slot spits out our IDs, and the gate screeches open. We step through onto a quarterdeck where the wing sergeant and wing officers are trying to dry themselves off from their last trip through the actual death row wings. Even with the air-conditioning in the main corridor and on this quarterdeck, the officers are drenched with sweat after each venture onto the walkways where the actual cells are located. The desk sergeant reverifies our identities and our authorizations with the same fervor that might have been used if no one else had bothered to check. Finally, he sets down the wing station phone and presents a clipboard for us to sign in.

Pastor Joe hand-signals that we will be starting all the way to the left and working our way across the floor. The sergeant grunts and nods. Then as we approach the solid steel door farthest to the left, the sergeant yells, "One left."

As Pastor Joe places his right hand on the huge brown metal door with a very narrow slit of security glass inset down one side, a loud slam echoes out from deep inside the wall. The lock has been released for five seconds. He yanks the door open, and we step inside into a corridor of Florida's death row.

It is as hot as I can imagine hell to be. The thermal intensity of the heat steals my breath. I find myself reaching for the wall to steady myself. Pastor Joe allows me a minute to arrive mentally, and I use the time to absorb my new surroundings.

To our far left is a beige exterior concrete wall, separated from us by a beige steel-barred wall. We are on a concrete path called the gate walk because it passes immediately in front of the cell doors that stretch out to our right. Those cell doors are also called gates. The concrete path on the other side of the steel-barred wall to our left, and right in front of the cranks that open and close the outside windows, is called the catwalk. The windows are translucent with security glass. They are cranked partially open.

The sun has been beating down on the exterior wall of this building all morning. That wall has become a radiator of intense heat. To our right extends a long string of fifteen maximum security cells. At the back of each cell is a ventilator fan sucking air. The effect is to suck in through the windows the superheated air off the outside wall to our left and, like a convection oven, circulate the heat across the walkway and into the cells. I realize that I have stepped into a solar furnace.

Cell by cell we greet each man inside, some white, some black, some Catholic, most not, some young, some old, but all dressed only in their shorts, the attire of choice for those living in a solar oven. Within minutes, Pastor Joe and I are both drenched with sweat. We still have hours to go.

As the sweat pours and the prayers flow, I find myself examining each of these men on the other side of the bars. We are able to shake hands through the steel bars. We do. We are able to lay hands on them through the bars as we pray. We do. We are able to give them Communion through the same slot in the bars that their food trays are passed through. We do. But the questions nag at me: *With whom am I shaking hands? With whom am I praying?*

Each cell looks the same—a bed, a stainless steel toilet, a locker that also serves as a sitting stool and a mirror. A space about six feet wide and ten feet deep. That is it. As we peer through the steel bars of each door into each cell, the only thing that changes is the face that meets us.

The death row cells are always only on one side of the corridor, so that from inside his cell, the man can never see another human face except for the faces of the officers and staff on the gate walk and those of religious volunteers at cell front. Like the heat and humidity, this deprivation of human contact is considered part of the punishment of death row.

Some men look grandfatherly. A couple are covered with demonic-looking tattoos from head to toe. One man who asks for prayer is covered with a full-body tattoo that appears to depict a human sacrifice. Another man who takes Communion has obscenities carved into his shoulder. The next man is too young to shave and looks like a neighbor kid who would help mow your lawn or shovel your snow.

I cannot tell for sure how much of it is the heat, but the pervading feeling in my mind is one of unreality. An obscuring dimness stands between me and each new face as definitively as do the cell doors. There also is a barrier woven of unanswered questions: *What did this man do? Why is he here? What would his victims reveal to us about him if they could speak now?*

Pastor Joe does not appear to be surmounting any such barrier. Either he knows the answers to such questions or he has long since stopped asking them. He has been coming here every week for fifteen years. He knows which men are Catholic, but the orders for this engagement are too big to fit into merely denominational support. We are charged by the bishops to be present for every single man, regardless of faith, or even if the man has no faith at all. Pastor Joe brings a warm smile and a greeting for every man in every cell, reading material for anyone who wants it and sacraments for those who are Catholic.

"Hey, how are you today?" he greets each man in each cell.

Almost all respond. One or two do not bother to look up, but no one sneers or reacts negatively.

We complete the first wing of fifteen and then complete another.

Halfway through the second wing of death row cells, I realize that I am adjusting. Even the shocking can become familiar far too quickly. I find myself troubled with another disturbing question: *Am I already becoming accustomed to holding hands in prayer with a condemned man in his shorts through a steel-barred door?*

My own voice in thought rebukes the question. These men are waiting to be killed, waiting to be burned to death in the electric chair. God forbid that I adjust to this.

Pastor Joe and I cover about ninety death row cells, all of north side upstairs. Then he tells me it is time for us to go to solitary confinement.

We work our way back out of the death row building, out through the fence tunnel and back into the main compound. We head toward another series of fences and electronically secure buildings. These are UCI's solitary confinement cells. The term *solitary confinement* has fallen out of favor because it sounds like excessive punishment. Now, the State uses the term *close management*, called CM for short.

Whether called CM or solitary, the reality is the same. In the unrelenting heat and humidity of rural north Florida, confinement is a hellhole of a different kind. It is not quite as hot as death row, but it is equally hellish.

We are in O-Dorm. Each corridor consists of a row of thirty cells, fifteen on each side. The cells here are just like the ones on death row, except they face another cell across the corridor and have solid steel doors with only a small Plexiglas window at face height. Also, each door has a feeding hole in the middle, about waist-high, to slide in the feeding tray. In prison slang the food hole is called a bean flap or a food flap.

Some men spend thirty days in confinement in one of these cells. Some spend years. As we walk into the corridors of O-Dorm, I again remember my prayer partner from the Panhandle. Kenny spent years in one of these cells, here in this prison. Then he was moved to a regular maximum security cell at the Rock. That is where he accepted Jesus Christ. I find myself looking through the little glass window of each cell and asking in my thoughts, *Is there another Kenny in that cell today?*

We are not allowed to open the cell doors, even for sacraments. Pastor Joe has the key that unlocks the padlock on the bean-flap in each door. That is only opened for those who are to receive Communion. For the others, we slip reading material through the quarter-inch space between the sides of the steel door and the concrete wall. That is called the gap, and it is the opening we use to talk to the man behind each door.

As Pastor Joe and I walk through each wing, cell by cell, the corridor echoes with screams and yells: "Gimmee a necklace! Gimmee a cross! Gimmee a magazine! Cap'n Chap, Cap'n Chap—over here! Gimmee . . . Gimmee . . ."

There are men here who are serious about faith. We pray with them and give Communion to the Catholics. A young man asks to go to confession and receive Communion. Pastor Joe opens the feeding hole in his door and bends to put his ear by the slot. The young man inside the cell kneels down on the other side of the door and places his mouth by the slot. I step two cells away to give them some sense of privacy.

While I am leaning against the opposite wall, hopelessly trying to wipe off my sweat, I hear a man's voice from my left.

"Brother, if you're a man of God, please talk to me."

Turning around I find the source of the voice. It is a tall black man, very tall, in the next cell. His face is scrunched against the quarter-inch gap between the door and the wall.

"Are you a Christian?" I ask while taking the one step right up to the crack. He is silent, but I can see his shadow nodding yes.

"Where are you at in your life with Jesus?" My lips are pressed against the rusted, foul metal of the gap and the moldy wall. He does not answer.

I break the silence and ask him if he would like me to lead him through a prayer.

He chokes down the trembling in his voice and manages a whisper. "Please."

He puts his hand on his side of the door; I place my hand on the outside of the door opposite his. Then he places his ear right up against the crack of the gap, and we pray. We pray for forgiveness, for healing, for deliverance, for protection, for hope and for perseverance. We pray the name that is our victory, the blood that is our protection, the empty tomb that is our hope and the Spirit that is our strength.

"Thank you, brother," he says softly after we finish. "I needed to pray so bad, but I didn't know how to get back. Thank you."

Pastor Joe and I finish both the downstairs and upstairs wings of O-Dorm. Then we move next door to N-Dorm, another confinement building. Next we go to another quadrant of the UCI prison complex.

This last unit is brand-new and is air-conditioned. It has to be because it is a psychiatric unit and holds men whose psychotropic medications could kill them in the heat. The doors in front of the cells are solid bulletproof, transparent plastic but still with a bean flap. As we walk down the corridor with the inmates on either side of us pressed up against their transparent doors, I cannot decide which is worse, the steel or the plastic. Hell is hell.

I also find myself wondering what is happening in our society that we are producing so many young men who are destined for this hell.

This unit has a request by a young man to go to Communion and confession. I step out off the wing corridor and stand in the hall between the confinement area and the guard station while Pastor Joe hears his confession. The guard who stands there with me turns out to be from my new hometown. He is a Christian, a Methodist.

He and I talk while Pastor Joe ministers the sacraments to the young inmate. I cannot help thinking how much grace from God a guard must need to work in this environment day after day after day, responsible to control young men who are behaving so badly. How much grace it must take to keep a sense of humanity and kindness, to treat as human those who are acting less than human. I make a promise to myself to pray for this guard and all the guards here every day for that grace.

Pastor Joe informs me that we are done for the day. The inmates are being counted by the guards.

We work our way back: back through the movement control guard stations, back across the compounds and past the hospital, one of the units we did not get to today because we ran out of time. We go back past the chapel hidden between the fortresses of lost souls, back past the hulking ghost of the Rock, back past the death row tunnel and its sidewalk covered by a three-sided fence. We find our way back to the entry station and the guardhouse and the rows of razor wire. We pass through the guard station, where everything in every bag is checked again as we leave. Finally we are in the parking lot. We are on the outside.

During the twenty-minute ride home, I ask Pastor Joe, "The needs are so great. There are so many men. Have you really been coming to death row for fifteen years all by yourself? Hasn't anyone else ever come to do this with you?"

He answers, "Yes, by myself. For fifteen years I've been praying for God to send someone to go with me. And you are finally here."

"And next week we go for my first time to Florida State Prison?"

"Yes," he says with a smile.

"Is it like this was today?"

"Oh no." He waves off the suggestion as ludicrous; but before I can exhale, he continues, "FSP is worse, much, much worse."

15

Inside the Belly of the Beast

IT IS SEPTEMBER OF 1998 and my first visit to Florida State
Prison, home to Florida's infamous electric chair, referred to as "old
Sparky." Security here is reputed to be stricter than at any other prison
in the state. Based upon my experience, that seems to be true.

Florida State Prison, usually called either FSP or Starke, is not
a campus. It is a huge, monolithic structure, painted pale green and
wrapped with razor wire–topped fences like an excess of ribbons
around a gift box on Christmas morning. I am with Pastor Joe and
a small group of religious volunteers. The volunteers will only attend
the church service in the chapel with a few inmates from general
population. I will be making rounds in the wings in the back.

As we approach from the parking lot, the redbrick one-story
administration building is to our left. It squats like an afterthought
next to the huge cavernous prison that looks to it for every permission and approval.

The prison building is on the right. We must enter through double gates, each surrounded and topped by razor wire. The dead spaces in between the fences are embedded with motion detectors and electrified elements. This prison is known in Florida for housing the worst of the worst. The highest levels of security are not a premium here. They are a necessity.

The outside gates are in the shadow of a turret tower that resembles the control tower at an airport. The guards inside are viewing us from about five stories up with loaded shotguns in immediate reach. Only one of the two gates can ever be opened at a time. The first grinds open, and we step into the space between the gates. The first shuts behind us, and then the second gate grinds open.

As we stand between thousands of pounds of moving metal and razor-sharp coils, I realize that there are some noises I have never heard anywhere except in prison. The grinding and clanging of gates is one such noise.

After passing through the double outside gates, we enter the olive green doors of the access point for the prison building, coming immediately to the first guard station, a short brown table outside the staff office. Regular visitors would register here for clearance. We are not regular visitors. We exchange greetings with the officers and process through the green doors into the first of several security entrances. Here, a guard in a bulletproof booth checks our identification, checks our names against the chapel list for gate passes and stamps our hands with a special fluorescent ink that can be read under a black light.

Then we process through another moving wall of steel bars, only to find ourselves standing before a narrow mechanical aperture, a metal detector that even registers the crowns on your teeth. I will nickname this particular metal detector the "eye of the needle." The metal detector is set at maximum sensitivity today. The guard on duty can monitor the level of sensitivity, so the setting may be because I am present. Anyone new is a security risk.

I take my keys, loose change and a roll of breath mints out of my pockets; wedding ring, wallet and watch all hit the table; off come the belt, my identification badge, my small metal replica of the San Damiano Cross from Assisi, my glasses (which are imitation wire-rims, plastic with metallic coating) and my walking shoes with metal arch supports.

As I stand barefoot and spread-eagled, hands against the wall, raising one unshod foot at a time, the gloved post guard pats me down, searching the insides of my shoes, my pockets, even the folds of my skin, joints and toes, to ensure that no contraband is clenched by body parts. My mind is on the mound of possessions stacked on the table. It is amazing how much stuff I carry around.

After clearing the eye of the needle, we wait for the beige gate to grind open. We step into a long beige corridor that ends at another guard station behind bulletproof glass and another beige metal gate. Again, this gate cannot be opened until the one behind us has ground closed. Once it opens, we step into the central core of the prison, a rectangular area surrounded by bars and barred moving walls referred to as "Time Square." The control room officer is on the phone, nodding and peering at my identification badge as she jots my name on the log.

Now we turn a corner into a beige corridor that is about a quarter mile long and three stories high. Here we meet another metal gate. This one swings open at the gentle nudging of the prison chaplain, who is there to greet us and to make sure we are in fact who we are supposed to be.

The chapel door is to our immediate right. That is where the church service will be. We have not yet come anywhere close to where the single cells on death row are. We are still close to the outside of the prison.

By the time I actually make my way to the far end of the beige corridor, I have spent twenty minutes processing into the bowels of FSP. Ten massive steel-barred doors and more than a quarter mile of corridor under electronic surveillance now separate me from the prison entrance. One more security door stands between me and death row.

All the wings in the prison are three stories high and are accessed at the mezzanine level from the main corridor through a heavy steel door. Each hall door has massive double locks. One lock can only be opened from outside the wing. The hall sergeant has the key for that lock. The other lock can only be opened from inside the wing. The wing sergeant has the key for that lock. The result is that, even if the inmates on a wing were able to overcome the security staff and take the wing sergeant's keys, they still could not get off the wing.

The hall sergeant escorts me to the death row wing door and knocks on the small Plexiglas window of the steel door. He waits until the sergeant inside shows his face in the door. Then, they simultaneously insert their keys and turn the locks. The sergeant on the wing stands in my path until he reads my badge and his assistant confirms my identity. Then he steps aside, nods and grunts.

"Thank you, sir." I acknowledge his "roger" and step through the portal into FSP's portion of death row. I can only hope that my appearance and voice do not reveal the depth of my fear. The only time I have seen security that requires simultaneous locks from different sides of a door is in documentaries about protecting nuclear weapons.

The inside and outside locks on the hall door are re-bolted. The wing sergeant hands me a sign-in log and directs me to the gate walk on mezzanine level left. As soon as I step onto the concrete ribbon that leads to the front of the cells, the heavy steel bolts in the barred door behind me clang shut, locking me in on the beige corridor of death row cells. Like a stray cosmic noise from another world, the spongy soles of my Rockports announce my arrival with muffled squeaks against the hot, damp concrete.

About fifteen solitary cells stretch to my right. The men immediately note the fall of my step and the noise of my shoes. A new guy is on the wing. Except for four hours a week of yard exercise, this short, narrow hall, with its six-by-nine-foot cages, is their whole world. Just as at UCI death row, there is nothing to see. All the cells face a wall of steel bar, backed by concrete and brick. They cannot see each other. It is a world of sounds. Nothing—not even the smallest squeak of upper-middle-class walking shoes—goes unnoticed.

With Pastor Joe starting at the far end of the corridor and progressing back in my direction, I work my way from cell to cell, starting at the front end. In a short time I am about five cells into the corridor, speaking to a young man who is about 25 years old. We bow our heads in prayer. Suddenly, there is a loud roar. The lights flicker out as the shriek accelerates into a shrill-pitched scream. I freeze like a deer in the dark that has been caught unawares by the headlights of a car bearing down.

"The generators for the electric chair," he explains with a shrug. "They test them every week."

"The generators are here?"

"Yeah. None of the power companies will provide the juice because they're afraid that radicals might bomb them to stop an execution."

"So we have an electrical generating station right here at FSP?" My experience with financing power generators for hospitals and universities tells me that such things are ghastly expensive, not just to build but also to maintain. And those systems do not need anywhere near the voltage the electric chair requires.

"Yup. We have our own FSP Electric Company, just for us."

My body stands frozen until the mechanical scream stops. Then, trying to look unruffled, I reach through the food flap to take his hands again. "Let's begin our little Communion service with the Lord's Prayer, okay?"

The overflow death row on Wing G is only a small part of Florida State Prison. Wing A is the medical clinic, with about five highly protected suicide-watch cells. Wing B houses the severely misbehaving. Still, none of the new experiences at FSP quite rival X Wing. The term used to describe the mezzanine and upstairs levels of X Wing is *maximum management.* What that means, literally, is total control of a person's environment by the State. That means control of all sensory input; in other words, maximum sensory deprivation. Each cell is literally encased inside another cell. When the solid steel door on the outer cell is shut and the light is turned off by the switch on the outside wall, the man in that cell cannot hear or see anything. Pastor Joe tells me that men go nuts inside those cells. He says that our regular presence there is absolutely necessary to make sure that nothing really, really bad happens.

Finally, there is the downstairs level of X Wing. We are not allowed to go down the stairs to the bottom today, but the guards allow us to stand on the landing midway down so Pastor Joe can point. This is the State of Florida's death house. These are the cells where men are held just ten or twenty feet from where they will be killed. This is the execution chamber with the electric chair. And on the other side of that wall, on the other side of the curtain-shrouded glass, is the execution witness room.

"I have witnessed four electrocutions." Pastor Joe shakes his head, speaking just above a whisper. "On the last one I witnessed, just last year, the man had flames shooting from his head. He died screaming, burned to death in the chair."

There are no words to answer such horror. I offer none.

"I still see it sometimes," he continues, "in my dreams."

I listen with a detached ear. To my mind, witnessing executions is connected with the sacrament of last rites, a job for the priest and way above my pay grade. Thank God I will never have dreams like that.

X Wing at one end, B Wing at the other end and the twelve hundred cells in the wings in between become part of my regular weekly rounds with Pastor Joe at FSP. Sunday has us in the chapels of both prisons with services for the general population inmates. Sunday afternoon and Saturdays find me on cell-front rounds at FSP. Monday and Tuesday are cell-front rounds at UCI. Little by little, I am becoming acquainted with each of the men on the other side of the doors.

○─○─○

During our family's time overseas, Kenny and I have continued to correspond. Now my family is living in northeast Florida near Jacksonville, and he is sitting in Holmes Correctional Institution in Bonifay, about one hour north of Panama City. Everyone calls it Holmes or Bonifay. With ideal weather and at the speed limit, Kenny is a four-hour drive west on Interstate 10.

By October 1998, my feet are planted firmly enough in our new situation for me to begin a monthly trek to see him at the prison chapel as his spiritual advisor. Everything is arranged through the chaplain, who is more than just a little curious about our friendship. On my first visit to Holmes he welcomes Kenny and me into his office.

"Let me get this straight, Chaplain Recinella," the Holmes prison chaplain begins, referring to me with the deferential title that goes with my spiritual advisor status. "Your chaplain at UCI tells me you are a lawyer. Is that right?"

"Yes, sir. But I agreed with the department not to practice law so long as I am serving the Church at UCI and FSP."

"By Church, you mean Catholic Church. Is that right?"

"Yes, sir. I serve under the Catholic Church at those two prisons."

"But inmate Kenny Cofield here is a Christian. Isn't that right?"

"Yes, sir." After pausing a moment to allow Kenny to answer the rhetorical question, I realize he has been in prison too long to jump into this line of questioning. He is happy to let me have at it. "Kenny is a Christian and is mighty serious about his faith."

"Well, Chaplain Recinella, and I don't mean no offense by this, but how can a Catholic be a spiritual advisor to a Christian?"

"Well, sir, we Catholics believe we are Christians. In fact, we believe that we are the original Christians." During the uncomfortable silence that answers my assertion of creed, I realize that this Panhandle chaplain has stacks of tracts on his desk, including a pile of the infamous anti-Catholic screed, "Ten Things to Say to a Catholic Priest." So I continue, "Have you heard tell any different, chaplain?"

"No, can't say that I have." He turns to look out his window and away from his tract-covered desk. "So, are you hoping to make inmate Cofield a Catholic?"

"No, sir. We have never even discussed such a thing. He is a baptized Christian, and so am I. We are prayer partners to share the Word and the Spirit. You know, chaplain, one baptism, one Spirit, one Lord, like it says in Scripture."

When Kenny and I are finally walking the short distance to the chapel assembly room where we will use two folding chairs for our meeting, Kenny smiles and shakes his head.

"Hey, man," I laugh as we set up our chairs, "I told you I would be back."

○─○─○

By the third week of January 1999, I have learned that, as hot as it gets on death row in the summer, it is that cold there in December and January. Sunday morning Communion rounds at FSP's death row wing find me standing at cell front while the man inside uses his toothbrush handle to break the thin layer of ice in his toilet bowl before using it. But it is the next thing I learn that is most jarring.

Pastor Joe needs to get out of this work. His physical health is failing. For the fifteen years before he was there, there had been a long succession of priests handling FSP and UCI. The usual tenure was about two years. He had been at it for fifteen years before we moved to Macclenny. The bishop has been unable to rotate him out to another location because no other priest will take the assignment. The physical and emotional environment at death row and solitary confinement is brutal. Even the specter of executions pales before the burden of week-in and week-out work at cell front. But now there may be a chance for Pastor Joe to get out of prison.

"Because you are here, we can make a change," he explains with full Indian expressions and hand gestures, as though I should be as excited as he is. "My nephew, Pastor Jose, he will come."

"And where will you go?"

"I don't know yet, but it doesn't matter." He is all smiles.

"So, what do you need from me?"

"A commitment to the bishop that you will stay long-term to do this."

"And based on that, your nephew will be willing to spring you from prison?"

"I told him, 'You have nothing to worry about because I am giving you Dale.'"

"You actually told him that? That you are giving me to him?"

"Of course. That is why he is willing to come."

By mid-June, Pastor Jose has moved into the rectory with his uncle and the changing of the guard is underway. Our former pastor will be gone before the end of June. It is a good time for me to take a vacation. I will be gone about four weeks, visiting friends and relatives around the Midwest and attending a wedding in Michigan. During the last few weeks before leaving, I inform the inmates at cell front and the guards at their stations of my planned return to FSP and UCI for services and rounds on Sunday morning, July 18.

O-O-O

On Sunday morning, July 18, I check in to FSP by all the normal procedures. There is a sense of great apprehension in the air, but no one says anything out of the ordinary. The FSP chaplain meets me at the chapel door and waves me inside without speaking. With ashen face and subdued affect he slides into his office chair and motions for me to sit in front of his desk. I drop into the rickety gray steel contraption that has long outlasted its chairness. The FSP chaplain came to this job after a career as a military chaplain. He knows the score and knows how to manage people. I assume he knows that this is my first day flying solo and he is going to hammer me into shape. I could not be more wrong.

"Nobody knows for sure what happened, Chaplain Recinella." His eyes are barely floating over the knuckles of his wringing hands. "I assumed he was alive when they took him out yesterday. There was no time to call for Catholic last rites before they took him out."

"Excuse me, sir?"

"Valdez. Surely you heard about Valdez. Yesterday."

"No, sir. You mean Frank Valdez? The death row inmate who is Catholic and whom I regularly give Communion every two weeks on X Wing?"

"Was Catholic," he corrects me without any hint of emotion. "He's dead. And nobody knows how."

"How? Was it natural causes?"

"Nobody knows how. It happened on X Wing. Nobody knows how."

"What should I do?"

"Do what you are here to do. Hold your Communion service and then make your rounds, just like normal."

As it turns out, the day is anything but normal. When the general population inmates pour in for the service, the anxiety level is off the charts. Everyone is speaking at once: "They killed him." "They beat him to death." "There are still more inmates back there."

We limp through the service, focusing on the answers our faith offers for dealing with such huge emotions and fears. Then it is time for my rounds in the back. My first stop is X Wing. The officers sign me in and wave me on through to the cell areas behind the locked access gates. It is as if everything is normal, at least until I step onto the floor where it happened.

Neon yellow tape is crisscrossed over the outer door to Valdez's inner cell. And bloodstains are everywhere, on the floor, on the door and on the walls. The men in the surrounding cells are screaming. I offer everything I have, prayer and Communion. By the time I step back to the quarterdeck, my comfortable notions of reality have been shaken to the core by the pleas of hardened men weeping on their knees.

"This is a h——l of a place, chap." The desk officer looks almost sympathetic as he signs me out. "One h——l of a place."

By Thursday, all the major newspapers in Florida are reporting that Valdez's death is being treated as a homicide. The *Orlando Sentinel* reports that he "suffered extensive injuries, every rib in his body was broken, and his corpse bore the imprints of three boot marks."

Pastor Joe has been gone for four weeks, but I cannot stop hearing his voice in my head saying that our regular presence as outsiders on X Wing is absolutely necessary to make sure that "nothing really, really bad happens." I vow to make my rounds on X Wing no matter what.

Just days before the Valdez incident upstairs on X Wing, a

gruesome and bloody event also occurred in the death house down-stairs, one that would change the course of Florida's use of the death penalty. On July 8, 1999, the execution of Allen Lee Davis in Florida's electric chair went very badly. Unlike the botched electrocutions of Jesse Tafero in 1990 and Pedro Medina in 1997, in which the men caught on fire and burned alive in the chair, Davis's electrocution causes his body to split open and blood to pour all over the place.

Within days of my return from vacation, FSP is swarming with Florida Department of Law Enforcement officials investigating the death of Frank Valdez and legislative types investigating the facts of Allen Davis's execution. The facts of that execution are being argued before the Florida Supreme Court in relation to cases asking for Florida's electric chair to be declared unconstitutional as cruel and unusual punishment.

Governor Jeb Bush is promising a total change of culture at FSP. As with most government makeovers, it starts with the cosmetic. The name *X Wing* is now infamous and synonymous with horror throughout Florida. Part of the reason is the Valdez killing, part is the Davis execution and part are the exposés in the Florida papers in the wake of those events. Investigative reports have found that men have become vegetables sitting in those X Wing cells with the door closed for more than a decade. X Wing is being renamed Q Wing.

To the governor's credit, real changes are also being made and fast. Institutional inspectors have reported to their prison warden, making it too tempting for them to be pressured to cover up illegal use of force. Now they will report to the inspector general in Tallahassee. Also, reviews of use of force will no longer be at the institutional and regional level. They will be at the state level with outside third-party involvement. All such actions must be videotaped, and the tapes will be reviewed. The department is implementing shift changes to reduce staff stress and burnout. A new policy requires that all use of force actions be immediately reported. They are to be followed by medical review. Finally, cameras are being installed on all confinement wings, including on the stairways and in the sally ports.

I begin to experience the changes immediately. The time needed for cell to cell rounds in solitary confinement explodes dramatically as the entire building becomes solitary. The five hundred general population cells in the wings have all been transformed. There are now twelve hundred solitary cells, plus death row and Q Wing. Two new dorms are being built outside in the back to house general population for the inmates who do the prison work. Everybody else must be serviced at cell front.

The halls of FSP are suddenly dancing with color. Newly hired women who are doctors, psychologists, nurses and psych technicians are waging an assault of street clothes against the beige brown corridors and uniforms that have held a monopoly on this inside space for decades. Day rooms and counseling offices are appearing out of nowhere. Overnight, FSP is becoming a psychiatric solitary confinement prison that just happens to hold the death house and the overflow death row.

"So what's happening here?" I ask an officer in the main hallway on a Saturday morning in the fall of 1999. "Are we going to start having room service?"

"Wouldn't surprise me one bit." He knows I'm pulling his chain and is happy to play along with a surly disposition. "Welcome to the new kinder, gentler FSP."

"So what do you think, sir?"

"What I know," he corrects me with an air of absolute certainty and authority, "is that they can build these psych hotels anywhere in the dad-gum state. But so long as we have executions, these jobs will stay here."

"So 'kinder, gentler' only goes so far?"

"Chaplain, you are not as dumb as you look." He winks.

"Thank you, sir."

By the end of 1999, there is fear in Tallahassee that the Florida Supreme Court may declare the electric chair unconstitutional. In a desperate move to save the Florida death penalty and, if prison scuttlebutt is right, the jobs at FSP and UCI, the Florida legislature makes lethal injection an alternative method of execution. The chair is still on the books, just in case lethal injection does not go well, so the weekly tests of the electric chair generators will continue.

In June of 2000 Florida's luck with lethal injection runs out, and the execution of Bennie Demps is badly botched. In his last words on the gurney, Demps tells the witnesses that the execution techs spent over half an hour butchering him, trying to find suitable veins, that his blood is all over the pre-execution room. The word in the halls of FSP is that it was even worse than he said.

Right on the heels of the botched lethal injection of Demps comes another execution that defies any logic or civilized thought. Thomas Provenzano was medically diagnosed as severely psychotic as a teenager, was severely psychotic when he committed his crime and is severely psychotic at the death row wing of FSP.

There is no dispute that Provenzano believes he is Jesus Christ and has believed it back to the time of his crime. Before his crime, his family had pleaded with the State of Florida to commit him to a State institution and were turned down because he had never been violent. Now they are begging the State to let him live out his life in prison.

The argument over whether it is ethical to execute a person who was certifiably crazy before his crime and was denied treatment by the State rises to the halls of the Florida legislature in Tallahassee. It is dismissed as merely coddling criminals. At a Florida House Criminal Justice and Corrections Council meeting, Rep. Howard Futch announces, "If he thinks he is Jesus Christ, why don't we just crucify him. I'd make him a cross and we could take it out there to Starke and nail him up."

Because Provenzano was raised Catholic, I make sure that Pastor Jose is given access to him for the last rites before his execution on June 21, 2000. That is all I can do.

I cannot do anything to stop the executions of the mentally ill in Florida or throughout the country. I cannot do anything to stop the slashing of civilian mental health services that result in so many mentally ill living on the streets and falling into our prison system. Almost no one I know believes the fact that it is cheaper to treat the mentally ill than it is to execute them.

By the time I have been ministering on Florida's death row for two years, I have not yet witnessed an execution, but my sleep is already not as sound as it used to be.

○─○─○

Meanwhile, in the fall of 2000, there is some good news from the western Panhandle of Florida with respect to Kenny. The chaplain at his prison asks to speak with me after my pastoral visit. I follow the chaplain into his office, immediately noting that there are no longer any tracts about Catholics on his desk.

"You know, Brother Dale," he begins, showing his acceptance of my Christianity, "you drive a powerful long way for just a one-hour visit in a small room."

"That's okay, chap. It's worth it."

"Oh, for sure, for sure. The Lord's burden is sweet. But I'm wondering if you all have considered being a Christian mentoring family for Kenny. You know, just get right on his visiting list and all."

"Is that allowed while my wife and I are religious volunteers at FSP and UCI?"

"Sure is. I checked with Tallahassee. They are real keen on getting

Christian mentoring families for inmates. It's a real thing with the secretary right now."

The Department of Corrections in Tallahassee confirms it all to me. So long as Kenny is not at FSP or UCI, we can be on his visiting list and show up on weekend days for six-hour visits. When I share this news with Susan and the children, they are enthusiastic about taking on this role as a family.

We could not imagine that this wonderful development would later be wielded as a weapon against us by the very same department that suggested and approved it.

16

"Thou Shalt Not Execute
an Innocent Man"

EXODUS 23:7

THE WEEK BEFORE THANKSGIVING of 2000, there is an unusual call from the chaplain at FSP. A death warrant has been signed for two weeks before Christmas. The condemned man has asked for me to be his spiritual advisor. Am I willing to do it?

"Yes."

"Good. Here are the names and phone numbers of his family members. Ready to copy?"

Over time I will learn that there are tremendous similarities to these calls. It is one thing to make cold calls to people one has never met. It is a whole different thing to make this kind of cold call. The area codes are unfamiliar to me. But the phone is ringing somewhere, in another time zone. Someone answers.

"Hello." I hear my voice as though it is as faraway as the distant receiver. "I'm Brother Dale, Catholic lay chaplain for Florida's death row."

There is always the moment of silence followed by a gasp, so clear that I can picture the hand starting reflexively for the chest or the cheek. I allow the unspoken meaning to penetrate. The subdued and apprehensive question is inevitable.

"Is everything all right?"

We both know everything is not all right. Things have not been all right for a long time. A brutal crime was committed. The loved ones of the murder victim died a thousand deaths trying to absorb that horror that hit them from out of the blue. Their son, their daughter, their mother, their father or their wife had been wrenched away in a brutal murder. A suspect was arrested and convicted. The man sits on death row. He also has loved ones. They also are in horror. They have been dreading my call for a decade or longer.

It takes five calls to inform all of this man's immediate family. My response to their questions feels like a script. It is the best I can do.

"The governor has signed a death warrant. Your son . . . your brother . . . your father . . . is scheduled to be killed two weeks before Christmas."

Even as they break down into sobs, I know that the echoes of their anguish will linger with me for a long time, like the smoke after a bonfire, subtle yet pervasive whispers of wrenching agony.

The man to be executed is from a large and devout family. His mother, nearly eighty years old but still a dynamo of energy and faith, has raised all her children by hard work. Most of them have attended college. This son has severe mental illness related to an industrial accident. In her younger days, she never dreamed she would receive a call like this one from me. The family pulls together quickly and makes arrangements to come to Florida to say good-bye to their loved one two weeks before Christmas.

This man is lucky. Some men have no one to come to their last days before execution. His family will be here. They will spend as much time with him as the State will allow. That means three hours per day for his last ten days of life. The day of execution, they must leave the prison at eleven A.M. I will be with him from one until five P.M. That is when the technicians start the preparations to kill him at six o'clock. He has asked me to be there for his execution. I will witness my first lethal injection. His family and friends are not allowed to be at the prison for his execution.

I cannot be in two places at once. So I meet with the FSP administration.

"Who will care for the family during the execution?"

"Sorry, Brother Dale, but that is not our job. We must ensure that they are off the property by eleven. That's it. The rest is not up to us."

My wife, Susan, steps forward and makes it her job to take care of this family. While I am at the execution, she will be with them at our church. She joins me to meet them at the church the day after they arrive in town. After about twenty minutes of introductions and small talk, Pastor Jose joins us. These are strong people. They are determined to see this through with eyes of faith. We all pray together.

Over the next several days, many details demand attention. Legal paper work for handling the remains and shipment for burial back home. Financial responsibility for various charges. Fortunately, there are others, like attorney Susan Cary, who assist with the legal needs of inmates nearing end of life. My call is to be present. I am present with the family in the mornings as they meet with him through a glass window speaking by a telephone. I am present for each of them as they take their turn to step away from the glass to the end of the hall and double over in pain and tears. I am present with him in the afternoons as he tries to pull the fabric of his life together and stay strong for them just as they are staying strong for him.

Finally it is the day. The fragments have been drawn together into a final walk up the front steps of the massive edifice called Florida State Prison. The State allows them a one-hour contact visit. They are allowed to touch each other. The elderly mother turns to the lieutenant on the death squad and asks, "May we form a prayer circle?"

He nods.

The family forms a circle with me and the condemned man included. Arm in arm, we pray the Lord's Prayer. After the amen each of the family members says good-bye. The last to let go is his mother. She kisses his forehead, and he is gone, escorted by the death squad to the first phase of preparation.

The family and I exit quietly together into the cavernous corridor of FSP. The family turns to me with another request. Is it possible that before leaving we could form a circle and pray again? I turn to the control officers who have heard the question. They are resolute but visibly touched.

"Yes."

The family forms a prayer circle again. We pray again for their loved one and for the healing of all those affected by the crimes, especially the families of the crime victims. Then the mother prays for the members of the death squad who will kill her son at six o'clock. One of the supervising officers looks quickly toward the ceiling, blinking back a tear. Who could not be moved by such faith?

After the noon-hour visit by Pastor Jose to administer the last rites, I am summoned from the prison chapel to the downstairs of Q Wing, the death house. Within a short period of time, a burly sergeant who is known at FSP to be an honest and straight-up guy, comes walking into the deathwatch area where I am sitting on a molded plastic chair between the gale force blow of a window air-conditioner and the bars of the condemned man's cell.

"Man, they are popsicling you all, aren't they?"

"Well, nobody knows who has the authority to turn it down." The death house station officer sounds a little defensive. We all know that his job is really to answer the phone, not climate control. "You know how that goes."

"No problem." The sergeant places both hands over his protruding belly. "I've got all the insulation I need. And I'll only be a moment."

"What's up, sergeant?" The condemned man smiles warmly at this officer who has always treated him with respect and dignity.

"I just wanted to say something." His jowls reveal a quiver as his hands move quickly to wipe both eyes. He steps right up to the bars and takes both hands of the man inside in his own. "I never knew you on the street. I don't know what you were like out there. But I've been knowing you since you came here almost twenty years ago."

The man in the cell bows his head to hide his eyes. I quickly hand him a tissue.

"And in all those times I been knowing you, I know that the man I've known inside these walls is more of a Christian than I am."

There is not a sound on the floor except the relentless blowing of the window unit. Even the peeling white brick walls seem to have faded out of sight.

"I wanted you to know that I refused to work second shift today because I don't want to be here when it happens." His eyes and the lift in his voice cue us that more is coming. "I know that you will get in heaven long before me, and I just hope that God will be merciful on me and allow me to see you there someday."

The two men, one in uniform brown and the other in condemned man white, one outside and one inside, one knowing the exact time when he will die and one having no certainty of the hour or the day, clasp hands and eyes firmly for the briefest moment. Then the sergeant wraps it. "Good-bye, good man."

The rest of my four hours at cell front blur into that instant when I am sitting in the witness room in the spiritual advisor seat, and the curtain opens. I am barely aware of the press and the ten State witnesses seated to my right and rear. I am sitting front row left. He is stretched out on the gurney less than three feet away. His feet are to the right. His arms and legs are strapped down. All he can move is his head. When he looks toward the window, I am staring right into his eyes.

On behalf of his family, I sign the words, "I love you."

He smiles, winks in acknowledgment and speaks his last words on earth.

"I ask that the good Lord forgive me my sins. I would like to apologize to the families of my victims."

Then, before thanking his family and friends who have shown him love and support, he pauses and looks at those who are there to carry out the execution, saying: "I ask the Lord to forgive them for they know not what they do."

In thirteen minutes he is dead. Killed right before our eyes.

Next thing I know, I am exiting a van, listening to official witnesses chat and laugh casually about Christmas party schedules. Twenty minutes and fifteen miles later, I am walking into the candlelit church where his mother and family have been kneeling in prayer with my wife for two hours. Only a tear in the fabric of time and space can describe the chasm.

First to them and then by phone to family not present, I hear my own voice: "It's finished. Your father . . . your son . . . your brother . . . is dead."

His family joins us at our home for a shared meal. By the time we see them off, we are truly saying good-bye to a piece of our own heart. Their life journey and ours have crossed in a way that has welded us together with a shared faith at the seams of shared experience.

Finally, I am sitting alone in my living room with the lit Christmas tree. It is about three A.M. on December 8, almost six hours since everyone left. Four hours ago my wife and children went to sleep. In the solitude of my living room, the blinking Christmas tree lights pulse with a solitary question: *What have we done?*

O—O—O

Even though I have agreed with the Department of Corrections not to practice law, my Florida law license remains active. That requires me to obtain continuing legal education credits (called CLEs) at the rate of ten hours per year. Since returning from Rome, I have been picking up CLEs based on convenience of scheduling and location, usually in a barely refurbished Howard Johnson's or in a dilapidated restaurant meeting room with inoperable folding chairs, tables with marred finishes and no fresh coffee. In 2001 I decide to get some CLEs in the area of death penalty law.

The first thing that catches my attention is that this death penalty CLE seminar, sponsored by the State, is scheduled at Lake Buena Vista near Disney World. That is different. When I arrive at the seminar room, I know this is big bucks and big business. At least 130 people are seated at three dozen rows of linen cloth–sheathed tables. To the rear of the room, stacks of high-tech equipment are clicking and chirping in preparation for teleconferencing. Front row center, alternating images of distant participants fade in and out on eight-foot jumbotrons that tower over each side of the podium. At the head table a Florida Supreme Court justice and a Florida State senator are scribbling notes for their introductory remarks. Peppered throughout the satellite-connected rooms around the state are familiar faces of prominent jurists, elected officials and attorneys. The emcee mounts the stage.

"This is the largest intrastate teleconference ever done in Florida. In addition to Orlando, we are teleconferencing with nine other locations, totaling hundreds of additional participants."

With a few quickly penciled sums, I rough cut the total dollar amount in State salaries that will be consumed today in an eight-hour conference attended by hundreds of Florida's best and brightest legal talents. This is the yearly gathering of one of Florida's most pervasive but invisible unofficial associations, the death penalty industry. For eight hours, all this talent, time, resources and potential will be squarely focused on the legal minutia of sentencing hearings in the miniscule percentage of criminal cases where the death penalty is constitutionally allowed. I am amazed.

As this monstrously expensive teleconference winds on, I cannot help but wonder if the public has any idea of the truth. By midafternoon, Seminole Circuit Court Judge O. H. Eaton Jr., Florida's resident judicial death penalty expert, relates that Florida jurors almost always believe that execution is cheaper than life imprisonment without possibility of parole. Laughter peals through the crowd present and over the teleconference screens. Everybody attending this conference knows that the truth is just the opposite: Execution can be two to three times more expensive than life imprisonment without possibility of parole at even the highest levels of security.

I look around to see if anybody besides me is not laughing. There are just a few who look very concerned.

o—o—o

In December of 2003, just before Christmas, Governor Bush signs a death warrant for the African American man mentioned at the beginning of this book. The condemned man is a Baptist Christian and asks for me as his spiritual advisor.

The execution takes place in February of 2004. Once seated in the witness room, I am right next to a murder victim family member, a niece of the victim, a young woman who appears to be in her thirties. After a horrendous wait for U.S. Supreme Court justices to vote on a stay, which is turned down by one vote, the curtain opens and the procedure begins. As soon as they pronounce the condemned man dead and close the curtain, this young woman erupts out of her seat.

"Is that it? Is that all there is?"

Both her fists are in the air. I am wondering whether we will need to restrain her to keep her from breaking the glass window. The young woman collects herself and walks out to the waiting witness van, shaking her head.

Bud Welch, whose daughter was killed in the bombing of the Murrah Federal Building in Oklahoma City, has told me of the long line of family members of the bombing victims who have come to him over the years since Timothy McVeigh's execution. They supported it and attended it because they believed what they were told, that seeing the death penalty carried out would bring healing. Now, after watching McVeigh die, they have had no healing, no closure. There is just another killing to contend with.

About 72 hours after the execution of that man and that moment of sad reality for the murder victim's niece, I arrive at a shack by the tracks in Deep South central Georgia. The executed man's lawyer is carrying the box with his cremains, which we must present to his newly widowed wife. This poor woman is literally dirt-poor. By now I have learned where to stand in these situations. After she welcomes us into her very small living room, I step to the other side of the coffee table, next to her, so I can catch her when she collapses.

The lawyer opens the cardboard box revealing the ashes inside.

The widow collapses into my arms, sobbing. Finally, when she regains the composure to speak through her tears, she says, "Other than my mother, he was the only person in my life that treated me well. Why did they have to kill him? Why couldn't they just let him live in prison for the rest of his life?"

○─○─○

My weekly rounds at FSP and UCI continue. The summers inside the cells and corridors on Florida's death row are as hot as I imagine hell would be, but with higher humidity. Outside temperatures have been hitting a hundred or higher, with humidity in the very high nineties.

My rounds reveal a constant procession of faces, men my age and even my dad's age, suffering in concrete and steel boxes with no air-conditioning, shade or air movement, in the middle of a former cow pasture in rural north Florida. They soak their sheets in the water of their toilet and then wrap themselves in them while they lie on the floor, hoping that some evaporation will occur, reducing their core body temperature. Some have passed out and split their head open against the metal sink in the cell.

The overriding issue is always the same: "What is our standard of care for men we are holding in cages until we kill them?" No one seems equipped to deal with this question. Nor are we equipped to deal with the problem of innocent people on death row. I experienced innocence in prison with Pops back at ACI in the early 1990s. But he was not facing the death penalty. Now at FSP and UCI, my rounds have acquainted me with others who are very likely to be innocent.

One such fellow always looks forward to seeing me on rounds. He is bright, articulate and persistently cheerful, even downright encouraging. As I approach his cell, there is the telltale pounding of his sneakers against the cement floor.

"How ya doing?" I call out over the din of his daily multi-mile workout.

"Still here," he banters back, wiping the sweat from hours of power walking in his six-by-ten-foot cage. "But it's good to see you. How's your family?"

This man has been on Florida's death row for over thirty years and has had more than one death warrant signed. From behind those beige bars he has watched scores of inmates, guards and politicians come and go. But one thing has never changed: his insistence that he is innocent, that he was a victim of the crime.

He worked in his long-standing family store and led an uneventful life until he spoke up for a friend who was falsely accused of a crime. Six months later his store suffered a brutal attack that killed his wife and in-laws. He was left for dead. Hours later, while this self-employed proprietor was in emergency surgery to save his life, someone turned the murder weapon in to the police and claimed the businessman had done the killing.

This Florida death penalty case is rife with fabricated evidence, inconsistent testimony and egregious State misconduct. The trial judge ordered Valium for the juror who was holding out against a guilty verdict. She took the drugs and changed her vote. A tape recording was discovered in possession of the State long after the trial. It recorded the State investigator offering eyewitnesses from Minnesota a free trip back to Florida if they changed their statements to support the State's case. They did not, and the jury never heard their testimony.

At first hearing of his innocence, I was incredulous. With all the media reports of endless death row appeals, I was sure that no one who was really innocent could be on death row. Now, after researching the facts, I am ashamed at what I and most lawyers, let alone laymen, do not know about how the death penalty really works in Florida and in America.

The legal principle this man is up against is called *procedural bar*, a common law doctrine that says no new evidence can be looked at by a court after a certain period of time has passed. Soon after the trial and penalty phase of a case are concluded, review by the courts becomes severely limited. Mostly the courts only determine whether proper procedures were followed. Consequently, even astounding evidence of innocence can be nearly impossible to review judicially, shortly after the original trial is concluded.

In death cases in Texas, the bar is eighteen months. In Florida it is 24 months, except for DNA evidence, which can be reviewed for up to 48 months after the original death sentence. The only exception is if one proves that the trial attorney was incompetent for not finding the evidence of innocence before the bar kicked in. If enough time has passed, evidence of innocence in a death penalty case is irrelevant. The courts are barred by procedural time limits from even hearing the new evidence.

Men and women with late-discovered evidence of innocence languish in prison or face execution, even when others have confessed to committing the crime. That is exactly what happened in the Herrera case in Texas. The courts allowed a man to be executed after another man had confessed to the murder. The dissenting opinion in the U.S. Supreme Court decision on Herrera said, "The execution of a man who can show he is innocent comes perilously close to simple murder."

The goal of procedural bar is admirable in principle, when only money is involved. But when procedural bar is applied in the criminal justice process, the result can be disastrous, as it is for this man on Florida's death row.

During our cell front visits I take his hands in mine, offering a prayer in Jesus Christ's name. His eyes are gentle. His words are deliberate, fervent. He prays for our families, for men on the row who are sick or away at court, for the staff and administration and for God's hand to move and the truth to be revealed. I find myself wondering how any human being could spend so long under such conditions in total innocence without being consumed by rancor. But there is not a trace.

The more I learn, the more I find myself deeply shaken by the reality of his predicament. He must sense it. After one of our prayers, he continues to clutch my hand. "I am innocent," he says, smiling gently. "Don't worry, I'm in God's hands."

Another former businessman on death row has a case that so astounds me I attend his Florida Supreme Court hearing. He has been on death row since 1986 and claims he was framed. In the oral arguments before the Florida Supreme Court, I am stunned when the prosecution actually admits that the State knew that an assistant State attorney went to the man's jail cell and solicited a $50,000 bribe for the judge. The State also admits that, during the trial, the judge in the case was removed from the bench in handcuffs, charged with taking bribes in other cases.

He is not granted a new trial. Instead, he is sent back to Miami for a resentencing hearing. Five death row corrections officers take annual leave and drive to Miami at their own expense to testify on this man's behalf. The twelve jurors are not allowed to hear about the State attorney's bribe attempt or about the corrupt judge. They are not allowed to hear about any of the corruption or irregularities behind his conviction. No witness is allowed to even suggest in front of the jury that this man never received a fair trial.

I am relieved when the jury returns with a life sentence. He is moved to south Florida and the Department of Corrections central office in Tallahassee provides me with a procedure number that allows me to continue to serve as his spiritual advisor by telephone so long as he is not assigned to a prison where Susan and I are volunteers. We begin accepting his weekly calls to our home.

o-o-o

Even with such experiences, it is not possible to be prepared to witness the execution of a man I believe is innocent. That is exactly what happens just before Christmas in 2005. The man's death warrant is signed, and he asks for me to be his spiritual advisor. He claims innocence and alleges that the State's star witness is in fact the one who committed the murder. His request for clemency to life in prison deserves serious consideration. He is a decorated Vietnam veteran who returned with PTSD and Agent Orange sickness. He was a single parent raising his children by working as a carpenter and, since coming to death row, has continued to be the parental figure in his daughters' lives through mail and visits. Moreover, his death sentence was handed down by a jury vote of just seven to five. One vote different and he would have been given a life sentence.

His three daughters beg Governor Bush to grant clemency, to commute his death sentence to life imprisonment because the evidence of his innocence has never been seen by a judge or a jury. But in practice there is no clemency in Florida in death penalty cases. The governor's lawyer simply asserts that the courts have properly applied procedural bar.

His appeals lawyers have collected boxes of sworn affidavits to the effect that his assertion is true and beg the Florida Supreme Court to order an evidentiary hearing that will allow the judge to hear from the witnesses under oath and under cross-examination. That will allow a determination of whether in fact he is innocent and was framed by the State's star witness.

The Florida Supreme Court refuses to consider the mess and hides behind the doctrine of procedural bar. It is too late to hear evidence of innocence. The only dissenter is Justice Harry Lee Anstead. His reasons, taken from the Court's slip opinion, are worth considering:

There can hardly be a more serious claim relating to a defendant's guilt or innocence than a claim that someone else has confessed to the crime for which the defendant was convicted and sentenced to death. With the possible exception of DNA evidence, the confession of another person raises the most compelling and fundamental doubt about a prior determination of guilt. Here, we have not only a claim that someone else has confessed, but we have sworn testimony attesting to its validity.

That sworn testimony will never be heard. It is procedurally barred. The sworn evidence of his innocence will sit in a box in the basement of a Panhandle courthouse while this man is being killed by the State. His execution is set for October of 2006.

My wife and I are seriously concerned about the well-being of the condemned man's three daughters, who range in age from twenty-two to thirty. Susan obtains permission to be present at the final family visit the morning of the execution. Susan and I arrive together at FSP at about seven o'clock. The noncontact visits, with a glass partition, last for two hours and are grueling. Then it gets worse. The contact visits require going through another security gate and then through two solid steel doors into an area down and across the hall. The one-hour contact visit is broken up into four fifteen-minute segments: first the brothers together, then the youngest daughter, then each of the other two daughters.

Each contact visit with a daughter ends with her holding on to her father for dear life and sobbing uncontrollably. One after another, I have to peel each daughter off her father, take her by both arms and lead her out of the room and into the hall. When the second steel security door closes from behind, each of them freeze in uncontrollable grief, doubling over, sobbing and crying, "Daddy, I love you. Why are they going to kill my daddy?"

Then I must almost carry her through the hall security gate and back to the gathering area. Susan takes her station with her, and I take the next one in. The daughters each crumple in a heap around the table by Susan, crying, "Why do they have to kill him? Why can't they just let him live in prison?"

After the good-byes, Susan and I gather them all together and escort them out of the prison to the parking lot, where we pray with them for a last time.

Then Susan prays with me before I return inside to the death house to take up my station with the condemned man at his cell, a dozen feet from the execution room, for the last five hours of his life.

At about five-thirty I go to the main lobby of the administration building of FSP. The announcement is made for the witnesses to load into the death vans. We ride around the back of FSP to the special entrance to the death house witness room. I take my spiritual advisor seat and wait for the curtain to open.

When the curtain opens, he is lying on the gurney in front of the window. I try to make eye contact with him, but the glare of the lights on the glass are interfering with his vision.

"Where is Brother Dale?" he calls out from the gurney.

I raise my hand hoping he will be able to see it despite the glare.

"I love you, man." He speaks clearly but softly, nodding directly at me.

All the witnesses hear him through the overhead mike. There is an immediate shift in the emotional feel of the entire room. In a split second those words have changed him from an object of scorn to a human being with connectedness to others. The effect is palpable.

Driving home from the execution, it occurs to me that watching an innocent man be killed may be all that is necessary to justify nightmares. At the moment it is beyond my imagination that things are already in motion to engulf me in a deeper level of horror in just a few weeks.

17

"What Has Been Done in Secret Will Be Revealed in the Light"

MARK 4:22

IN MARCH OF 2006 Susan and I submit separate letters to the Florida Parole Commission, requesting consideration for Kenny's parole request. We join with Rev. Ken Cooper and express our support for Kenny's participation in Rev. Cooper's faith-based reentry program for inmates who have been confined for long periods of time. A critical part of this step will be Kenny's participation in the prerelease program at Everglades Correctional Institution, known as Everglades, at the far southern end of Florida, south of Miami and just off Krome Avenue. Round trip for visits will be about 860 miles. If Kenny is allowed to enroll in that unique program, the sheer distance will require that we curtail our monthly visits to quarterly visits and make up the contact through increased telephone calls and correspondence.

We both appear before the Florida Parole Commission in

Tallahassee to present our commitment to Kenny in person. The Commission is supportive but wants to move slowly, with an intermediate step. Kenny is moved from Holmes to a pre-prerelease program at Sumter Correctional Institution, just off Interstate 75 between Ocala and Tampa. Our monthly family visits continue at Kenny's new prison in Central Florida.

○─●─○

By the week of Thanksgiving, 2006, Susan and I have been through three executions in nine weeks. It is a gubernatorial election year in Florida. There are usually at least three executions in the fall leading up to a November gubernatorial election day, so the heavy load is not a surprise. We assume that the gurney in Starke is done for the year.

Then, just two days before Thanksgiving, Angel Diaz is pulled into the death house. His family is notified the day before Thanksgiving, and they are driving up from Miami overnight in multiple vehicles for an all-day deathwatch visit with him. They will meet Susan and me at FSP at five o'clock on Thanksgiving Day.

On Thanksgiving Day, Chris and Addie are troupers. After we all have our fill of the first Thanksgiving meal, they jump in and help with reload. At quarter to five Susan and I are standing at the steps of FSP inside the gates, waiting for this new family. They are warm and gentle people. It seems that we and they are the only ones out driving that evening. The multiple vans follow us easily on the deserted county roads to our home in town. Soon they are gathered around our table, great-aunt, brother, sister, nieces and nephews, cousins and grandchildren playing on the floor while the adults talk and eat. This is a middle-class family just like us. They never dreamed they would be at FSP on Thanksgiving for deathwatch visits. The execution date is set for December 13.

On the morning of the execution, I meet the family at FSP about ninety minutes before the noncontact visits. It is an unusually cold day for north Florida, even in December. The noncontact visits and contact visits are by the book. The family leaves on time.

Pastor Jose arrives for last rites at noon. When he returns to the chapel, I make the trek downstairs on Q Wing to take my station at Angel Diaz's death cell. At about four-thirty we close in prayer, and I head to the administration building to join the official witnesses. Soon, the witnesses are all seated in front of the curtain. At six o'clock the curtain opens.

Angel Diaz gives his last words in Spanish. "The State of Florida is killing an innocent person. The State of Florida is committing a crime because I am innocent. The death penalty is a form of vengeance but also a cowardly act by humans. I am sorry for what is happening to me and my family who have been put through this."

The warden reads the death warrant and orders the procedure to start. Within minutes I know that something is horribly wrong.

By the time it is over and I exit the death van, bedlam is overtaking the crowds outside. Word of the botched execution and its duration has already leaked. There is nothing I can add to this crisis. While I am leaning against my car in the FSP parking lot to assess whether my stomach will stay in place for the drive home, Diaz's lawyer approaches me.

"Will you be willing to testify to what you just watched?"

"Only under subpoena and under oath," I respond robotically with the formula that I have memorized for just such an occasion.

"You'll be hearing from me."

It takes almost twelve miles driving north on State Road 121 to get into cell phone range. As soon as the bars pop up on my phone screen, I press the speed-dial button for Susan.

"Susan . . ."

"Dale, is this you?" she asks falteringly.

"Yes, why?"

"Honey, I had no idea it was you. You don't sound at all like you. What happened?"

"Susan, I just watched a man be tortured to death."

By the next morning, the entire death penalty industry in Florida is in an uproar. Some Florida politicians who have virtually no basis for reelection except their fealty to executions go on record that the only witnesses who will think Diaz suffered are those who oppose the death penalty. Meanwhile, the Florida Supreme Court grants an eight A.M. motion for independent medical personnel to be present at the autopsy and to forestall any attempt at cremation of the body before the investigation is completed.

The medical reports are not pretty. Although the State originally claimed that the execution just took longer because Diaz's liver was damaged from bad life choices, the autopsy reveals that his liver is fine. It is his arms that are horribly burned, with a twelve-by-five-inch chemical burn on his right arm and an eleven-by-seven-inch chemical burn on his left arm. The autopsy shows that the lethal injection catheters pierced the front and back walls of his veins, pumping the chemicals into underlying soft tissues.

My nightmares start very soon after the botched execution. At first I refuse to own them.

"Susan, it's not like with Pastor Joe, where he watched a man burn to death in the electric chair."

"Really? Then tell me, Dale, what's the difference between watching a man burn to death from the outside in with electricity and watching a man burn to death from the inside out with chemicals?"

I know she is right. There is almost no difference. My nightmares are mine, and I had better deal with them.

But not everyone in Florida's death penalty industry is ready to accept the reality of what had been done to Angel Diaz. There is no point in guessing at the motives of those whose livelihood and political survival depend upon keeping the death house in Starke in business. We must look at what they do.

Governor Bush has only a few days left in office. He really does not have a dog in this fight. He issues Executive Order 06-260 to create a Commission on Administration of Lethal Injection to review the method in which the lethal injection protocols are administered by the Department of Corrections and "to ensure the method is consistent with the Eighth Amendment of the United States Constitution and its prohibition against cruel and unusual punishment."

My instincts warn me that all those gray- and blue-suited State lawyers and politicians who were in those rooms around Florida for the Lake Buena Vista Death Penalty Conference may not be interested in finding out whether Angel Diaz suffered. The State's entire invisible death penalty industry could be on the line. The press reporters who were in the witness room are prohibited from testifying by journalistic ethics. The lawyer for Diaz who was in the witness room will be discounted as being biased. Everybody else present inside the execution room and in the witness room depends on the State for their livelihood. I am the only truly independent witness. This could get really bad.

I retain Robert Link as my personal lawyer to represent me in this mess. His main job is to be my human shield against the mortar rounds that will soon be headed in my direction. The immediate critical factor is whether testimony before the Commission will be under subpoena and under oath. Without those two elements, any State employee or religious volunteer could be suspended or terminated if the department does not like their testimony. The State's argument would be that such a witness was not under legal obligation to testify and therefore volunteered to go against the department's interests. For an employee it would be the end of their jobs. For me, it would be the end of my ministry service.

If all those who testify are subpoenaed and placed under oath, their testimony is protected by law, and there cannot be any repercussions against them for telling the truth. This religious volunteer will only testify under subpoena and under oath. Period. But even that is not a guaranteed safe haven. In such a highly charged us-versus-them public and political arena, even the refusal to testify could have drastic repercussions. The State's perception could be that if you are not with us, then you are against us, and you must be dealt with.

The call from the Commission comes. It is referred to my lawyer. He gives them my conditions: under subpoena and under oath. I am not surprised to learn that Florida's Commission on Administration of Lethal Injection refuses to subpoena anyone and refuses to put anyone under oath. That means any employee or volunteer who gives testimony that the State does not like will do so at his or her own peril. My lawyer mentions to me that the Commission is very unhappy about my refusal to testify without a subpoena.

On Thursday, March 1, 2007, the Commission delivers its report to newly elected Governor Charlie Crist. The report sanctifies and protects Florida's death penalty and, presumably, the livelihoods of all the high-priced lawyers and politicians who owe their living to the State's invisible death penalty industry. Just four days later, on Monday, March 5, 2007, the control room at the access gate to UCI holds me outside while they wait for the chaplain to come down.

The man who comes is an assistant chaplain. His face is grim. He reaches through the bars of the gate and hands me an envelope containing the official document that permanently expels me and my wife from ever entering a Florida Department of Corrections prison for the rest of our lives. The grounds it claims for our expulsion are my spiritual advisor phone calls with the former death row inmate serving life in south Florida and the calls, letters and visits we have made as a Christian mentoring family with Kenny.

"Chaplain, the phone calls were approved, and the Christian mentoring relationship was suggested and approved by the department. This is nuts."

"Brother Dale, I cannot do anything about it. You do what you can. I'll pray. God bless you, man."

My lawyer is not surprised and reminds me how upset the Commission was at my refusal to testify without a subpoena and not under oath. We reflect on the fact that this expulsion has been issued by UCI and not from FSP, where the botched execution took place. It turns out that I have not been expelled by FSP at all. This could just be chance, but we must assume that such an arrangement has been thought out and strategized.

If we are able to overturn the expulsion, FSP could claim the botched execution had nothing to do with the expulsion in the first place. If we exhaust our appeals and do not get the UCI expulsion overturned, Susan and I will be banned from all the State prisons in Florida, including FSP. Someone could have planned this out very carefully. Regardless, it will take one heck of a fight to get this overturned.

When Susan arrives home from work, I show her the letter and bring her up to date. Her response is pitch-perfect. "We need to pray. We need to pray a lot and to pray real hard."

As we fall on our knees together in the living room, she reminds me of the old Christian maxim, "God will not take you where His power cannot keep you."

"Lord, turn on the juice," I pray out loud. "We need a flood of Your power, Lord. Please, God, don't hold anything back."

I prepare the written appeals and supporting documentation within just a few days. Everything is sent by Federal Express to Tallahassee. This battle will be both legal and political. The legal part requires showing that the allegations are trumped up and do not hold any water. Fortunately, I have the original papers for our family approval as visitors to Kenny. They show our very clear and unambiguous disclosure of our status as religious volunteers at FSP and UCI. They are stamped "approved" by the Department of Corrections in Tallahassee. Also, we have all the copies of paper work and procedures that went into my research before accepting the change in status from spiritual advisors to Christian mentoring family. All that is only legal.

The real battle is political. This is about the job security of all those people in expensive suits on the State side who were attending the Lake Buena Vista Death Penalty Conference. This is about the punishment they must mete out to anyone who does not salute the Florida death penalty. The official representatives of our church are fully engaged in my behalf. By the end of April, a friend of a friend leaks the information that every phone call I have ever had with Kenny has been recorded and preserved. Now those tapes have been transcribed and teams of State lawyers are combing through every word, looking for a basis to sustain our expulsion.

I am truly impressed at this level of desperation to keep the Florida death penalty. It is common knowledge that Florida would save well over $50 million a year by reverting to life in prison without possibility of parole as the maximum punishment. It is generally believed that most of those savings would come from money paid to lawyers, especially on the State side. The State lawyers in expensive suits who are combing through years of transcripts of my prayers over the phone with Kenny must be some of the ones who would lose their jobs if Florida loses the death penalty. Susan and I thought we were already praying hard. We start praying even harder.

◯–◯–◯

A lawsuit is filed by Angel Diaz's lawyers to end the use of lethal injection in Florida. I am subpoenaed and will be put under oath. The hearing will be in Ocala in front of a circuit judge. In Florida circuit judges are the ones who hand down death sentences. On May

18, 2007, my attorney and I drive together to the Marion County Courthouse in Ocala. It is a modernized southern courthouse with glass skin and a rounded central façade, dominated by a shiny steel exoskeleton.

The elevator dumps us into an upper-floor lobby, where we are expected. The bailiffs usher us into the courtroom and seal the doors. I will be the first witness to testify. The judge orders me to be put under oath. The following excerpts are from the official transcript of the case, except that procedural arguments are omitted and names of prison staff have been replaced by their titles.

> Witness, Dale Recinella, having been produced and first duly sworn as a witness, testified as follows (under direct examination by Diaz's Attorney):

Judge: You may proceed.

. . .

Q: Do you recall what time the curtains opened during the execution procedures of Mr. Diaz?

A: As I recall, this one started right on time at 6:00 P.M.

Q: And once the curtains open can you describe what your view of Mr. Diaz was?

A: Because of where I'm sitting, his entire body is in my vision, so I can see his head and his torso and then his legs to the end of the gurney and that's my primary scope of vision. So he's right in front of me, probably six or seven feet from the window.

Q: Are you able to see both of his arms?

A: No. I can only see his right arm, which is on my side. He's lying flat and so I would not be able to see his left arm; his right arm is on my side. His left arm would be on the other side of his body and I would not be able to see that clearly.

Q: Were you able to see if Mr. Diaz was restrained in any way?

A: Yes. He was restrained exactly the way the men always are at the time the curtain opens. His hands are tethered to the gurney and his feet are strapped down and there is a strap over his head, over his forehead. . . .

Q: Were you able to observe the IV site in the right arm?

A: I could—I saw the IV tube going up this arm but I don't recall actually seeing the site where the injection was.

Q: But you could see the tubing?

A: I could see the tube on the side of him that was facing me.

Q: And can you describe where that tubing was?

A: It came down and then up to his arm, the tubing did.

Q: Do you know where the tubing came from?

A: I don't recall. I don't recall if it went around the head or went underneath. I don't recall.

Q: Can you also describe what you saw in terms of other persons in the chamber?

A: There was an officer at the head of the gurney and then an officer on the opposite side.

Q: Would that be where Mr. Diaz's head was?

A: Yes, and then there was an officer right about midway.

Q: Is that on Mr. Diaz's left side?

A: Mr. Diaz's left side. And then there were administration officials at the foot. There was a third officer, a female officer, and I don't remember exactly where she was standing.

. . .

Q: If you can describe what you witnessed when the curtain opened?

A: When the curtain opened Mr. Diaz was asked if he had any last words and he did speak words in Spanish, which I do not understand. When he finished his last words the procedure started.

Q: Was there any signal to you that the procedure had started?

A: No. It was clear though that the microphone had been turned off and that was how I knew the procedure was starting.

Q: Had you witnessed executions prior to Mr. Diaz's?

A: Yes, this was my fifth time witnessing an execution all the way through.

Q: And so once the microphone is turned off and the procedure had started, can you explain to the Court what you saw?

A: Several minutes into the procedure I knew something was wrong.

Q: How did you know something was wrong?

A: Because in the other executions that I had witnessed, usually within two, three minutes any movement of the person on the gurney stops. In this case it was already several minutes into the procedure and Mr. Diaz was still blinking. He was still showing much movement in his throat and I do remember that it just came out of me spontaneously in a whisper to myself, something's wrong.

Q: You stated that there was still movement several minutes. Can you—do you have any specific recollection as to how many minutes it was into the procedure?

A: The movement continued all the way through until close to the end, so I noticed it probably about three minutes into the procedure but he continued to move. He at some point looked to me, looking through the glass but without being able to hear, as though he was trying to speak in a very forceful way. I mean, the lines of stress in his cheeks and in his throat at the speaking, it was not just normal speaking, to the staff and then he began to show signs of his body arching. So if you have someone who's lying flat on a table and their arms cannot move, but yet his body, his torso was arching.

Q: You're saying that he began to arch his back. Was his body moving in any other way at that time?

A: Well, his head was also going back. And in fact, at one point the strap fell toward the top of his head and the officer that was at the head of the gurney very gently put it back up on his forehead.

Q: At the point that you said to yourself something's wrong, do you know what time it was at that point?

A: I believe that would have been about three minutes into the procedure.

Q: And you said that it looked like he was trying to speak; is that correct?

A: Yes.

Q: And you believed that or you saw that it looked like he was trying to speak why?

A: Well, you could see his mouth moving. And there was, it was moving with force, the kind of force that makes stress in your cheeks and in your throat.

Q: And you indicated that there was a lot of movement in his neck. Can you describe that movement?

A: Yes. Well, it was really of two kinds. There was the movement of the tension again and again and again, but there also was the Adam's apple continually going up and down. That continued as long as he kept breathing in a less pronounced way, but it continued throughout.

Q: And how long did he continue to breathe?

A: It seemed to me that total cessation of the movement in his neck didn't occur until a couple of minutes before they pronounced him dead; perhaps two to three minutes before they pronounced him dead.

Q: Were you able to see the IV tubing during this process?

A: The IV tube was there but the only time I noticed it distinctly was at some point in the process it was clear that fluid was moving through it again.

Q: Do you know at what point that was?

A: I would have to say . . . it must have been about fifteen to eighteen minutes into the procedure.

Q: Did you make any observations when you saw the IV fluid begin to flow through the tube?

A: Well, at this point I knew that whatever was taking place was quite different from all the other executions I had witnessed, that something new was being done. I didn't know what.

Q: Now, you indicated that the fluid rushed sometime between 6:13 and 6:20 P.M. Can you describe what you were seeing still at 6:20 P.M.?

A: His breathing was still extremely labored. The breaths were with great signs of tension in the neck and under the chin. I believe at that point his head was no longer moving, his body was no longer arching. But there was still the movement of breathing, labored, labored breathing like someone's trying to get air.

. . .

Q: And when did that finally cease?

A: I believe that continued, already less and less and less, until about two or three minutes before he was pronounced dead.

. . .

Q: How long in all did this procedure take?

A: I believe it was concluded at about 6:34 P.M. So it was thirty-four minutes.

Q: Did Mr. Diaz give a rather lengthy last statement or would you determine it as brief?

A: It was not lengthy, it was pretty typical. Certainly a minute or less.

Q: And you've stated that you've seen other executions. Have the other executions taken as long?

A: The other four executions I have witnessed the person was pronounced dead usually by around 6:11 or 6:13 P.M.

Q: And you indicated that at some point death was pronounced? Can you describe how you know that?

A: Yes. The, I assume they're doctors, the men in the hazmat suits came out one at a time and looked into his eyes and it appeared they were checking his heartbeat and then the curtain closed.

Q: What do you mean the hazmat suits?

A: It's a suit like you would see people wearing in a hazmat cleanup. It's from head to toe in bright color with a hood and a plastic over the face so that the person inside is completely unrecognizable.

Q: Once the curtain to the window is closed, what happens next?

A: The officer asks the official witnesses to please file out into the vans. And we get back into the vans and we are taken back to the administration building to leave.

Q: Was there any conversation in that ride in the van?

A: There was not and that is unusual.

Q: Why do you say that is unusual?

A: My experience is that there's usually the kind of chitchat that you would expect from people who have just watched somebody be killed. Another December execution I witnessed people were talking about Christmas party schedules, but on this one it was absolutely dead silent; no one said a word.

Q: Once the van brings you back, to the administration building, what did you do at that point?

A: At that point Mr. Diaz's attorney asked me if I would be willing to testify to what I had seen, and I told him I will not testify without a subpoena.

Q: Let me ask you why you wouldn't testify without a subpoena?

A: It's not part of my work for the Church to be a witness in court, and I work very hard to preserve my ability to minister, not just to the inmates, but also to the staff. And so, I would never testify and have refused to do so in other circumstances without being under oath and the compulsion of the subpoena, because both are important for me to protect my ability to minister to the people inside those buildings. . . .

Q: At what point did you leave the prison that evening?

A: I would have left the prison about 6:45, 6:50 P.M. I drove over to the other side of Highway 16 because I know that's where the family was going to be. However, at that point the situation was quite emotional and people were all moving in mass over to the press tent and so I realized there was absolutely nothing I could do ministry-wise for anybody in that situation and I went home.

Q: Did you call your wife in the car to tell her what had happened?

A: I did call my wife as soon as I got into cell phone range. My voice evidently was not sounding like me and in response to her question of what had happened, I told her: I just watched a man be tortured to death.

Attorney: I have no further questions, Your Honor.

After the attorney from the Florida Attorney General's office cross-examines me, the attorney for Mr. Diaz asks her final questions on redirect to clarify the reason why I did not volunteer to testify in front of the Florida Commission on the Administration of Lethal Injection. I am clear that my refusal was to avoid being expelled from death row prison ministry if the Department of Corrections did not like my testimony.

At this point the attorney from the Florida Attorney General's office asks his final questions of me:

Q: You're still carrying on your ministry at the Florida Department of Corrections, UCI and Florida State Prison, aren't you, sir?

A: Florida State Prison.

Q: You're only at FSP, Florida State Prison now?

A: Right now.

I can tell from the attorney's expression that he has no idea that I have been expelled by UCI. He is a career trial lawyer. He knows better than to ask any more questions without knowing what my answers will be, but his demeanor gives me a wealth of information.

If the Department of Corrections thought there were solid

grounds for my expulsion, it would have hand-delivered the supporting evidence for those grounds to the attorney general's office for use to impeach me on cross-examination at this trial. They did not give any such information to the attorney general's office. Not only that, but they did not even tell the attorney general's office that they had expelled me. The most likely reason for this is that the department knows the allegations supporting my expulsion are bogus, so bogus, in fact, that if the charges were aired by them in court it could damage the State's case for trying to keep the death penalty!

This realization gives me renewed hope for a successful appeal of our expulsion. Despite the emotional strain of the two hours of testimony just completed, I feel encouraged as the judge releases me from the witness stand.

Judge: The witness is excused.
A: Thank you, sir.

18

"Take Off the Grave Clothes and Let Him Go"

JOHN 11:44

EARLY MORNING ON JUNE 28, 2007, Susan and I head west on Interstate 10 for our meeting in Tallahassee at the Office of the Secretary of the Department of Corrections. It happens that at this time the department is in crisis, with many issues in addition to its death penalty policies. Florida's inmate population is burgeoning past ninety thousand, and the department is still reeling from a major scandal at the highest levels. Before leaving office, Governor Bush had brought in a tough new secretary to clean house in Tallahassee and at the local level. The new secretary, Colonel James R. McDonough, is a man of strong Christian faith and impeccable integrity. He is brilliant, with degrees from both MIT and the U.S. Military Academy. He is comfortable with command and has on-the-ground experience from the platoon level in Vietnam to brigade command in Bosnia.

In addition to three Bronze Stars and a Purple Heart, he is the West Point boxing champion for the years 1968 and 1969.

Susan and I know that the Florida prison system is in crisis, and the balance of power between the local institutions and the central office is the pressure point. We have no expectation that someone will jeopardize the bigger picture over the death row ministry of a couple of lay volunteers from a small town somewhere near the Georgia border. Our hope is for a fair hearing and an honest assessment leading to the inevitable conclusion that a mistake has been made in our case, and it must be corrected. We believe this secretary is capable of doing that.

We find ourselves meeting with Colonel McDonough's number one, Dr. Laura Bedard. She is cut from the same cloth. With experience as a university professor and as an actual prison warden in Florida, she is fully at ease discussing the whys, the wherefores and the hows. She knows our case inside out before we even sit down in her office. She believes we can be reinstated, but there will need to be some concessions on our part.

Susan and I understand that the politics of the situation require that both parties show some bruises. Our being readmitted to minister at UCI, in and of itself, will show bruises on the local institution. It turns out that our bruises are going to be rough on Kenny as well as on us. We must go back to spiritual advisor status, and we will not be allowed to have any phone calls or even to correspond with him. Also, no more family visits on the weekend at the visiting park. From now on our only contact with Kenny can be one-hour visits at the chapel on weekdays, arranged through the chaplain at his facility. This will also be true for the former death row inmate that I am spiritual advisor for at a prison in Miami.

"There is only one question for today," says Deputy Secretary Dr. Bedard as she looks at Susan and me from behind a mountain of Department of Corrections files that are so urgent they have all made it to a pile on her desk. "Are you willing to accept that?"

"So the question is not whether that is productive, or even consistent with the secretary's own policies?" I probe for any crack or crevice in the rock.

There is no hint of acknowledgment of my words. She appears patiently resigned to the fact that because I am a lawyer, I had to at least ask. She sits quietly, waiting for me to answer her question, which is the only question that counts.

"Of course we will accept that."

"Good. Then I think we are done."

"I do have one request."

"Sure, Chaplain Recinella. What is it?"

"Can I have one more visit with Kenny to explain to him what the new rules will be, so he will understand why this is happening? This is going to be a real drastic loss of support for him."

"Yes, that would be a good idea. But you must do it right away, before we request that the institution readmit you."

"I will go this weekend, and then call your office next Monday to confirm that it is done."

○-○-○

On Sunday morning, July 1, 2007, Kenny is sitting across the table from me in the huge visiting park at Sumter, quietly sorting through the ramifications of these new restrictions. The powerful odor of fresh chicken manure from the farms across the highway has invaded every nook and cranny of the prison. Even air-conditioning cannot keep it out. Our breathing is light and shallow.

"Man, oh man. This is going to be tough." He shakes his head with folded hands. "I have really gotten used to talking to you guys and praying with you on the phone. When things are hard in here, I tell myself, 'Kenny, you can handle it because Dale and Miss Susan are going to pray with you about this tonight or tomorrow or next week.' And I know I'll be seeing you guys here in the visiting park for hours. Now that's all gone."

"I'm sorry, man. I wish there was another way."

"If the institution refuses to readmit you, then what? Can we stay the way we are?"

"Do you think that's what God wants?"

"No, I know what God wants. God wants you bringing His love to those guys on death row. Excepting for that one vote on my jury, I would be there, and I would need for you to be coming in to see me. I know what God wants. It just feels so hard to accept right now."

"And if you get moved from this pre-prerelease program to the actual prerelease program at Everglades, I will only be able to come for a one-hour pastoral once every three or four months. It is over 860 miles round trip and must be scheduled during the week. This is going to be hard, Kenny, but you and God are up to it. You must be, or He wouldn't allow it."

"Man, oh man." He quickly wipes his moist eyes with a blue sleeve.

"Don't worry," I say with a laugh. "With the smell from those blasted chickens, everyone in here will be crying soon."

"You shoulda been here on Thursday." He shakes his head and joins me in laughter. "Unbelievable. What can they possibly do to those poor chickens to make them smell so bad?"

We both need the brief interlude. He sighs and returns to the subject at hand.

"It feels like when you moved to Rome. All of a sudden I was all by myself again."

"And what happened?"

"God and I got a whole lot closer." He pauses and chuckles. "Well, at least we got closer after I finished being mad at Him."

"Kenny, God knows that you have to know your security is in Him, not in us or in any other flesh. Only in Him."

We close, as always, with a prayer before he steps to the blue door at the end of the visiting room.

"Kenny, what do you want to pray for today?"

"I want to pray that you and Miss Susan get readmitted to death row ministry, and that God will give me what I need to deal with it."

○―○―○

On Thursday afternoon, July 19, 2007, I am escorted from the control gate at UCI to the warden's office for my three o'clock reinstatement meeting. It will be attended by the acting warden and the senior chaplain, the two men who expelled me in the first place.

The meeting goes as well as such a meeting can. They make it clear that this expulsion was not their idea, that they were in fact ordered to do it by the regional office. At the very end, however, they bring up my position on the death penalty. I explain that I used to support it, but now, because of my Christian faith, I can no longer support it.

"How can a Christian justify being opposed to the law of the land?" they ask in unison. "The death penalty is the law of the land."

"So is legalized abortion," I note and shrug, "and as a Christian I must be against that as well."

There is a long silence before the acting warden closes up with the necessary administrative pronouncement.

"You can start back to work here on July twenty-fourth, and your wife too, as soon as her paper work from Tallahassee comes in."

On Tuesday, July 24, I return to rounds at the death row building at UCI for the first time since the end of February. Some of the officers seem shell-shocked to see me, so much so that one officer pulls me aside.

He smiles. "Give them a little time. You wouldn't believe the rumors that have been floated around here about the reasons for your expulsion."

"Such as . . ."

"Such as never mind. That will all pass, because if any of it was true, you would not be here." He pats me on the shoulder. "It's good to have you back, chap. Now, get back to work."

In August the circuit judge in Ocala orders the Department of Corrections to show cause why the death penalty by lethal injection in Florida should not be declared unconstitutional as cruel and unusual punishment. However, the window of hope closes quickly, just a month later. In September the same judge issues a final ruling that the Diaz execution cannot be called a botched execution because the goal was to kill the inmate, and Diaz is dead. The judge also notes that it would be inappropriate for a circuit judge in just one county to render a decision that would take away the death penalty from all of Florida. That should be done, he decides, only by the Florida Supreme Court.

The Florida Supreme Court pretends the judge did not say that last part. It simply affirms his ruling that Florida's lethal injections can continue. The State's invisible death penalty industry is safe for another day.

○─●─○

It is time for Susan and me to turn our attention to Kenny's request for parole. When he was sentenced for his crime in 1983, he received a natural life sentence with a mandatory minimum of 25 years. In the trade that's called life with a mandatory quarter. He is asking to be considered for release from prison after the mandatory 25 years is completed. For the hearings on Kenny's parole request, Susan and I are headed back to Tallahassee to the same buildings where we met on the appeal of our expulsion.

Rev. Ken Cooper is offering to house, feed and find employment for Kenny through his faith-based ministry program in Jacksonville. Susan and I are committing to be Kenny's family, to serve as an emotional and spiritual support for him in his new life on the outside. Even so, that is nowhere near enough for him to be considered for release.

In his 25 years in prison Kenny has maintained an exemplary behavior record and has availed himself of every opportunity on the inside to learn, to serve, to teach, to attend and to facilitate programs that prepare an inmate for reentry into society. This includes life skills, job skills, successful work habits, addiction recovery and—the program most dreaded on the inside—identifying and overcoming criminal thinking. He has worked in every job made available to him and has accumulated reams of recommendations from bosses, chaplains and even staff. He has agreed to regular psychological batteries and tests by the department's own people and is being recommended for consideration.

That still might not be enough. One vociferous objection from anyone involved in the prosecution of his case, from the family of the victim or from the judge who sentenced him, would be enough to derail his consideration.

On our first appearance before the Florida Parole Commission on Kenny's behalf, Susan and I are amazed at the thoroughness and integrity of the process. For years, we had the impression from the media that prisoners were just strolling out on parole without any critical evaluation. That does not describe this process. This is rigorous.

Our slot on the full morning agenda is just before lunch. The meeting starts at nine o'clock. For over two hours, we listen to what these commissioners listen to every week, the pleadings by the family and friends of the inmate, asking for a second chance. There is gut-wrenching testimony from the crime victim or, in the case of murder, from the family of the victim. There are impassioned pleas by the attorneys on both sides, frequently accompanied by blowup photos of the crime scene and the victim found there. We are shocked at the level of suffering and horror that the Commission members must routinely endure. We make a personal commitment to pray daily for them and their staff.

After two hours of listening to the horror, we are almost too wrung-out to speak, but it is time for us to stand for Kenny. Rev. Cooper goes first. He himself was granted parole by this Commission in the 1980s. He is a nationally reputed success story for their process. They welcome him and accept his renewed thanks for their trust in his second chance. Then he outlines the parole plan and how he and we will assist Kenny. My words are brief, basically recounting my history with Kenny as set forth in my letter. Then it is Susan's turn.

The people on this Commission really want to hear from Susan. It may not be startling for a volunteer prison chaplain to speak on behalf of an inmate's release. Apparently it is quite exceptional for a volunteer chaplain's spouse, a professional woman in her own right, to take time from her job to travel to appear before the Commission to make her commitment to serve as part of the family for a man in prison. They have questions: "Why are you doing this? What do you see in this man that gives you hope for his success on the outside? How has he changed over the many years that you have known him? How have you experienced him in your visits, in your correspondence, in your phone calls? What precisely is your commitment to his successful transition?" The time limits for our presentation do not apply to commissioners' questions or to Susan's answers to their questions. I know now why they put us at the end of the morning agenda.

The conclusion is favorable. This does not mean that Kenny will be released. It only means that he will be moved from Sumter to the prerelease Corrections Transition Program created by this

Commission and operated in far south Florida at Everglades by Dr. Regina Shearn and Florida International University. A whole new slate of classes, learning, preparation and work will begin. The environment will not be easy. To sum up the philosophy, it is better for a man to lose it in prison than for him to lose it after release. So put him in an environment in which, if he is ever going to lose it, he will lose it now.

Kenny will be navigating this without our calls, without our letters and without our monthly visits. It will truly be him and God in the test by fire.

○─○─○

The rounds at death row continue. The executions continue. The rounds in solitary confinement continue. Starting in the summer of 2008, Marcus Hepburn and Michael Savage, the two men who joined me in prison ministry in the early 1990s just outside Tallahassee, begin accompanying me on death row and in solitary one day a month. For their first visit, they make the early morning two-hour drive from Tallahassee in time to meet me at the church at seven o'clock. Then, after a true country breakfast at a local feeding hole, we make the cell-to-cell visits. After six hours of delivering Fuller-Brush Christianity at cell front, we are seated in a local restaurant renowned across four counties for its barbeque.

"So what surprised you the most?" I ask, hoping to get the two of them talking so I can eat. "What was most different from your experiences at a regular prison?"

"The smell," Michael answers immediately, "the overpowering smell in the three-story-high atriums of the solitary wings at FSP."

"What smell?" My innocence is not pretense. I no longer am aware of the smell in the prison or on my clothes when I return home.

"Man, you've got to be kidding," Mike responds, shaking his

head, "the smell from all the men in the hundred cells in that wing. The smell of sweat and . . . and . . ."

"And their toilets." Marcus grimaces but dutifully completes Mike's sentence. "Should we really be talking about this during lunch, especially barbecue? And by the way, what's the deal with the buttons?"

"You mean the button on the wall outside each cell in solitary?" I am not getting to eat as much as I had hoped.

"Yeah. The button that flushes the toilet that is inside the cell. What is up with that?"

"It is a security item. If a man has contraband in his cell and hears a guard opening his door, he could try to flush the contraband down the toilet. With the flush button on the wall outside the cell, nobody can flush their own toilet. Only the staff and volunteers can flush the toilets."

"So, Marcus, how many toilets did you flush today?" Mike cannot help poking at the subject that Marcus has asked us to drop.

"I stopped counting after a few hundred. I should have stopped sooner. I think that pushing all those buttons with my thumb has given me a repetitive stress injury."

"You should apply for workers' comp." Mike is on a roll.

"We are volunteers."

"Even better." I try to sound like a television ad lawyer. "I bet they will pay your full volunteer salary for as long as you're unable to flush prison toilets."

"So, Dale," Mike adds, deftly deflecting all blame for the subject of flushing in my direction. "Do you have any other great questions?"

"Just one: Are you guys going to come back and do this again?"

The long pause without response makes it clear that there will be a two-hour discussion on that subject all the way back to Tallahassee. I know that only God can call people to this ministry. Friendship is not enough. Fortunately, God does call Marcus and Mike to be regulars at cell front in FSP and UCI.

Another surprise regular is retired Bishop John Snyder. Most men who retire at age 75 with a basketful of accomplishments, including having a large high school named after them, might feel entitled to rest or play golf or travel. Not Bishop Snyder. He plays golf a little but spends most of his time in volunteer ministry to those struggling to overcome drugs and to the disabled. Two days a month, he is with me at cell front.

The first August he accompanied me at FSP, we were standing on the bottom floor of the three-story atrium in a solitary confinement wing. He has just prayed with a man at cell front and realizes he cannot even hear his own words over the incessant din of agony cascading down upon us from the entire wing. The atrium, radiating heat like a Bessemer furnace, is echoing with the thuds of men in a hundred cells throwing themselves against their doors and screaming against the heat. He pauses to absorb the reality surrounding us.

"This . . . all of this," he remarks to sum up our surroundings through the open atrium from floor one up to floor three, "this is the seventh level of Dante's Hell."

We also have better experiences, such as the fellow with severe mental illness who, despite the ravages of his illness, works steadily for four years to understand the faith. Finally, it is the morning for his efforts to be rewarded. The bishop is here to baptize and confirm him and offer his first Communion. We will do it right at cell front in solitary confinement.

Six officers in full protective gear accompany us to his cell. The shields and batons, close at hand, are a testimony to the damage this man can do with his body. The cell door opens. We enter with the six officers immediately around us.

The inmate is in shackles and waist cuffs with his hands in black box handcuffs. He is wearing a butting helmet and both spit and bite shields. The officers remove the helmet and pull back the shields to expose his mouth so he can receive the sacraments. Then they fall back about one foot, flanking us with a semicircle of observant protection.

Bishop Snyder begins the rite of baptism. As the biblical words of salvation fall from the bishop's lips, the man begins to tremble. By the time the water is poured upon his head, he is flowing with tears, whispering over and over, "Thank You, Jesus. Thank You, Jesus." Finally, after receiving confirmation and Communion, the inmate speaks softly, looking toward his feet and the floor. "This is the first time in my life I did the right thing."

o—o—o

In April of 2009 Susan and I make the long drive to Everglades, where Kenny is now in his second year in the prerelease program. We will attend the program's Saturday evening commencement ceremony. In addition to receiving his completion certificate, Kenny is also the master of ceremonies for the event. We are here for him at the invitation of the program directors.

After clearing Everglades security, we are shepherded with the other guests into the visiting park. Earlier that day, this room was full of visitors for the men who live at this prison. Tonight it is filled with long folding tables, covered with special place mats and flanked on every side by the beaming faces of the almost one hundred men who are in the program. They are called the men who are going home. Some will, some will not. The program is zero tolerance, because making it outside is zero tolerance. But for those who do go home, the statistics show that, out of the last 125 men released, only one has come back for re-offending.

It is a tough evening to pull together and to pull off. Everything that could go wrong has gone wrong. Props for the skit have disappeared. The guest speaker does not show and does not call to say why.

The food is delayed because of bureaucratic hassles. Inmate counts disrupt the flow like speed bumps on a highway. Yet it unfolds well, and Kenny shows no anxiety whatsoever.

"How did you stay so calm with all the problems?" I ask him later, as we say good-bye.

"Well, at first I was worrying. Then I asked myself, 'Can I trust God with this evening?'" He laughs deeply, the way he does when he is laughing at himself. "That's when it occurred to me that of all the things I'm asking God to do these days, this evening is the easiest thing for Him to handle."

"How did you feel then?"

"It was like, 'Let's have at it and have a good time.'"

On the way from the reception at the Everglades visiting park back to our hotel, Susan and I talk about how good Kenny looks, how calm he was and how poised he has become.

"He has worked so hard, Dale." Susan's voice is brimming with pride. "Do you think they will give him a chance?"

"Only God knows that answer. We just have to trust in how much God loves Kenny and leave it up to Him."

In July of 2009 we send new letters to the members of the Florida Parole Commission, updating them on our commitment and on our willingness to proceed as Kenny's sponsors and mentoring family if they allow him to be released to Rev. Cooper's program. We attend the hearing with Rev. Cooper in Tallahassee in August. It goes extremely well. Another hearing is set for September. We update our letters and attend the hearing in Tallahassee. It goes extremely well. Another hearing is set for October. Rev. Cooper attends without us because we have a prior commitment downstate for the church. Cooper's call comes immediately after the hearing.

"November 17. You can pick him up at Everglades on November 17."

Neither Susan nor I have much memory of the drive to south

Florida on November 16, nor of the room where we stayed that night, nor even of whether we ate breakfast the next morning.

Our memory starts with presentation of our identification at the control gate at Everglades on the morning of the seventeenth. After confirming our identities and that Kenny is to be released that morning, they ask us to sit about thirty feet away from the gate under a visitor's umbrella. It is about eight-thirty.

We pray and chat. Mostly we are quiet, flooded with our own thoughts and memories. Every time an electric gate clicks within earshot, we jump and look quickly at the control gate. Each time, it is not for us.

As the hours pass, I find myself fingering the paper in my pocket with the emergency number in Tallahassee I can call in case the prison says he cannot be released today. As I stare at the gate, I imagine face after face of men who never got this chance. I imagine them standing just inside it, men I last saw on the gurney or in a prison hospital. The gate of a second chance did not click open for them in this life, but sometimes it does. God gave me a second chance with school and a second chance with my life. We pray that this time, for this man, God will see fit to do it.

Floods of memories of prayers and tears and shared journey with Kenny pour through my thoughts. I think of our visits, our struggles, our times of separation and reunion, our times sharing family and laughs. It has been eighteen years since the first time I sat down across from him in that card room and said, "What would you like Jesus to do for you today?"

It is almost eleven-thirty when we hear a loud clang resound from the sally port adjacent to the control room. Then suddenly, there he is, Kenny, standing inside the gate, in jeans and sneakers and a double-knit shirt.

Susan and I both stand and step forward.

The sergeant raises a gentle but firm hand, motioning us to stay put.

We freeze and wait, barely able to breathe.

Someone is on a phone inside the control booth. Someone is speaking loudly.

My thoughts are racing. *Oh God, please do not let it come undone here, not now.*

A man in a white shirt enters the control room and takes the phone. He is reading something into the phone. Finally, he hangs up and nods. The loud report of the electric lock in the control gate hits us like a punch.

The gate opens. Kenny steps through. He is walking very deliberately, like a man who might be awake but is not sure he is not asleep.

His steps bring him straight to us and into our outstretched arms as we both join in giving him a solitary hug.

"Kenny." Susan smiles through her tears. "Kenny, this is the first day of the rest of your life."

And we stand together under that umbrella, and we pray.

Epilogue

IT IS SPRING OF 2010. Susan and I are sitting with Kenny on the dock of Riverhouse, the residential program where he now lives with the loving support of Rev. Ken and June Cooper. The dark green waters of the Trout River are so calm that not even the lick or lap of a stray wave breaks the silent beauty splashed around us in lively shades of blue, green and brown. This is natural northeast Florida at its best.

"So, Kenny, how would you sum up your first six months on the outside?" I ask. My voice is hushed so as not to disturb the moment's peace. "What are your days like?"

"Well, you are looking at where my day starts and ends—right here by this river. I haven't seen anything this beautiful in almost thirty years."

"What time do you set your alarm for?" The lawyer in me is always pushing for the facts.

"Are you kidding? Who needs an alarm!" His arms gesture out in an attempt to embrace the length of the river. "This is my alarm. I've been in prison for almost thirty years. Now, when that sun starts to come up, I'm awake and out here watching it rise."

"Sounds like the river is calling your name," Susan responds with a gentle smile.

"In the prisons I never saw a sunrise or a sunset. We had to be in before dark and couldn't come out until after light."

"That's for security, you know." My inflection betrays a need to defend the State's need to impose such a deprivation.

"Brother, you don't have to be telling me nothing about security." Kenny is laughing so hard he almost slips off his perch on the dock railing. "I got me a graduate degree in security."

We laugh too, before he continues. "Now I never miss a sunrise or a sunset. I'm making up for all the ones that I didn't get to see."

"And what do you feel when you see this beauty around you?" Susan's arms motion to the expanse of the river from east to west. "What does this say to you?"

"God is good. God is good all the time." The corners of his eyes betray small tears. "He was good when I was inside, and He is good now. He made all this—" The words catch in his throat.

"It's okay." Susan encourages him with a hand on the shoulder. "We are overwhelmed too."

"He made all this because He loves us. He loves me. And I was so focused on myself that it took being caged inside a fence for me to be able to see how good He is."

"So, how would you sum up the difference between life inside prison and life now?"

"Brother Dale, it's like this. My worst day on the outside is better than my best day on the inside. It don't matter what goes wrong, who yells at me or whether the bus to the parole office gets a flat tire and I have to walk three miles in the heat with no lunch. Nothing changes the fact that this life is better than the life I'd made for myself."

"And this life?" My question hangs in the air, begging for the only possible answer.

"This life is grace, man. This life is a resurrection from the dead. I'm like Lazarus. My life now is a gift from God, who gave me a second chance even though there was nothing I could do to deserve it."

My gaze strays to the west, where the four-lane bridge over the river is just far enough away to protect us from the buzz of the constant traffic streaming by. *I wonder how many of the motorists speeding by have noticed this river today? I wonder how many have noticed that they are whipping past a resurrection event?*

Hours later, Susan and I are sitting in our living room with coffee and our Bibles. A beautiful framed print of Jesus at the Last Supper is illuminated by a small light on the wall opposite our chairs. He is depicted looking up into the eyes of His Father in heaven. Our days begin and end before that picture.

"Susan, I'm more like Kenny than I realized."

"Really?"

"Yeah. I was imprisoned in a life I had made for myself, and God resurrected me and gave me a second chance."

"We were both in that old life, Dale, and now we are both free of it."

"I honestly can say the same thing Kenny said. My worst day in this new life is better than my best day in the old life I had made for myself. I was so blinded with rage at the suffering in the world and angry that God allows it. I simply could not believe that God is good. I could not see the goodness of what He made. I was like those motorists zooming by on the bridge today. I didn't really see anything beautiful. I just kept moving, faster and faster."

"I wondered what you were thinking when you were staring at the bridge."

I shake my head in mock despair. "Once a psychologist, always a psychologist."

"You think you've got it bad, honey?" Susan never misses a beat. "You should try living with a lawyer."

As these new insights sift in with our laughter, our focus returns to the opposite wall, to the eyes of Jesus gazing into the face of His Father.

"There is so much suffering, Dale. So many good people suffer. Some from disease or from accidents. Some from crime. Some from evil. There is no denying it. We are immersed in suffering."

"I know. But I don't believe anymore that God desires it. I used to think He did. I used to curse God for it. But that cannot be true. The Father Jesus describes is the God Kenny described today, always good, all the time."

"It's a mystery, honey." Susan sighs into her coffee. "We all know that suffering is a mystery."

My thoughts stream through a collage of faces. My mom with my sister Janet. Pops struggling against dementia until he can return to his wife. The mother of my first AIDS buddy, and scores of others. None cursed God. They all trusted in His providence.

"Susan, if I've learned anything from the faith of so many suffering people that God has put in our path, it is that Job was right."

Susan is already flipping her Bible open to the passage that we have read aloud to each other so often, usually in the grips of our suffering alongside others who are suffering. She knows that the printed letters of that verse in my Bible have become smeared to illegibility from tearful readings. I do not even open my book. Susan motions for me to relax. "I'll read; you listen."

Then she reads aloud Job 19:25–27, the poor man's profoundest words, even though uttered in the absolute depth of his suffering and abandonment:

I know that my Redeemer lives, and that in the end he will stand upon the earth. And after my skin has been destroyed, yet in my flesh I will see God; I myself will see him with my own eyes—I, and not another. How my heart yearns within me!

"That is the endgame, Susan," I whisper, as she sets her book on the side table and retakes my hand. "That is the silver lining of joyful hope that triumphs over suffering."

She nods softly. "Yes, it is. There is really nothing more to say."

Our gazes return to the eyes of Jesus in the picture before us.

DALE S. RECINELLA, formerly a lawyer handling Wall Street finance in the public and private sectors, is a licensed Florida attorney and has taught international law and business ethics at the undergraduate and graduate levels.

For twenty years he has served as a spiritual counselor and Catholic lay chaplain in Florida's prisons. In 1998 he began ministering cell to cell to the approximately four hundred men on Florida's death row and the approximately two thousand men in Florida's long-term solitary confinement. He and his wife, Dr. Susan Recinella, minister as a team during executions. He serves as spiritual advisor to the condemned, and Susan assists the condemned's family and loved ones. They also minister to the families and loved ones of murder victims.

He presents the weekly two-hour program for the faith-and-character-based dorm at Union Correctional Institution, Raiford, Florida, and was named "Citizen Volunteer of the Year" for 2000 by the chaplains of that prison. In 1997 he was named a University of Notre Dame "Exemplar" for modeling faith and citizenship in action. He appears frequently on radio. The Recinellas travel extensively to address audiences throughout the United States and in Europe.

Mr. Recinella received a Masters in Theological Studies *summa cum laude* from Ave Maria University's Institute for Pastoral Theology (2009) and a law degree *magna cum laude* from Notre Dame University Law School (1976).

Mr. Recinella can be reached at P.O. Box 541, Macclenny, FL 32063, U.S.A. or by email at dalereci@nefcom.net.